NANTUCKET GENEALOGIES

by
ALEXANDER STARBUCK

CLEARFIELD

Originally published
as pages 653–832 and 853–871 of
*The History of Nantucket County, Island, and Town
Including Genealogies of First Settlers*
(Rutland, Vermont)

Reprinted for
Clearfield Company, Inc. by
Genealogical Publishing Co., Inc.
Baltimore, Maryland
2001

International Standard Book Number: 0-8063-5106-3
Made in the United States of America

Note:
The subject index, whaling index, and addendum
(original pages 833–843, 845–852 and 873–874)
were deleted from this reprinted edition.

CHAPTER XIX

GENEALOGY

A study of the First Purchasers (as the original twenty owners of Nantucket were called) shows them to have been men of marked ability in the communities in which they dwelt.*

THOMAS MACY,

whom traditions all seem to unite in according the credit of being the first permanent English settler, is said to have come from Chilmark, Co Witshire, England, to Newbury. He was made a freeman September 6, 1639.†. He was as appears from the records one of the original settlers of Salisbury.‡ He and Robert Pike were two of the seven selectmen "to order all the affairs of the town of Salisbury (excepting giving out of lands)" elected on the 4th of the 3d mo. 1643, for six months. He was again chosen one of the Selector Prudential men on the 7th 12 mo. 1652. He was Deputy to the General Court in 1654. The General Court prior to 1658 had enacted a law forbidding preaching by any save regularly licensed and ordained ministers. A division of the town of Salisbury in May, 1658, seemed to make it more convenient that those in the new town should worship by themselves and Joseph Peasely officiated for them. Evidently Mr. Macy was instrumental in this breach of discipline which took away material support for the old meeting and the Court issued a summons for them to appear October 26 to answer for "disorderly practices."**

---

*It is a little singular if the early settlers fled to Nantucket to enjoy religious freedom that the only churches known upon the Island until early in the 18th century were Indian churches. Thomas Macy had preached some, Edward Starbuck had been punished for Anabaptism and yet so far as is known neither of them lived to see an English church in Nantucket.
†Savage's General Dict.
‡Macy's Genealogy, p. 11.
**Mass. Archives, Vol. 10, p. 92.
Mr. Sylvanus Macy in his Macy Genealogy says (p.11) that his distinguished progenitor was a Baptist and "would frequently on the Sabbath exhort the people." When Macy and Peasely were fined it was because Peasely was not duly licensed and the Puritans were averse to dividing congregations and not because of unorthodox doctrines. The evidence does not really show that Mr. Macy did any preaching, but rather that he actively encouraged Peasely.
Patronymica Britannica spells the name Macey and traces it to Macie near Avranches in Normandy; also an old Norman form of Matthew.

Not only did he seem to be a forceful man, frequently called on for public service in Salisbury, but he was also a well to-do citizen. Obed Macy says (p. 13) that he was the owner of 1000 acres of land, "a good house and considerable stock."* It is not recorded that he lost any of these. In a letter to the Governor at New York under date of May 9, 1676, he mentions Thomas Mayhew as "my honored cousin." In the original scheme for the settlement of Nantucket that relationship may have had some bearing.

Thomas Macy married Sarah Hopcott, who was born in Chilmark, England, in 1612.† While the record does not seem to show the date of the marriage it probably occurred in 1643. The children were all born in Salisbury and were. Sarah born July 9, 1644; died 1645. Sarah, born August 1, 1646; died at Nantucket, 1701. Mary, born December 4. 1648; died at Nantucket, 1729. Bethiah, born about 1650, died at Nantucket 1732. Thomas, born September 22, 1653; died at Nantucket, December 3, 1675. John, born July 14, 1655; died at Nantucket, October 14, 1691. Francis born about 1657; died at Salisbury 1658.

TRISTRAM COFFIN

As already stated Tristram Coffin appears to have been the Moses sent out to view the promised land and see what opportunities it offered for new settlers. He was, as Mr. Barney says,‡ the most prominent and influential of the First Purchasers. He was born in Brixton, County Devonshire, England, the son of Peter Coffin and Joanna Thember, in 1605. He married Dionis daughter of Robert Stevens, also of Brixton probably in 1630. They came to America with five children in 1642, accompanied by his mother and two sisters, Eunice and Mary. "The family," according to Sylvanus J. Macy,** "is one of those which have always used arms in this country, though unable to prove a right to them, inherited from ancestors ranking among the gentry of England. In Prince's 'Worthies of Devonshire' may be read an account of the family of the name of Coffin which claims to have been seated at Portledge, in the Parish of Alwington, in the northern part of that county, since the time of the Norman conquest.†† The family sent off branches into different parts of Devonshire, and it is highly prob-

---

*Mr. Macy's own statement regarding his not appearing at Court is that he neither had a horse nor could procure one, so he wrote a letter.
†Macy Genealogy, p. 67.
‡Unpublished M. S. of Nathaniel Barney.
**N. E. Historical and Genealogical Register 1870.
††Allen Coffin Esq. in his Coffin Family, (p. 9) seems to trace the family back as early as about 1110. Mr. Coffin says, however, (p. 17) "While many have searched for the pedigree of our ancestor, Tristram Coffyn, among the records of Devonshire, no one has yet been able to trace his pedigree beyond that of his grandfather, Nicholas Coffyn."

able that the Coffins of this country are descended from some such branch, but the connection has not yet been proved.

"Smith's M. S. Promptuarium Armorum contains a drawing of the arms borne by "'Sir William Coffin of Portledge in Devon of ye Privy Cha. to K. H. 8"—Vert, five cross—crosslets argent, between four plates,—Heraldic Journal, vol III—These are the arms used by the family in this country."

Tristram Coffin and his family made a brief stay at Salisbury, removing the same year to Pentucket.* According to Mr. Coffin ("The Coffin Family" p 23) he was the first person to plough land in Pentucket, using a plough of his own construction. In 1648-9 he removed to Newbury, thence, in 1654-5, to Salisbury. In 1644 he was allowed to keep an ordinary, sell wine and keep a ferry on Newbury side, and George Carr on Salisbury side of Carr's Island.† December 26, 1647 he received a renewal of his permit "to keep an ordinary and retayle wine" and maintain the ferry.‡ In September, 1653, his wife, Dionis, was complained of for selling beer at the ordinary for three pence per quart. The complaint was brought under the law of 1645, which provided that "Every person licensed to keep an ordinary, shall always be provided with good wholesome beer of four bushels of malt to the hogshead, which he shall not sell above two pence the ale quart, on penalty of forty shillings the first offence and for the second offence shall lose his license."** Dionis, however, as a defence, proved that she put six bushels of malt into the hogshead and the Court considered the defence a valid one and discharged the defendant.†† It may fairly be presumed that Tristram Coffin was not necessarily actuated by a sentiment of persecution or of religious restriction in changing his abode, and yet he seems to have been the pioneer in the movement for the purchase of Nantucket.

He and Dionis had as children‡‡—Peter, born in England in 1631, who married Abigail, daughter of Edward and Katharine Starbuck; Tristram Jr., born in England in 1632, married in Newbury March 2, 1652 Judith Somerby, widow of Henry and daughter of Edmund and Sarah Greenleaf; Elizabeth, born in England in 1634-5 probably, married in Newbury November 13, 1651. Capt. Stephen Greenleaf son of Edmund; James, born in England, August 12, 1640, who married Mary, daughter of John and Abigail Severance; John and Deborah, who died in infancy; Mary, born in Haverhill February 20. 1645, married in 1662 Nathaniel Starbuck, son of Edward and Katherine Starbuck; Lieut John Coffin born in

---
*Haverhill.
†Coffin's History of Newbury, p. 43. It would seem by the record that Mr. Coffin's sojourn in Pentucket must have been quite brief.
‡General Statutes.
**Hist. of Newbury, p. 49.
††Hist. of Newbury, p. 57.
‡‡His mother, Joan Coffin, does not appear to have resided on Nantucket. It is said that she died in Boston in May 1661 (The Coffin Family p. 31).

Haverhill October 30, 1647, married Deborah daughter of Joseph and Sarah (Starbuck) Austin; Stephen, born in Newbury May 10, 1652, married Mary, daughter of George and Jane (Godfrey) Bunker. An examination of the record of marriages, particularly of the children of Tristram Coffin, will perhaps account for many of the group of First Purchasers.*

EDWARD STARBUCK

Probably the next in importance among the so-called First Purchasers will by general agreement be admitted to be Edward Starbuck. Although not of the original ten he accompanied Tristram Coffin on his first voyage to the Island and was also a companion of Thomas Macy when he left Salisbury to make a new home at Nantucket. When the original ten selected ten others as partners, Thomas Macy selected him.

He was born in 1604, a native of Derbyshire, England.† He married Katharine‡ Reynolds of Wales, and migrated to America about 1635, settling at Dover, now in New Hampshire but then a part of the Province of Massachusetts Bay. The first mention made of him on the record is in 1643 when he is recorded to have received "a grant of forty acres of land on each side of the Fresh River at Cutchechoe * * * and also one platt of Marsh above Cutchechoe great Marsh, that the brook that runs out of the river runs through, first discovered by Richard Walderne, Edward Colcord, Edward Starbuck and William Furber."** Various other grants were made to him and he is recorded several times as called on to be one of the "lot-layers." He was Representative in the General Court in 1643 and 1646, was an Elder in the church and in other ways enjoyed the respect and esteem of his fellow-citizens.††

In 1644 an act was passed by the General Court of Massachusetts Bay banishing from the Colony all who should either openly or privately oppose the baptism of infants.‡‡ While the punishment

---

*The name Coffin seems to be from the Hebrew, signifying a small basket or it may be synonyonous with Coffer. Patronymica Britannica traces it to Colvin or Colvinus who held lands under Edward the Confessor.

†The name Starbuck is Scandinavian and signifies a person of imposing appearance, great or grand bearing bokki meaning "vis grandis corpore et animo. Ferguson gives it Starbocki, from Star, great "vir imperiosus." It is not improbable that the family was of Danish origin and settled in England in the days of what is historically known as the Danish Invasion. Patronymica Brittannica says in "O. Norse bokk; means "vir grandis, corpose et' animo." Hence **Starbocki** from **Stor,** great." vir imperivsus."

‡Some authorities state the given name to be Eunice, but the more commonly accepted version is Katharine.

**N. E. Hist. & Geneal. Register, vol. viii, p. 68, Alonzo H. Quint.

††On the 20th, 2 mo. 1644 it was ordered that Mr. Edward Starbuck, Richard Walderne & Wm. Furber be wearesmen for Cotcheco fall & river during their lives or so long as inhabitants. N. E. Hist. & Geneal. Register, vol. iv, p. 31.

‡‡Beginnings of New England, John Fiske, p. 195.

meted out to some of the offenders was severe, banishment was not always inflicted.

Edward Starbuck was one of those who subscribed to the proscribed doctrine and the record of the General Court, under date of October 18, 1648, says: "This Court, being informed of great misdemener committed by Edward Starbucke, of Douer, with p'fession of Anabaptisme, for which he is to be p'ceeded agaynst at the next Court of Assistants, if evidence can be p'pared by that time, & it beinge very farre for wittnesses to travill to Boston at that season of the yeare, it is therefore ordered by this Court that the secritary shall give commission to Capt. Thomas Wiggan & Mr. Edw. Smith to send for such p'rsons as they shall haue notice of which are able to testifie in the s'd cause & to take theire testimonie uppon oath & certifie the same to the secritary so soone as may be, that further p'ceedings may be therein if the cause shall so require."*

There seems to be no indication from the record that the complaint was prosecuted, notwithstanding the severe penalty contemplated by the law. The action of the Court did not seem to affect his standing in his community for he continued to be called upon to lay out land.

In Edward Starbuck's case, while what it would seem he considered his theological rights were interfered with, there does not appear that his removal to Nantucket was in any sense a result of such interference. It would not be unreasonable to think, however, that in making the change he was entirely satisfied to remove from the jurisdiction of the Massachusetts Bay Colony but he resided at Hampton eleven years nearly after he had committed an offence against the Orthodox opinions of the Court. As has been stated, he accompanied Tristram Coffin on his voyage of discovery and Thomas Macy on his voyage of settlement. It is stated that he returned to Salisbury and vicinity in 1660 and then went back permanently to Nantucket accompanied by eight or ten families.†

---

*On Oct. 18, 1649 the General Court drew up and sent to the authorities of the Plymouth Colony a letter expressing the hope they once entertained that the Anabaptists in that Colony would be turned "againe into the right way." The Court expresses also that the leniency of the Plymouth authorities results in increase of the erring. "Lett it not, wee pray you, seeme presumption in vs to minde you heerof, nor that wee earnestly intreate you to take care as well of the suppressing of errors, as of maintenance of truth, God equally requiring the p'formance of both at the hands of Christian magistrat, but rather that you will consider our interest is concerned therein. The infeccon of such disease, being so heue vs, are likely to spread into our jurisdiccon. * * * by faith, by neighborhood, by fellowship in our sufferings as exiles, and by other Christian bonds, and wee hope neither Sathan nor any of his instruments shall, by this or any other errors, disvnite vs, and that wee shall neuer have cawse to repent vs of our so neere conjunction with yow, but that wee shall both so a equally and zealously vphold all the truths of God revealed, that wee may render a comfortable accompt to Him that to **Him that bath** sett vs in our places, and betrusted vs with the keeping of both tables."

†Macy's Hist. p. 17. Mr. Macy gives no authority for this statement which seems to rest largely on tradition. The Town Records do not seem to confirm the statement, neither do they disprove it. It is likely that some of the First Purchasers returned with him or came soon after.

"His influence over the Indians was so great," says Nathaniel Barney, "that if at any time a suspicion or alarm arose among the early settlers, he was always in requisition to explain the apparent cause thereof, and to suggest a palliation for their rude and inexplicable action, which served to allay the fears of the more timid."*

His wife doubtless died in Dover; at what time is not recorded. He died on the 4th of the 12th month 1690. Their children were—Nathaniel, who married Mary Coffin, daughter of Tristram and from whom all American Starbucks descend; Jethro, who was killed at the age of twelve years by being run over by a cart; Sarah, who married first, William Story, second Joseph Austin, third Humphrey Varney (as his second wife); Dorcas, who married William Gayer; Abigail, who married Peter Coffin, son of Tristram; and Esther, who was the first wife of Humphrey Varney.

RICHARD SWAIN

according to Savage† embarked in London on the Truelove September 17, 1635, for America. Savage says that in April, perhaps, he had sent his wife Elizabeth† in the Planter, his sons William and Francis in the Rebecca and daughter Elizabeth in the Susan & Ellen, under the care of various friends. He was then 34 years old. He was settled in Rowley in 1639; was made a freeman March 13, 1639; had liberty, with others, to plant in Hampton in 1638; and in the following year was authorized to settle small causes in Hampton. The date of the death of his first wife does not appear to be given, but in 1658 or 1659 he married Jane, widow of George Bunker. Soon after he and his wife removed to Nantucket, bringing the Bunker children with them. These were Elizabeth, the wife of Thomas Look; William, who married Mary Macy, daughter of Thomas Sen'r; Mary, who married Stephen Coffin, son of Tristram Sen'r; Ann, who married Joseph Coleman, son of Thomas Sen'r; Martha, who married Stephen Hussey, son of Christopher. He had by his first wife a son John, who married Mary, the daughter of Nathaniel and Sarah Wyer. He probably came to Nantucket at or about the same time that his father did.

---

*Unpublished M. S. There is a tradition that at one time an uprising among the Indians seemed imminent. They appeared to be gathering in hostile groups and as they greatly outnumbered the whites it was a serious affair. In this juncture Edward Starbuck went unhestatingly among them and soon succeeded in quieting them. The deed of Coatue to him by the Sachems as a "free and voluntary" gift shows their esteem for him.
†Genealogical Dictionary. Mr. Barney says "the name of his first wife is not known" (unpublished M. S.). This, according to Patronymica Brittannica is a Scandinavian personal name of great antiquity, introduced into England under Danish rule and originally applied to a pastoral servant.

Richard Swain's second wife (Jane) died October 31. 1662; he died in 1682.

WILLIAM BUNKER

the son of George and Jane (Godfrey) Bunker was of Huguenot* origin and was born in 1649. He came to Nantucket with his stepfather Richard Swain. He settled at the east end of the Island. There is an interesting tradition concerning him. His residence was quite isolated from his fellow islanders. Early one night, after the family had gone to bed, the house was surrounded by Frenchmen in search of plunder. A vessel had been sighted in the afternoon a short distance from the shore, but as that was not an uncommon circumstance so especial attention had been paid to it. In the evening the large oven was heated with a blazing fire and the light from it served as a beacon to the marauders. England and France at that period were at war with each other. Late in the evening the toothsome rye and indian bread, pumpkin pies and other culinary nicities were taken from the oven and were left smoking and odorously hot when the family retired. Suddenly a door was lifted from its hinges and in walked the undesired and unwelcome visitors.

"Nothing could be more grateful to the wretches than the contents of that oven spread in profusion around them, and, 'nothing loth,' they purloined the whole batch. Nor did they stop here; they took beds and bedding, clothing, and, indeed, everyhing which their rapacity demanded, and then added to their insolence, by demanding that the good farmer himself should go on board their craft which they had left near the shore, and pilot her into the Vineyard Sound. He had no alternative but to go, and after an absence of a few days, he returned to his distressed family. His wife was a woman of indomitable perseverance, and she sustained herself throughout the loneliness of that memorable night, and after surveying their rifled tenement, cast around her that she might repair the ravages as best she could. Her friends did not forget her necessity, and she had cause to remember their kindness, even though she was heard to say, that the 'loss of her twenty pair of sheets was never wholly repaired.' "†

The children of William and Mary Bunker were; Daniel; George who married Deborah Coffin, daughter of James Sen'r; John; Jonathan, who married Elizabeth Coffin, daughter of James Senr; Peleg, who married Susanna Coffin, daughter of Stephen Sen'r; Jabez, who married Hannah Gardner, daughter of Nathaniel Sen'r; Thomas, who married Priscilla Arthur, granddaughter of John Gardner; Benjamin, who married Deborah Paddack, at Yar-

---

*The name originally was Bon Coeur synonymous with Good heart or Great heart. Patronymica Britannica.
†Unpublished M. S. of Nathaniel Barney

mouth; Mary, who married Tristram Coffin (of the Vineyard); Abigail, who married Nathaniel Paddack; Jane, who married Shubael Pinkham, son of Richard; Christian, who married (1) Robert Wilson, (2) Isaac Coleman.

JOHN SWAIN

the son of Richard, seems to have been the only child by the first wife who came to Nantucket, and it is quite likely that he accompanied his father to the Island. At first his residence was at the west end of the Island. The record shows under date of February 15, 1667 that "John Swain had his house lot layed out by the Lot layers aforesaid being sixty Rod square bounded on the South with the first Lot of Richard Swain and on the North with the highway that leads into the Longwoods, on the East and West by the common, more or Less, as it is laid out." The section laid out at that time to the First Purchasers seems to have been west of the Wesco lots. Subsequently he removed to the east side of the Island. It was his dwelling house that Thomas Story refers to as being raised on the occasion of his visit to Swain on the 17th of the 5 mo. 1704 and that date probably indicates very nearly the time when John Swain settled at Polpis.

The children of John and Mary Swain were; Mary, who married Joseph Nason; John, who married Experience Folger; Stephen; Sarah, who married Joseph Norton; Joseph, who married Mary Sibley, of Salem; Elizabeth, who married Joseph Sevolle; Benjamin, who married Mary Taylor; Hannah, who married Joseph Tallman; Patience, who married Samuel Gardner. He died in 1715. His son John, born September 1, 1664, was the first male English child born on Nantucket.

THOMAS BARNARD

never removed to Nantucket although one of the original ten purchasers. He was one of the early settlers of Amesbury. He was one of the signatories to articles of agreement between the inhabitants of the "Old Town" and the "New Town" in May 1654* in company with Thomas Macy, John Severance and others.† He transferred

---
*Hoyt's "Old Families of Salisbury and Amesbury," p. 13.
†A careful study of the lives of the First Purchasers, their business relations and intermarriages will explain matters connected with the original purchase and with subsequent civil complications.

one-half of his share to his brother Robert, and his son Nathaniel represented him on the Island in the other half share. Nathaniel, who married Mary Barnard, daughter of his uncle Robert.* He was highly esteemed among the early inhabitants, and died in Nantucket in 1718. His children were—Mary, who married John Folger; Hannah; John, who married Sarah Macy; Nathaniel, who married (1) Elizabeth, widow of Peter Coffin 2d and daughter of Nathaniel Starbuck, Sen'r, (2) Dorcas Manning, (3) Judith Folger; Stephen, who married ——— Hopcott; Sarah, who married ——— Carrier;† Eleanor, who married Ebenezer Coffin, son of James Sen'r; Benjamin, who married Judith Gardner, daughter of Nathaniel Sen'r; Ebenezer, who married Mary Worth, widow of John Worth and daughter of Stephen Hussey; Abigail, who married Abraham Chase of Martha's Vineyard.

ROBERT BARNARD,

who purchased a half share of his brother Thomas, came to the Island at an early period. The Town Records show that on the 5th 12 mo. 1663, "John Bishop, Mr. Coffin, Robert Barnard and Peter Folger are appointed to view and consider of Land in order to the Laying out thereof for cornfields or other use." He married Joanna Harvey. His only son John married Bethiah, daughter of Peter Folger, February 26, 1668. On the 6th of June, 1669, they were returning from the Vineyard where they had been in pursuit of furniture, in company with Eleazer Folger Sen'r, Isaac Coleman, son of Thomas, and an Indian, when the canoe upset and all perished except Eleazer Folger. He clung to the boat till in crossing a shoal where he could touch bottom he succeeded in uprighting it. With a plough-share which was fastened to it, he managed to free it from water. His sufferings and fatigue had been such that sleep now overcame him, and on waking he found the canoe had drifted on to Norris Island. It was then that he realized how great had been his preservation, and that he alone was left to tell the story of the sufferings through which he and his unfortunate companions had passed.‡

Robert Barnard died on Nantucket in 1682. His wife Joanna died March 31, 1705.

CHRISTOPHER HUSSEY,

probably came from Dorking, County Surrey, England, in the William & Francis, June 5, 1632. He came with the family of Stephen

*Unpublished M. S. of Nathaniel Barney.
†Mr. Barney says he was "an Eastern man."
‡Unpublished M. S. There is a tradition that at one time an up-

Batchelder, whose daughter, Theodate, he married in Lynn, where he originally settled and where their son Stephen was born, the second child to be born in that town* In 1639 he removed with his family to Hampton. He also is said to have participated in the settlement of Haverhill. His daughter Huldah married John Smith. Christopher Hussey was a sea-faring man and was cast away and died on the coast of Florida, March 6, 1686. He never came to Nantucket. He also incurred the displeasure of the General Court by petitioning, with others, for a mitigation of the sentence of Capt. Robert Pike for seeming to uphold speaking in public without a license. He was a deputy for Hampton in 1658.

THOMAS MAYHEW

never was a resident of Nantucket and no detailed biography of him seems needed. Briefly he came to America in the Griffin in 1633, settling at Watertown where he was an active and honored citizen until his removal to Martha's Vineyard in 1647. Both he and his son Thomas were preachers to the Indians there. He died in 1681.

PETER COFFIN

was the son of Tristram and married Abigail daughter of Edward Starbuck. He was born in England in 1631. He was made a freeman at Dover in 1666. He was a very prominent citizen of New Hampshire, attaining the rank of Chief Justice of the Supreme Court. His sojourn in Nantucket was brief and met with considerable opposition from the John Gardner faction during the so-called "Insurrection."

STEPHEN GREENLEAF

never removed to Nantucket. He married, November 13, 1651, Elizabeth Coffin, daughter of Tristram Sen'r. He married subsequently Esther Swett, daughter of Nathaniel Weare or Wyer and widow of Capt Benjamin Swett. He sold his share to his brother-in-law, Nathaniel Starbuck.

*Savage's Genealogical Dictionary; also unpublished M. S. of Nath'l Barney.

WILLIAM PILE

did not come to Nantucket. He sold his share to Reuben Swain and William Bunker and his sisters.*

ROBERT PIKE

If any one of the twenty original purchasers had reason to remove outside the Massachusetts Bay Colony that man was Robert Pike; and yet he never removed to Nantucket nor without the Massachusetts jurisdiction. He was one of the original settlers of Salisbury and was on terms of intimate friendship with Thomas Macy. The New England Historic Genealogical Register represents him as opposed to the election of Sir Harry Vane as Governor and as going on foot from Newbury with Thomas Coleman and eight others to qualify themselves to vote by taking the freeman's oath, so as to vote for Winthrop. He was a very prominent man in his community. He seems to have been a trial justice, was Deputy from Salisbury for several terms an Assistant six terms, a Captain and Major of militia and held other positions of trust and responsibility. He made trouble for himself by declaring that the General Court exceeded its authority in forbidding public speaking by any not duly licensed and was disfranchised. He was also prohibited "settling small causes," pleading in Court any cause but his own, and put under bonds for his good behavior.

May 10, 1661, at a meeting of the First Purchasers at Salisbury he was appointed to keep the Records at Salisbury and Thomas Macy to keep them at Nantucket.

TRISTRAM COFFIN JR.

was a resident of Newbury and married Judith Somerby, widow of Henry and daughter of Edmund and Sarah Greenleaf. He never was a resident of Nantucket.

JAMES COFFIN

son of Tristram Sen'r. was one of the Associate Proprietors, and was the partner selected by his brother Peter. He became promi-

---

*Savage says he removed to Nantucket but by July 1663 he had removed again to Dover. There is no mention of him in the Town Records.

nent in the Islands' affairs and is said to have been the first one on Nantucket appointed to a Probate judgeship. He was appointed in 1680. He died July 28, 1720.* Allen Coffin Esq says he came to the Island with the earliest settlers, but removed to Dover, was a member of the church there and there made a freeman May 31, 1671, soon after which he returned to Nantucket where he resided up to the time of his death.† From him descended the Coffins who were loyalists during the Revolution among whom were General John Coffin and Admiral Sir Isaac Coffin.‡

Lucretia Mott also descended from this branch. He had fourteen children; i. Mary, born in Nantucket, April 18, 1665, married (1) Richard Pinkham, of Portsmouth, N. H., (2) James, son of Richard and Sarah Gardner, and died in Nantucket February 1, 1741; ii. James Jun'r, born probably in Dover, N. H., married (1) Love, daughter of Richard and Sarah Gardner, (2) Ruth, daughter of John and Priscilla Gardner—died in Nantucket October 2, 1741; iii. Nathaniel, born in Dover, 1671, married (August 17,1692) Damaris, daughter of William Gayer—died August 29, 1721; iv John born in Nantucket, married Hope, daughter of Richard Gardner—died July 1, 1747; v. Dinah, born in Nantucket, married (November 20, 1690); vi. Nathaniel Starbuck, Jr. —died August 1, 1750; vii. Deborah, born in Nantucket, married (October 10, 1695) George, son of William Bunker—died October 8, 1767; viii Ebenezer, born in Nantucket March 30, 1678, married (December 12, 1700) Eleanor, daughter of Nathaniel Barnard—died October 17, 1730; ix. Joseph, born in Nantucket, February 4, 1680, married Bethia, daughter of John Macy—died July 14, 1719; x. Elizabeth, born in Nantucket, married (1) Jonathan, son of William and Mary Bunker, (2) Thomas Clark—died March 30, 1769; xi Benjamin, born in Nantucket August 28, 1683—lost overboard between Nantucket and Martha's Vineyard; xii. Ruth,, born in Nantucket, married Joseph son of Richard and Mary Gardner—died May 28, 1748; xiii. Abigail, born in Nantucket, married Nathaniel, son of Richard and Sarah Gardner—died March 15, 1709; xiv. Experience, born in Nantucket—died young; xv. Jonathan, born in Nantucket, August 28, 1692, married Hephzibah, daughter of Ebenezer Harker,—died February 5, 1773.

THOMAS COLEMAN

Mr Barney in his unpublished M. S. says it is not known at what time Thomas Coleman came to Nantucket. It is said that he arrived in Boston from England June 3, 1635. According to Coffin's

---

*"Early Settlers of Nantucket"—Hinchman, p. 28.
†"The Coffin Family," p. 55.
‡Ib. p. 55.

History of Newbury he was three times married—(1) Susanna—who died November 17, 1650; (2) Mary, widow of Edmund Johnson July 11, 1651, who died in Hampton, January 30, 1663; (3) Margery———*. He seems to have resided in Newbury and Hampton until late in life. The Town Records under date of March 4, 1663, say "it was agreed that John Coleman shall have land Layd out on the North side of the Lot of Robert Barnard for the use of the said John Coleman his father Thomas Coleman having given half of his accommodation on the Island half the house lot to be Layd out in the place before mentioned for John Coleman, the aforesaid Thomas Coleman doth Lay down one half of his Lot already layd out." In February 1667 the Record says a house lot was laid out to him "abutting on the long woods." The first time his name appears in the Records in such a way as to show his residence on the Island is on the 23d 3 mo 1672, when it was "Voted by the Town that Thomas Coleman is to keep the cattle upon the playns from comming unto the Nack at Richard Swains for fourteen days for which he is to have eighteen pence a day." He died in 1685, aged 83 years. His children by his first wife, were i. Joseph, born December 2, 1642, married Ann, daughter of George Bunker, Sen'r; Isaac, born February 20, 1647, who was drowned in going from Marthas Vineyard to Nantucket in 1669; ii. John, who married Joanna Folger, daughter of Peter. By the second wife there seems to have been no children. By the third wife there was a son iii. Tobias, who removed with his family from the Island. Joseph had but one son who was drowned in his boyhood.†

NATHANIEL STARBUCK

son of Edward, married Mary, daughter of Tristram Coffin, previously to removing to Nantucket and was the chosen partner of his father-in-law as one of the First Purchasers. Mary, daughter of Nathaniel and Mary was the first English child born on Nantucket. He was a man of marked ability and his wife was a woman of such excellent judgment that as Thomas Story noted in his Journal she was " a wise and discreet woman, well read in Scripture and not attached to any sect, but in great reputation throughout the Island for her knowledge in matters of religion, and an Oracle among them on that account, insomuch that they would not do anything without her advice and consent therein." Their children were—i. Mary who married James, son of Richard Gardner Sen'r;

---

*Mrs. Hinchman says some authorities give her family name as Ashbourne.
†Mrs. Hinchman in "The Early Settlers of Nantucket" p. 61, records a son Benjamin, born May 1, 1640, and a daughter Joanna, evidently by the third wife.

ii. Elizabeth, who married (1) Peter Coffin Jr. (2) Nathaniel Barnard Jr.; iii. Nathániel who married Dinah daughter of James Coffin; iv. Jethro, who married Dorcas, daughter of William Gayer; v. Eunice, who married George, son of John Gardner Sen'r; vi. Priscilla, who married John Coleman Jun'r; vii Hepzibeth, who married Thomas Hathaway, of Dartmouth; viii Barnabas, who did not marry; and ix. Anna and x. Paul who died young. He died on the 6th 6 mo 1719.

THOMAS LOOK

was the partner of Richard Swain. He married Elizabeth, daughter of George Bunker. It is not clear at what time he took up his residence in Nantucket. Nathaniel Barney says that "after residing at Nantucket a number of years, he removed to Martha's Vineyard." His children were mostly daughters and four of them were born on Nantucket between 1672 and 1680. His daughter, Experience married her cousin, Stephen Coffin Jun'r, grandson of Tristram.

JOHN SMITH

It does not appear clearly whether John Smith ever resided on Nantucket. He was partner of Thomas Mayhew Sen'r and had land laid out to him on the Island. There are several items in the records of the General Court referring to John Smith but it is difficult to determine whether they refer to this particular John or not.

The foregoing biographical sketches will give an idea of the kind of men the First Purchasers were. They were a sturdy, God-fearing race, everyone of them prominent in the community in which he lived. Many of them had experienced the severity of the Puritan laws, laws made to preserve, as the makers believed, the rights they fled from England to enjoy, and not the presumed rights of peoples in general, for the Puritans were not and did not assume to be religious emancipationists,* and yet of the First Purchasers

---

*John Fiske in "Beginnings of New England." Mr. Fiske attributes much of the severity against the Quakers to the determination not to allow any interference with the theories and methods they came to America to maintain for themselves and not for humanity at large only so far as new comers coincided with their views.

those who were the severest penalized remained under the jurisdiction of the Massachusett Bay Colony and, so far as we know, did not even visit Nantucket. As before noted, knowing how many interests they had in common, the many intermarriages and the intimacies which must have existed among them about the time the purchase was made, and soon after, we can more readily account for their partnership and for subsequent alliances in the civil government of the Island.

The First Purchasers were not unacquainted with each other. They did not live far apart and several of them had been members of the General Court. Tristram Coffin, Thomas Macy, Christopher Hussey, Peter Coffin, Stephen Greenleaf, Thomas Barnard and William Pile were, or had been, residents of Salisbury or Newbury. Peter Coffin was a son of Tristram. Stephen Greenleaf married Elizabeth Coffin, daughter of Tristram. Peter Coffin married Abigail Starbuck, daughter of Edward. Hampton was not far off and the Swains evidently were interested in the projected settlement. Thomas Mayhew owned Martha's Vineyard and Nantucket and had been a resident of the former island at the time he sold Nantucket for about 15 or 16 years. The partners who the original purchases took were similarly neighbors and interested through marriage or acquaintance. Tristram Coffin took as his partner Nathaniel Starbuck, his son-in-law; Thomas Macy took Edward Starbuck whose son Nathaniel married Mary Coffin and daughter Abigail married Peter Coffin, both children of Tristram and Dionis; Richard Swain took Thomas Look, whose daughter. Experience, married her cousin Stephen Coffin, Jr. grandson of Tristram; John Swain took Thomas Coleman who had resided near him in Hampton; Thomas Barnard took his brother Robert; Peter Coffin took his brother James; Christopher Hussey* took Robert Pike, a resident of Salisbury; Thomas Mayhew took John Smith, who had been otherwise associated with him. It was no chance acquaintance then which brought them together.

The principal intricacies met in the genealogy of the descendants of the First Purchasers arise from the persistency of the intermarriages and the duplication of given names. Of course that becomes increasingly troublesome with each succeeding generation. The situation becomes relieved somewhat after 1750 when the use of middle names began and other means were adopted to particularly designate individuals, but progress in that direction was very

---

*Christopher Hussey and John Bishop had been punished for taking sides with Robert Pike who had espoused the cause of Macy and Peasley.

slow. The Friends Records are a God-send to the worker in that field because they give the details in marriage of the parents of the contracting parties.

What may be, perhaps not inaptly, termed the clannishness of the descendants of the First Purchasers, is illustrated by a little doggerel written by some one who had no fear of tribal displeasure nor any respect for the family pride of those he lampoons.* It appeared in two stanzas, published about 1834 and the irreverent writer thus characterized his victims:

> "The Rays and Russels, coopers are,
> The knowing Folgers lazy,
> A lying Coleman very rare,
> And scarce a learned Hussey.
>
> The Coffins noisy, fractious, loud,
> The silent Gardners plodding,
> The Mitchells good, the Barkers proud,
> The Macys eat the pudding."

As though that was not enough, some super-reckless individual added the following for good measure:

> "The Swains are swinish, clownish called,
> The Barnards very civil,
> The Starbucks they are loud to bawl,
> And Pinkhams beat the devil."†

In a large part of the early history of the Island the rule has been to follow the dates as shown by the Records. Those, after so large a number of the residents had become Friends, followed the custom of the Friends in using numerals to express the months.

---

*Presumably it was written, or at least the first two stanzas were written by Hart the author of Miriam Coffin. It has also been attributed to Phineas Fanning who married Kezia Coffin, daughter of John and Kezia.

†Illustrative of one of the results of the intermarriage among the Islanders is a little story of Prof. Maria Mitchell told by Mrs. Hinckman in her "Early Settlers of Nantucket (p. 12). When connected with Vassar College, someone said to her "Miss Mitchell, I met a cousin of yours the other day." "Where?" was the natural question, "on Nantucket" was the expected reply. Miss Mitchell quickly said "Oh, very likely; I have five thousand cousins on Nantucket." At that time that was the Island's population. Similarly Rev. Dr. Ferdinand C. Ewer humorously once said—"I found that my precious blood was chemically composed of the following old Nantucket elements, for every one of which I am humbly grateful, viz—Silicate of Trott, 2 per cent; Bicarbonate of Burnell, 2 per cent; Protoxide of Swain, 3 per cent; Nitrate of Worth, 3 per cent; Chloride of Cartwright, 11 per cent; Sulphate of Starbuck, 11 per cent; Hydrated Sulphuric Acid of Ewer, 11 per cent; Super phosphate of Coffin, 12 per cent; Hydrated Dentoxide of Gardner, 15 per cent; Aurate of Folger, 20 per cent; Traces of Tobey, Wing and Macy, 1 per cent; total 100 per cent." Godpey's Hand Book, pp 105-6.

This statement is particularly applicable to the Genealogical portion of the work which relies very much, and with excellent reason, on the Records of the Friends. Naturally the question arises when was the change made in the Friends' Records to make January the first month instead of the eleventh.

According to the Record, as stated by the custodian,*—"There was a Monthly Meeting held the 30th of 1st month 1752, and the next was held the 27th of 4th month, 1752. There is a minute which states 'that an epistle has been received from the Meeting for Sufferings in London, wherein is contained the advice of Friends concerning the reducing the year to New Style according to act of Parliament &c was read in this meeting and ordered to be read in first Day meeting." The change was made therefore that year. Dates then prior to 1753 make March the first month and from 1753 January has been the first month. The general rule which has been followed in this work is to follow the record.

The intention of the compiler of this genealogy was to cover only the first 100 years after the settlement of the Island, or to the year 1760.

---

*Mr. James W. Oliver, of Sharon. In this compilation, as in other portions of the History, the intention has been to follow the record using either the name of the month or the numeral, as there given.

BARNARD

Thomas Barnard, the first apparently of that surname in America, came to this country about 1650. He settled in Salisbury but appears to have been one of those who founded the new town of Amesbury. He never removed to Nantucket. He was brother to Robert who is named among the first ten purchasers and selected by Robert as his partner. His son Nathaniel came to Nantucket and assumed his father's interests. Robert married Joanna Harvey and came to Nantucket in 1663. They had but one son, John, who married, (February 26, 1668) Bethiah Folger, daughter of Peter. He and his wife were drowned, with Isaac Coleman and an Indian, June 6. 1669, when returning with Eleazer Folger in a canoe from Marthas Vineyard, where they had been to purchase some furniture.* Robert and Joanna had one daughter, Mary, who married her cousin Nathaniel, son of Thomas.†

Mr. Worth says of Nathaniel Barnard‡—"He was very prominent in Town and public affairs, having been chosen many times to serve in all the important offices. He was a trader, and the court records show that he was fined in 1709 for selling liquor to the Indians."

Regarding his home Mr. Worth says—** "East of the Elihu Coleman house is the Mill-Brook, and a short distance further east, on the south side of the road near a cluster of willow trees, was once a house which was the homestead of Thomas Barnard. Directly across the road lived Nathaniel Barnard. The present road was merely a path for many years later. The house lot of Thomas Barnard on which the house of Nathaniel was located, was about 1000 feet square, and southwest of it was the lot of Robert Barnard. These lots extended northeast and southwest, and comprised twenty acres each. The house of Robert cannot be exactly located, neither can the bounds of the lots be identified. But the high land between the Mill-Brook swamp and the Indian boundary line was substantially comprised within the two Barnard lots."††

NATHANIEL [1]

The children of Nathaniel and Mary were—

    i **Mary**, born February 24, 1667; married John Folger, son of Peter and Mary.
   ii **Hannah**, born July 19, 1669; probably never married.
  iii **John**, born February 24, 1670; married Sarah Macy, daughter of John and Deborah.

---

*Unpublished M. S.
†Mary died 17th 1 mo 1717-8. Nathaniel Sr. died 3d 4m. 1718. Jane (or Joanna), wife of Robert, died March 31, 1705.
‡Nantucket Lands and Land Owners, p. 61.
**Ibid, p. 62.
††Patronymica Britannica calls the name a "well-known personal name" probably of occupational origin.

iv **Nathaniel,** born November 24, 1672; died 28th 2 mo. 1718; married—first (1706) Dorcas Barnard; Second (1st 12 mo 1709) Judith Folger, daughter of Stephen and Mary Coffin.
v **Stephen,** born February 16, 1674; married——Hapcott
vi **Sarah,** born March 23, 1677; married——Carrier, "an Eastern man."
vii **Eleanor,** born June 18, 1679; married (December 12, 1700) Ebenezer Coffin, son of James and Mary.
viii **Benjamin** married (3d 11mo. 1711) Judith Gardner daughter of Nathaniel and Abigail. She died 17th 9 mo. 1765.
ix **Ebenezer** married (24th 3mo. 1722) Mary widow of Jonathan Worth and daughter of Stephen and Martha Hussey.
x **Abigail** married Abraham Chase of Martha's Vineyard.*

JOHN [2] (Nathaniel [1])

born February 24, 1670; married Sarah Macy, daughter of John and Deborah. Their children were:

i **Jemima,** born 14th. 9 mo, 1699; married (6th 10 mo. 1720) Elihu Coleman, son of John and Priscilla.
ii **Robert,** born 14th 11 mo. 1702; married (1st. 6 mo. 1726) Hepzibah Coffin, daughter of Stephen and Experience.
iii **Matthew,** born 7th 9 mo. 1705; married (29th 10 mo. 1726) Mary Tebbets, daughter of Ephraim and Rose.
iv **Samuel,** born 3d. 7 mo. 1707.
v **Hannah,** born 7th 7mo 1711; died in 1784, probably unmarried. John's will was probated June 8. 1748.

NATHANIEL [2] (Nathaniel [1])

born November 24, 1672: died 28th 2 mo. 1718; married——first (1706) Dorcas Barnard: second (1st. 12 mo. 1709) Judith Folger,

---

*All of the name of Barnard in Nantucket descend from Nathaniel and Mary. In his will, which was executed April 7, 1718, and probated June 11, 1718, Nathaniel devises land in Wesco, received from his father-in-law, Robert Barnard, to "my grandson Nathaniel Barnard." Nathaniel Senior was one of the seven men designated under the Dongan patent to form the first Board of Trustees. His estate inventoried £2460.

widow of Peter and daughter of Stephen and Mary Coffin.* It would seem by the Probate Records (vol 1 p 54) that Nathaniel Jr and Nathaniel Sr. must have died very nearly at the same time as the Records show that an inventory of his (Nathaniel Jr's) estate taken January 27, 1719, totaled £405,7.6, while the estate of his father totaled, as reported December 28, 1728, £2460. The Friends' Records show that the Junior Nathaniel died 28th 2 mo 1718 and the Town Records show that the Senior Nathaniel "departed this liffe in great peace" 3d. 4 mo of the same year. Mary, wife of the elder Nathaniel, died 17th 1 mo 1717-18. The children of Nathaniel Jr were—by his first wife:

    i Dorcas, born 9th 10 mo. 1707, who married (8th 7 mo. 1726) Jacob Barney of Newport† R. I.

By his second wife:

    ii Elizabeth, born 11th 7 mo. 1710, who married (3d 11 mo. 1728) Barnabas Coleman, son of John and Priscilla.
    iii Peter, born 5th 1 mo. 1713; married (10th 11 mo 1733-34) Anna Starbuck, daughter of Nathaniel and Dinah.
    iv Nathaniel, born 2d 2 mo. 1717; died 1743.
    v Eunice, born 7th 6 mo. 1714.

STEPHEN [2] (Nathaniel [1])

born February 16, 1674: married (———) Hapcott———. They had—

    i Thomas born,———; married (2d 10 mo. 1735) Sarah Hoag, daughter of Benjamin and Sarah. He removed from the Island 26th. 10 mo. 1772.

BENJAMIN [2] (Nathaniel [1])

married (3d 11mo 1711) Judith Gardner, daughter of Nathaniel and Abigail. Their children were:

    i Timothy, born 3d 8 mo 1712; married (2d. 1 mo. 173½) Mary Bunker, daughter of Peleg and Susanna.
    ii Abigail, born 12th 5mo. 1714; married (3d 11mo 1731) Robert Macy, son of Thomas and Deborah.

---

*His widow Judith married (31st 6mo. 1722) Stephen Wilcox (or Wilcock). She died in 1760.
†This marriage is the only one on record where the event is recorded in the full form adopted by the Friends and signed by all the witnesses.

 iii **Ruth** born 2d 7 mo. 1717; married first (30th 11 mo 1734-5) Peter Clark son of Thomas and Mary; second (28th 3 mo. 1758) Joseph Jenkins son of Matthew and Mary.
 iv **Francis**, born 6th 8 mo. 1718; married (14th. 11mo. 1741) Elizabeth Macy daughter of Thomas and Deborah.
 v **John**, born—11mo 1720; probably married (July 20, 1744) Mary Ellis.
 vi **Abishai**, born 2d 12 mo 1722; married (15th 10 mo 1743) Hannah Coffin, daughter of Peter and Hope.
 vii **Nathaniel**, born ——— 1727.
 viii **Mary**, born 18th 8 mo. 1729; married (12th 10 mo. 1751) Christopher Starbuck, son of Tristram and Deborah. Benjamin died 8th mo 1739;* his wife died 17th 9 mo. 1765.

EBENEZER [2] (Nathaniel [1])

married (24th 3mo. 1722) Mary Worth, widow of Jonathan and daughter of Stephen and Martha Hussey. He died 4th 5 mo. 1767; she died 8th, 1mo. 1771. Their children were—

 i **Stephen**, born 14th, 6 mo. 1723; married, first (3d 11 mo. 1744) Eunice Starbuck, daughter of William and Anna; second (25th 2mo 1754) Phebe Swain, daughter of George and Love.
 ii **William**, born 23d 9 mo. 1724; married (5d 11mo. 1743) Mary Coffin, daughter of Samuel and Miriam.
 iii **Jemima**, born 19th 1 mo. 1726; married (8th 1 mo 1743-4) Tristram Coffin, son of Peter and Hope.
 iv **Lydia**, born 2d 12 mo. 1730; married (20th 10 mo 1750) Jonathan Folger son of Jonathan and Margaret.
 v **Martha**, born 18th 2 mo. 1733; died 30th 9 mo. 1733.

ROBERT [3] (John [2] Nathaniel [1])

born 14th. 11mo. 1702; married (1st, 6 mo. 1726) Hepzibah Coffin, daughter of Stephen and Experience; he died 10th 7 mo. 1765; she died 28th 9 mo. 1782. Their children were—

---

*There would appear to be an error in this date which is taken from the Friends' Records, for the Records of the Probate Court show that his widow was appointed administratrix of his estate February 7, 1734-5. The estate inventoried £2610, 8, 8¼.

    i **Anna**, born probably in 1727; died young.
   ii **Eunice**, born 26th 6 mo. 1728; married—first (14th 11 mo. 1747) Jonathan Coffin, son of Tristram and Mary; second (10th 7mo. 1760) Samuel Ray, son of Samuel and Mary; third (1769) Jonathan Gardner, son of Barnabas and Mary.
  iii **Elizabeth**, born 23d 8 mo. 1731.
  iv **Jonathan**, born 28th 1 mo. 1734; married (8th 1 mo 1756) Mary Coffin, daughter of Tristram and Mary.
   v **Hepzibah**, born 24th 2 mo. 1736; married (16th 1 mo. 1755) Richard Mitchell son of Richard and Mary.
  vi **Sarah**, born 10th 4 mo 1738; married (1781) William Ellis, son of John and Dinah.
 vii **Nathaniel**, born 19th 5 mo. 1740; died 26th 7 mo. 1768.
viii **Matthew**, born 4th. 7 mo. 1742; married (2d 1 mo. 1766) Deborah Coffin, daughter of David and Mary.
  ix **Anna**, born 29th, 1 mo. 1745; married (28th, 5 mo. 1767) Reuben Macy son of Francis and Judith.
   x **Robert**, born 24th 10 mo. 1748; married (December 18, 1766) Margaret Whitney.
  xi **Abishai**, born 25th 8 mo. 1751; removed from the Island 26th. 9 mo. 1785; married (3d. 4 mo. 1772) Susanna Paddack, daughter of Stephen and Eunice.
 xii **Shubael**, born 8th, 5 mo. 1754.

MATTHEW [3] (John [2] Nathaniel [1])

married (29th 10 mo. 1726) Mary Tebbets, daughter of Ephraim and Rose; he died 5th 8 mo. 1788; she died 4th 4 mo. 1785. Their children were—

   i **Benjamin**, born —— 1728; married (2d. 12 mo. 1748) Judith Folger, daughter of Barzillai and Phebe; He died 28th 8 mo. 1779.
  ii **Shubael**, born 13th, 1 mo. 1730; married—first (2d, 1 mo.1748-9) Susanna Gardner, daughter of Ebenezer and Judith; second (28th, 11 mo. 1765) Ruth Myrick, daughter of James and Bethiah Bunker.
  iii **Joseph**, born 25th, 2 mo. 1732; married (April 15, 1752) Mary Gardner.
  iv **Abigail**, born —— 1734; probably married (June 6, 1753) Christopher Folger.
   v **Ann**, born 25th, 1 mo. 1737; married (24th, 3 mo. 1757) Joseph Nichols, son of William and Bethiah.

HISTORY OF NANTUCKET 675

- vi Rose, born 18th, 3 mo. 1739; married (2d, 12 mo. 1756) Stephen Hussey, son of Daniel and Sarah.
- vii Mary, born 27th, 1 mo. 1741; married (3d, 12 mo. 1761) Thomas Jenkins, son of Thomas and Judith.
- viii John, born ———— 1745; married (1st, 1 mo. 1767) Mary Russell, daughter of William and Mary.
- ix Elizabeth, born ———— 1747; married (10th 1 mo. 1765) Sheffield Coffin, son of Nathaniel and Mary.
- x Matthew, born ———— 1749; married first (30th, 8 mo. 1774) Elizabeth Swain, daughter of Reuben and Elizabeth; second, (2d, 4 mo. 1783) Avis Folger, daughter of John Slocumb and Martha.
- xi Hepzibah, born ———— 1754; married (23d, 9 mo. 1773) Daniel Paddack, son of Stephen and Eunice.

PETER [3] (Nathaniel [2] Nathaniel [1])
married (10th, 11 mo. 1733-4) Anna Starbuck, daughter of Nathaniel and Dinah; he died 27th, 4 mo. 1775; she died 18th, 12 mo. 1785. Their children were—

- i Christopher, born 26th, 5 mo. 1737; married (28th, 1 mo. 1762) Judith Swain, daughter of Caleb and Margaret.
- ii Elizabeth, born 26th, 4 mo. 1739; married (8th, 12 mo. 1757) Alexander Ray, son of Samuel and Mary.
- iii Nathaniel, born 8th, 2 mo. 1741; married (6th, 12 mo. 1764) Margaret Swain, daughter of Caleb and Margaret.
- iv Hezekiah, born 10th, 2 mo. 1743.
- v Judith, born 7th, 5 mo. 1745; married 9th, 12 mo. 1779) Jonathan Barney, son of Jonathan and Mary.
- vi Peter, born 2d, 3 mo. 1747.
- vii Eunice, born 8th, 12 mo. 1749; married (31st, 10 mo. 1765) Nathaniel Starbuck son of Joseph and Ruth.
- viii David, born 27th, 11 mo. 1752; married (November 1, 1771) Abigail Starbuck daughter of Sylvanus and Mary.
- ix Elisha, born 30th, 1 mo. 1754; married (October 7, 1775) Lydia Starbuck, daughter of Sylvanus and Mary.
- x Lydia, born 17th, 10 mo. 1756.

THOMAS, [3] (Stephen [2] Nathaniel [1])
born————; married (2d 10 mo. 1735) Sarah Hoag. daughter of Benjamin and Sarah. Their children were—

i Mary, born probably in 1736; died 1st 7 mo. 1767; married (4th 12 mo. 1753) Jethro Folger, son of Jethro and Mary.
ii Hopcot.
iii Stephen, lost at sea 1772; married (31st. 12 mo 1761) Hephzibah Paddack, daughter of Paul and Anna.
iv Benjamin
v Thomas, married (1st 12 mo. 1768) Ruth Macy, daughter of Zaccheus and Hepzibah.
vi Valentine, married (28th 12 mo. 1769) Anna Coffin, daughter of Peleg and Hepzibah.
vii Judith.

Thomas Senior and his wife removed from the Island 26th 10 mo. 1772; Thomas junior. Valentine and Judith removed in 1773.

TIMOTHY [3] (Benjamin [2] Nathaniel [1])

married (2d, 1 mo. 1731-2) Mary Bunker, daughter of Peleg and Susanna who died 18th, 9 mo. 1750. The Probate Records show that his will, executed in May 1743, was probated September 9, 1748. At the time the will was probated his widow Mary, and five children survived him—

i Benjamin, born probably in 1732, or 1733, who married (9th, 1 mo. 1755) Eunice Fitch, daughter of Beriah and Deborah, and removed from the Island in 1773.
ii Judith, born September 30, 1735; married (5th, 12 mo. 1754) Benjamin Folger, son of Shubael and Jerusha.
iii Timothy, born about 1738; removed from the Island 1773; married (8th, 2 mo. 1759) Love Swain, daughter of George and Love.
iv Mary, born 1742; probably married (February 6, 1766) Benjamin Barnard, son of Matthew and Deborah.
v Susanna, born 24th, 11 mo. 1744; married (3d, 12 mo. 1767) Seth Coffin, son of David and Ruth.
vi William, born probably about 1744; married (4th, 6 mo. 1772) Hepzibah Gardner, daughter of Charles and Anna.

FRANCIS [3] (Benjamin [2] Nathaniel [1])

born 6th, 8 mo. 1718; married (14th, 11 mo. 1741) Elizabeth

Macy, daughter of Thomas and Deborah; he died 20th, 4 mo. 1800; she died 1st, 6 mo. 1765. Their children were—

    i **Reuben**, born 24th, 1 mo. 1743; married (December 4, 1767) Phebe Coleman, removed from the Island 26th, 10 mo. 1778.
    ii **Deborah**, born 3d, 6 mo. 1745; died 15th, 8 mo. 1790; married (11th, 6 mo. 1767) Prince Gardner, son of Robert and Jedidah.
    iii **Francis**, born 4th, 7 mo. 1747; removed from the Island 29th, 8 mo. 1774; married (16th, 3 mo. 1769) Katherine Osborne, daughter of James and Anna.
    iv **Elizabeth**, born 13th, 4 mo. 1749; died 27th, 11 mo. 1764.
    v **Nathaniel**, born 27th, 3 mo. 1751; died 10th, 11 mo. 1752.
    vi **Anna**, born 16th, 6 mo. 1755; removed from the Island 19th, 9 mo. 1799; married (9th, 11 mo. 1775) Christopher Gardner, son of Robert and Jedidah.
    vii **Judith**, born 9th, 3 mo. 1753; removed from the Island 29th, 8 mo. 1785.
    viii **Jemima**, born 21st, 8 mo. 1757; died young.
    ix **Lydia**, born 25th, 12 mo. 1759; removed from the Island 27th, 6 mo. 1785.
    x **Abigail** born 6th, 3 mo. 1762.

ABISHAI [3] (Benjamin [2] Nathaniel [1]) born 2d, 12 mo. 1722, married (15th, 10 mo. 1743) Hannah Coffin, daughter of Peter and Hope. His will was probated December 9, 1790, and he probably died in November of that year; his wife died 14th, 2 mo. 1797. Their children were—

    i **Phebe**, born 11th, 7 mo. 1744.
    ii **Jonathan**, born 11th, 7 mo. 1746; married (21st, 2 mo. 1770) Sarah Joy, daughter of David and Sarah; died 25th, 11 mo. 1775.
    iii **Tristram**, born 17th, 9 mo. 1748.
    iv **Nathaniel**, born 2d, 10 mo. 1752.
    v **Abishai**, born 2d, 8 mo. 1755; married (5th, 9 mo. 1776) Phebe Swain, daughter of Tristram and Anna. Lost at sea 1781.
    vi **Rhoda**, born 26th, 5 mo. 1757.
    vii **Elizabeth**, born 29th, 2 mo. 1759.
    viii **Isaiah**, born 9th, 11 mo. 1763; lost at sea 1781.
    ix **Rebecca**, born 9th, 11 mo. 1767.

STEPHEN [3] (Ebenezer [2] Nathaniel [1])

born 14th, 6 mo. 1723; married—first (3d, 11 mo. 1744) Eunice Starbuck, daughter of William and Anna; second (25th, 2 mo. 1754) Phebe Swain, daughter of George and Love; he died 4th, 2 mo. 1813; his first wife died 26th, 4 mo. 1750, and his second 8th, 1 mo. 1794. His children were—

By Eunice:

    i **Jethro**, born 8th, 7 mo. 1745.*
    ii **Ebenezer**, born 10th, 6 mo. 1747; died 9th, 9 mo. 1830.†

By Phebe:

    iii **George**, born 19th, 11 mo. 1754; lost at sea 1777.
    iv **Stephen**, born 19th, 11 mo. 1756; died 21st, 8 mo. 1759.
    v **Seth**, born 2d, 9 mo. 1760; died 6 mo. 1771.
    vi **Charles**, born 21st, 12 mo. 1762; died 17th, 9 mo. 1763.
    vii **Eunice**, born 1st, 1 mo. 1766.
    viii **Henry**, born 17th, 10 mo. 1769.

WILLIAM [3] (Ebenezer [2] Nathaniel [1])

born 23d, 9 mo. 1724; married (3d, 11 mo. 1743) Mary Coffin, daughter of Samuel and Miriam. He died 11th, 7 mo. 1771; she died 28th, 8 mo. 1777.

    i **Tristram**, removed from the Island 23d, 9 mo. 1773; married (2d, 1 mo. 1766) Margaret Folger, daughter of Reuben and Dinah.
    ii **Miriam**, removed from the Island 28th, 11 mo. 1785; married (31st, 10 mo. 1765) Tristram Macy, son of Nathaniel and Abigail.
    iii **Lydia**, removed from the Island 23d, 9 mo. 1773.
    iv **Paul**, lost at sea; married (9th, 7 mo. 1778) Phebe Macy, daughter of Nathaniel and Abigail.
    v **Eunice**, removed from the Island 24th, 4 mo. 1780.
    vi **Obed**, removed from the Island 27th, 12 mo. 1784.
    vii **Mary**, removed from the Island 25th, 10 mo. 1773.
    viii **Phebe**, born 28th, 12 mo. 1763; married (30th, 11 mo. 1780) Gilbert Coffin, son of Micajah and Abigail.

---

*There is a slight discrepancy between the Town Records and those of the Friends; the Town Records give Jethro's birth as June (4 mo.) 27th 1745 and Ebenezer's as May (3 mo.) 30, 1747.

†Phebe is the only one of the children whose age is recorded in the Friend's Records. In his will, dated April 5, 1771, William calls himself a cooper

JONATHAN [4] (Robert [3] John [2] Nathaniel [1])
born 28th, 1 mo. 1734; married (8th, 1 mo. 1756) Mary Coffin, daughter of Tristram and Mary. Their children were—

    i William, born 28th, 10 mo. 1756.
    ii Hepzibah, born 29th, 7 mo. 1758.
    iii Jonathan, born 17th, 10 mo. 1760.
    iv Henry, born 4th, 10 mo. 1762; died 14th. 9 mo. 1763.
    v Libni, born 22d, 3 mo. 1765.
    vi Andrew, born 4th, 7 mo. 1767.
    vii Cromwell, born 22d 9 mo. 1769.*
    viii Tristram, born 17th 8 mo. 1771.
    ix Thomas, born 4th, 10 mo. 1774.

MATTHEW [4] (Robert [3] John [2] Nathaniel [1])
born 4th, 7 mo. 1742; married (2d, 1 mo. 1766) Deborah Coffin, daughter of David and Mary. Their children were—

    i Abigail.
    ii Timothy.
    iii Elizabeth.
    iv Mary.
    v David.
    vi Deborah.

ABISHAI [4] (Robert [3] John [2] Nathaniel [1])
born 25th, 8 mo. 1751; married (3d, 4 mo. 1772) Susanna Paddack, daughter of Stephen and Eunice. Their children were—

    i Eunice.
    ii Anna.
    iii Susanna and iv. Hepzibah. The family removed from the Island 30th, 5 mo. 1785.

---

*Cromwell was father of Major Moses J. Barnard of the Voltigeur Regiment, who was cited for conspicuous gallantry in the Mexican War at the battle of Chapultepec. In his official report Gen. Pillow said "To the Voltigeur Regiment belongs the honor of having first planted its colors upon the parapet. The color bearer of the regiment having been shot down, the colors were immediately seized by the gallant and fearless Capt. Barnard who scaled the parapet and unfurled the flag under a terrible fire, from which he received two wounds." (Ex. Doc. 1st Session 30th Cong. p. 402.) In his report Col. T. P. Andrews of the Voltigeurs said "The Voltigeurs had the honor of planting the first flag, which was fairly riddled by shot, on the lower battlements, inside of the main fortifications. Capt. Barnard, after being twice smartly wounded, was the commissioned officer inside the works and planted the flag of his regiment." The citizens of his native town presented him with a sword and the Captain was awarded the brevet rank of Major.

BENJAMIN [4] (Matthew [3] John [2] Nathaniel [1])
born 1728; married (2d, 12 mo. 1748) Judith Folger, daughter of
Barzillai and Phebe; he died 28th, 8 mo. 1779; she died 17th, 9
mo. 1765. Their children were—

    i **Benjamin,** born 24th, 5 mo. 1751; died 28th, 11 mo. 1786; married (7th, 2 mo. 1771) Lydia Swain, daughter of Tristram and Phebe.
    ii **Judith,** born, 3d 3 mo. 1754.
    iii **Reuben,** born 15th, 3 mo. 1756.
    iv **Phebe,** born 27th, 5 mo. 1758; perhaps married (July 13, 1774) Daniel Killey.
    v **Elizabeth,** born 30th, 6 mo. 1760.
    vi **Obed,** born 26th, 8 mo. 1762; probably married (July 28, 1786) Susanna Hussey.

SHUBAEL [4] (Matthew [3] John [2] Nathaniel [1])
born 13th, 1 mo. 1730; married—first (2d, 1 mo. 1748-9) Susanna
Gardner, daughter of Ebenezer and Judith; second (28th, 11 mo.
1765) Ruth Myrick, widow of John and daughter of James and
Bethiah Bunker. Their children were—

By Susanna:

    i **Eunice,** born 7th, 1 mo. 1750; died 12th, 1 mo. 1779; married (1st, 1 mo. 1767) George Russell, son of John and Ruth.
    ii **Lydia,** born 5th, 11 mo. 1751; died 24th, 2 mo. 1772; married (1st, 3 mo. 1770) Abishai Swain, son of Tristram and Phebe.
    iii **Rose,** born 26th, 7 mo. 1756; died 18th, 6 mo. 1775; married (10th, 12 mo. 1772) Matthew Starbuck, son of Edward and Damaris.
    iv **Shubael,** born 15th, 7 mo. 1759; died 21st, 6 mo. 1778.
    v **Susannah,** born 20th, 12 mo. 1761; married (28th 8 mo. 1788) Latham Bunker, son of Peleg and Lydia.

By Ruth:

    vi **Mary,** born 14th, 6 mo. 1766; married (28th, 9 mo. 1786) Valentine Swain, son of David and Martha.
    vii **Anna,** born 23d, 1 mo. 1769; died 22d, 5 mo. 1795; married (31st, 7 mo. 1794) Hezekiah Barnard, son of Nathaniel and Margaret.
    viii **Sarah,** born 12th, 1 mo. 1771; died 20th, 9 mo. 1798.
    ix **James,** born 7th, 3 mo. 1774. Probably married in 1799 Hepzibah Bunker.

x Thomas, born 26th, 7 mo. 1777; died 23d, 5 mo. 1808; married (4th, 4 mo. 1799) Alice Freeborn, daughter of George and Susanna.
xi Shubael, born 19th, 10 mo. 1780.
xii Lydia, born 28th, 4 mo. 1785; removed from the Island 30th, 8 mo. 1804.

JOSEPH [4] (Matthew [3] John [2] Nathaniel [1])
born 25th, 2 mo. 1732; married (April 15, 1752) Mary Gardner. By an incomplete entry in the Friend's Records their children appear to have been—

i Eunice, who married (30th, 4 mo. 1778) Joseph Coffin, son of Peleg and Elizabeth.
ii Hannah, who married (31st, 5 mo. 1781) Gideon Gardner, son of Hezekiah and Sarah.
iii Joseph.
iv Enoch.
v Abigail, who married (31st, 5 mo. 1770) William Coleman, son of Barnabas and Rachel.

JOHN [4] (Matthew [3] John [2] Nathaniel [1])
born 1745; married (1st, 1 mo. 1767) Mary Russell, daughter of William and Mary.

MATTHEW [4] (Matthew [3] John [2] Nathaniel [1])
born 1749; married (30th, 8 mo. 1774) Elizabeth Swain, daughter of Reuben and Elizabeth.

CHRISTOPHER [4] (Peter [3] Nathaniel [2] Nathaniel [1])
born 26th, 7 mo. 1737; married (28th, 1 mo. 1762) Judith Swain, daughter of Caleb and Margaret; he was lost at sea in 1767; she removed from the Island in 1775. Their children were—

i Christopher, born 27th, 3 mo. 1765.

ii **Lydia,** born 30th, 11 mo. 1762. Married (2d, 10 mo. 1783) John Hussey, son of Stephen and Elizabeth.
iii **Anna,** born 1st, 12 mo. 1766.

NATHANIEL [4])Peter [3] Nathaniel [2] Nathaniel [1])
born 8th, 4 mo. 1741; married (6th 12 mo. 1764) Margaret Swain, daughter of Caleb and Margaret; he died 30th. 5 mo. 1718; she died 22d, 10 mo. 1811. Their children were—

    i **Hepzibah,** born 7th, 10 mo. 1765; died 27th, 9 mo. 1766.
    ii **Margaret,** born 25th, 7 mo. 1767; died 25th, 7 mo. 1768.
    iii **Hezekiah,** born 30th, 4 mo. 1769.
    iv **Abisha** and v **Christopher,** twins, born 29th, 3 mo. 1771.
    vi **Margaret,** born 27th, 6 mo. 1774.
    vii **Eunice,** born 1st, 12 mo. 1776; died 19th, 6 mo. 1777.
    viii **Samuel,** born 7th, 10 mo. 1782; died abroad 10th, 9 mo. 1805.

STEPHEN [4] (Thomas [3] Stephen [2] Nathaniel [1])
married (31st, 12 mo. 1761) Hepzibah Paddack, daughter of Paul and Anna. Their children were—

    i **Ruth,** born 16th, 12 mo. 1766.
    ii **Hepzibah,** born 30th, 11 mo. 1768.
    iii **Lucretia,** born 9th, 7 mo. 1771; died 22d, 8 mo. 1776.

BENJAMIN [4] (Timothy [3] Benjamin [2] Nathaniel [1])
born probably in 1732 or 1733; married (9th, 1 mo. 1755) Eunice Fitch, daughter of Beriah and Deborah. He removed from the Island 23d, 9 mo. 1773. Presumably his wife died prior to that time as the record says nothing about her going. Their children were—

    i **Timothy,** born probably in 1756; removed from the Island 25th, 4 mo. 1774.
    ii **Mary,** removed from the Island 29th, 1 mo. 1776.
    iii **Lydia,** removed from the Island 23d, 9 mo. 1773.

TIMOTHY [4] (Timothy [3] Benjamin [2] Nathaniel [1])
born probably in 1738; removed from the Island 1773; married
(8th, 2 mo. 1759) Love Swain, daughter of George and Love. Their
children were—

    i Uriah, probably born in 1760.
    ii Job, removed from the Island with his father 23d, 9 mo. 1773.
    iii Barzillai.
    iv Gilbert.

REUBEN [4] (Francis [3] Benjamin [2] Nathaniel [1])
born 24th, 1 mo. 1743; married (4th, 12 mo. 1767) Phebe Coleman. The entire family removed from the Island 26th, 10 mo. 1778. Their children were—

    i Elizabeth.
    ii Lucretia.
    iii Phebe.
    iv Deborah.
    v Mary.

BUNKER

Savage states* that George Bunker, the first of the name in America, resided at Ipswich. He was the son of William, a French Huguenot, who fled to England to avoid the religious persecution to which he was subjected in France. In its original the name was Bon Coeur; corrupted into Bunker doubtless through the phonetic spelling of the time. George married Jane Godfrey, probably about 1645. He died May 16, 1658, leaving five children: Elizabeth, aged twelve; William, ten; Mary, six; Ann, four; and Martha, eighteen months. The widow married Richard Swain, then of Rowley, and soon after the entire family removed to Nantucket. She died here October 31, 1662, her death being the earliest recorded in the Town Records.

Elizabeth married Thomas Look; William married (April 11, 1669) Mary, daughter of Thomas and Sarah Macy; Mary married (29th, 2 mo. 1714) Tristram Coffin; Ann married Joseph Coleman, son of Thomas; and Martha married (October 8, 1676) Stephen Hussey, son of Christopher and Theodate.

According to H. B. Worth,† William's first houselot was included in that of his step father, as he was a minor at the time of the allotment. A few years later he was allotted ten acres north of No Bottom Pond. The lot set off to him, according to Mr. Worth, was bounded on the north by the road which is the present West Chester street extended, and which was the first road established, with a westerly boundary by the land of William Worth. After his decease, which occurred June 6, 1712, the Proprietors allotted to his heirs land in lieu of land of theirs taken for a Town House. "This" Mr. Worth says, "indicates that the church, Town House and jail were * * * placed on the hill north from No Bottom Pond." At the west end of this hill was erected the first school-house mentioned in the Records. William Bunker was appointed keeper of the jail in 1686. The children of William and Mary were—

  i George, born April 22, 1671; married (October 10, 1695) Deborah Coffin, daughter of James and Mary.‡
  ii John, born July 23, 1673; married (February 13, 1725-6) Mary Coffin, daughter of James and Ruth.
  iii Jonathan, born February 25, 1675; married Elizabeth Coffin, daughter of James and Mary.
  iv Peleg, born December 15, 1676; married (January 9, 1700) Susanna Coffin, daughter of Stephen and Mary.

---

*Genealogical Dictionary.
†Nantucket Land and Land Owners, p. 63.
‡Deborah, widow of George, married (29th 6 mo. 1728) Jonathan Folger, son of John and Mary.

HISTORY OF NANTUCKET 685

    v **Jabez**, born November 7, 1678; married (November 19, 1706) Hannah Gardner, daughter of Nathaniel and Abigail.
    vi **Thomas**, born April 18, 1680; probably never married.*
    vii **Benjamin**, born May 28, 1683; married (3d, 8 mo. 1709) Deborah Paddack, of Yarmouth.

GEORGE [3] (William [2] George [1])

born April 22, 1671; married (October 10, 1695) Deborah Coffin, daughter of James and Mary. He died in 1743.† Their children were—

    i **Daniel**, born August 16, 1696; married (November 14, 1717) Piiscilla Swain, daughter of John and Experience.
    ii **John**, born December 27, 1697; married (February 13, 1725-6) Mary Coffin, daughter of James and Love.
    iii **Caleb**, born November 2, 1699; married (October 3, 1725) Priscilla Coffin.

JOHN [3] (William [2] George [1]

born July 23, 1673; married (February 13, 1725-6) Mary Coffin, daughter of James and Love. According to the Probate Records he must have died in December, 1760, intestate, leaving a widow and seven children, namely—

    i **Christopher**, married (January 3, 1765) Abigail Worth, daughter of John and Mary.
    ii **Joshua**, married (January 17, 1750) Margaret Brock.
    iii **John**.
    iv **George**, married (January 4, 1763) Phebe Barnard.
    v **Elisha**, married (December 20, 1770) Margaret Gardner.
    vi **Abigail**, married (February 19, 1750) George Coffin, son of Nathan and Lydia.
    vii **Mary**, married, possibly (January 7, 1750) Thomas Carr.

---

*According to the Probate Records the estate of Thomas was administered on by his brothers George, Peleg and Jabez, in September, 1721. It was inventoried at £802. 13s and by order of the Court was apportioned to Mary and George Bunker, children of Jonathan (deceased); Peleg and Jabez Bunker, children of Benjamin (deceased); Ann Paddack, Jane Wadson (Watson) wife of Robert; Abigail Pinkham, wife of Shubael; and Mary Coffin, wife of Tristram. This would show that he had no immediate family.

†He was for several years Judge of Probate Court.

JONATHAN [3] (William [2] George [1])
born February 25, 1675; married Elizabeth Coffin, daughter of James and Mary.* His will was probated September 13, 1721, and was executed August 16, 1719. His wife survived him. The children named in the will are—†

    i **Zacchariah**, married (September 2, 1728) Desire Gorham.
    ii **Simeon**, married (2d, 11 mo. 1734-5) Huldah Hussey.* daughter of Bachelor and Abigail.
    iii **George**, married (1st, 4 mo. 1738) Abigail Worth, daughter of Joseph and Lydia.
    iv **James**, married (30th, 3 mo. 1737) Bethiah Jenkins, daughter of Matthew and Mary.
    v **Lydia**, married (March 5, 1717) Nathan Coffin, son of James and Ruth.
    vi **Ruth**, married (November 20, 1718); Richard Coffin, son of John and Hope.
    vii **Patience**, married (14th, 8 mo. 1723) Jonathan Gardner.
    viii **Abigail**, married (9th, 9 mo. 1712) Shubael Pinkham.
    ix **Judith**, married (January 12, 1737-8) Alexander Coffin, son of Ebenezer and Eleanor.

PELEG [3] (William [2] George [1])
born December 15, 1676; died June 1, 1730; married (January 9, 1700) Susanna Coffin, daughter of Stephen and Mary. Their children were—

    i **Judith**, born September 21, 1701; married (January 1, 1718-9) Bartlett Coffin, son of Peter and Christian.
    ii **Priscilla**, born December 8, 1703; married (April 3, 1721) Joshua Coffin, son of James and Ruth.
    iii **Dinah**, born January 25, 1705; married (April 3, 1721) Elisha Coffin, son of James and Ruth; he died in 1722.
    iv **Mary**, born ————; married (2d, 1 mo, 1731-2) Timothy Barnard, son of Benjamin and Judith.
    v **Jonathan**, born ————; married (6th, 11mo. 1742) Judith Macy, daughter of Richard and Deborah.

---

*Simeon died at sea in 1751 and his widow married (6th 12mo. 1753). Benjamin Barney, son of Jonathan and Sarah.
†The widow of Jonathan married for her second husband (30th 11 mo. 1723-4) Thomas Clark.

JABEZ [3] (William [2] George [1])
born November 7, 1678; married (November 19, 1706) Hannah Gardner, daughter of Nathaniel and Abigail. He died July 6, 1750; she died March 25, 1773. Their children were—

    i Naomi, born 4th, 11 mo. 1709; died 31st, 5 mo. 1792; married (9th, 9 mo. 1726) Eliphalet Paddack, son of Joseph and Sarah.
    ii Samuel, born 5th, 9 mo. 1711; died 3d, 9 mo. 1786; married (7th, 11 mo. 1731-2) Priscilla Coleman, daughter of John and Priscilla.
    iii Paul,* born 16th, 8 mo. 1713; died 20th, 8 mo. 1795; married (3d, 1 mo. 1736-7) Hannah Gardner, daughter of Samuel and Patience.
    iv Silas,* born 16th, 8 mo. 1713; died 18th, 11 mo. 1714.
    v Lydia, born 1717; lived about 18 months.
    vi Abner, born 30th, 2 mo. 1719; died 17th, 11 mo. 1780.
    vii Benjamin, born 14th, 4 mo. 1721; removed from the Island 29th, 9 mo. 1788; married (9th, 12 mo. 1743-4) Abigail Bunker, widow of George and daughter of Joseph and Lydia Worth.
    viii Hannah, born 1st, 1 mo. 1722-3; died 25th, 9 mo. 1806; married (3d, 4 mo. 1766) Benjamin Coffin. son of James and Ruth.
    ix Peter, born 8th, 1 mo. 1724-5; lost at sea 1755; married (9th, 1st mo. 1748-9) Judith Gardner, daughter of Jethro and Kezia.
    x Peleg, born 19th, 4 mo. 1727; removed from the Island 27th, 11 mo. 1786; married (8th, 12 mo. 1749) Lydia Worth, daughter of Joseph and Lydia.

BENJAMIN [3] (William [2] George [1])
born May 28, 1683; married (3d 8 mo. 1709) Deborah Paddack of Yarmouth. He died 16th 5 mo. 1721, of small pox. Their children were—

    i Reuben, born 4th 4mo. 1710.
    ii Obed, born 14th, 2 mo. 1714; married (October 19, 1738) Mary Duanna.
    iii David, born 19th 1 mo. 1716; married (14th 6 mo. 1740) Elizabeth Gorham, daughter of Stephen and Elizabeth.
    iv Nathaniel, born 9th. 9 mo. 1718.

*Twins.

  v **Thomas,** born 1st 5 mo. 1719; married (23d 12 mo. 1741) Anna Swain, daughter of Richard and Elizabeth.*

DANIEL [4] (George, [3] William, [2] George [1])
born August 16. 1696; married (November 14, 1717) Priscilla Swain, daughter of John and Experience. Their children were—

  i **Ruth,** born July 23, 1721; married (April 27. 1738) Uriah Gardner, son of Ebenezer and Eunice.
  ii **Joseph,** born August 25, 1727; married (February 4, 1747) Phebe Pinkham, daughter of Shubael and Abigail.
  iii **Deborah,** born February 20, 1729-30; married (March 6, 1746) Ichabod Clark.
  iv **Silvanus,** born February 24, 1732-3; married (October 17, 1754) Hepzibah Swain.

The settlement of his estate in February, 1747, mentions a son [V] Tristram, under 14 years of age.

CALEB [4] (George, [3] William, [2] George [1])
born November 2, 1699; married (October 3, 1725) Priscilla Coffin. In his will, probated July 4. 1777, and executed March 20 of the same year, he names his wife, Priscilla; his daughter [i] **Anna** (Brock) deceased; his son [ii] William (deceased) born July 14, 1726; and the children of Anna born August 18, 1728, and William. The Town Records give also a son [iii] Caleb born March 31, 1736 who appears to have married (December 18, 1755) Eunice Gardner. It would appear by the record that William married (February 24 1745-6) Mary Russell. Anna was married March 13, 1746.

ZACHARIAH [4] (Jonathan, William, George [1])
born———; married (September 2. 1728) Desire Gorham. Their children were—

---

 *Richard, son of Thomas and Anna, married (15th. 12mo. 1768) Eunice Mitchell daughter of Richard and Mary.

HISTORY OF NANTUCKET 689

 i **Jonathan,** born April 2, 1729.
 ii **Shubael,** born August 9. 1731; married (7th 12 mo. 1750) Lydia Paddack, daughter of Daniel and Susanna.
 iii **James,** born August 21, 1733.
 iv **Simeon,** born March 21, 1736.
 v **Elizabeth,** born September 18, 1738; married (July 25 1756) Robert Rider.
 vi **Desire,** born August 16, 1741; married (May 1, 1766) John Benthall.
 vii **Zachariah,** born March 11. 1744; married (1st 1 mo. 1767) Judith Folger, daughter of William and Ruth.
 viii **Francis,** born August 29, 1746.
 ix **Andrew,** born August 30, 1752.

SIMEON, [4] (Jonathan, [3] William, [2] George [1]) married (2d. 11 mo. 1734-5), Huldah Hussey, daughter of Bachelor and Abigail. Their children were—

 i **Bachelor,** born 10th 3 mo. 1738; married (February 11, 1759) Bethiah Hussey, daughter of John and Jedidah.
 ii **Simeon,** born 15th, 7 mo. 1747; married—first (January 27 1766) Mary Swain daughter of ——————— second (January 1, 1769) Lydia Hussey.

Simeon senior died at sea in 1751; his widow subsequently married Benjamin Barney, son of Jonathan and Sarah and died 3d 4 mo. 1798. Benjamin Coffin "schoolmaster" was appointed guardian for Simeon, and Bachelor, who was old enough to choose for himself, selected his uncle Richard Coffin. The inventory would indicate that Simeon was a tradesman.

GEORGE [4] (Jonathan, [3] William, [2] George [1]) married (1st 4 mo. 1738) Abigail Worth, daughter of Joseph and Lydia. They appear to have had but one child, a daughter [1]. **Lydia** born probably in 1739, married (5th 1 mo. 1757) Shubael Folger, son of Shubael and Jerusha.

JAMES [4] (Jonathan [3] William [2] George [1]) married (30th 3 mo. 1737) Bethiah Jenkins, daughter of Matthew and Mary. Their children were—

  i **Matthew**, born 29th 5 mo, 1738; married (5th 1 mo. 1764) Bethiah Coffin, daughter of Zaccheus and Mary.
 ii **Ruth**, born 27th. 8 mo. 1740; married (February 12 1761), John Myrick.
 iii **Nathaniel**, born 5th 9 mo. 1742; died abroad; married (probably) (June 24, 1766) Anna Swain.
 iv **William**, born 16th 1 mo. 1745.
 v **Elisha**, born 7th 11 mo. 1747; died abroad; probably married (December 20, 1770) Margaret Gardner.

JONATHAN [4] (Peleg, [3] William [2] George [1]) born ———; married (6th. 11 mo. 1742) Judith Macy, daughter of Richard and Deborah; he died 20th 10 mo. 1778. Their children were—

 i **Peleg**, born probably 1743; married (7th. 1mo. 1768) Kezia Bunker, daughter of Peter and Judith.
 ii **Susannah**, removed from the Island 14th 3 mo. 1776; married (8th 12 mo 1763) Paul Coffin, son of Zephaniah and Abigail.
 iii **Deborah**, removed from the Island 28th 12 mo. 1778; married (8th. 12 mo. 1763) Silas Bunker, son of Samuel and Priscilla.
 iv **William**, removed from the Island 25th 4 mo. 1774; married (9th 12 mo. 1773) Miriam Bunker, daughter of Abishai and Dinah.
 v **Hepzibah**, removed from the Island 30th. 11 mo. 1798; married (7th. 1 mo. 1768) Zephaniah Coffin, son of Zephaniah and Abigail.
 vi **Judith**, removed from the Island 26th 10 mo. 1778.
 vii **Lydia**, removed from the Island 29th 6 mo. 1779.
 viii **Jonathan**, removed from the Island 31st 5 mo 1779.

SAMUEL [4] (Jabez, [3] William, [2] George [1]) born 5th 9 mo. 1711; married (17th. 11 mo. 1731-2) Priscilla Coleman, daughter of John and Priscilla; died 3d 9 mo. 1786. She died 11th. 7 mo 1797. Their children were——

 i **Phebe**, born 1st 7 mo. 1732; married (1st 12 mo. 1749) William Clasby, son of William and Abial; died 28th 8 mo. 1750.

ii **Abishai,** born 21st 5 mo., 1734; married first (29th 10 mo. 1753) Dinah Coffin, daughter of Zephaniah and Miriam; second (8th 12 mo 1757) Hephzibah Allen, daughter of Daniel and Elizabeth; died 17th 6 mo. 1761.
iii **Mary,** born 10th 7 mo 1736; married (30th. 11 mo. 1751-2 Stephen Coffin, son of Zephaniah and Miriam.
iv **Abigail,** born 22d, 8 mo. 1738; married (7th 2 mo 1760) Francis Coleman, son of Solomon and Deliverance; died 27th 6 mo. 1812.
v **Charles,** born 9th 5 mo. 1740; married (11th 12 mo 1760) Mary Coffin, daughter of Zephaniah and Abigail; died 27th 5 mo. 1813.
vi **Silas,** born 28th 9 mo. 1742; married (8th 12 mo. 1763) Deborah Bunker, daughter of Jonathan and Judith; removed from the Island 28th 12 mo. 1778.
vii **Priscilla,** born 14th. 4 mo. 1745; married (3d 12mo 1761) Abraham Macy, son of Abraham and Anna; removed from the Island 25th 4 mo. 1774.
viii **Elihu,** born 18th, 3 mo. 1748; married (1st 12 mo. 1768) Phebe Starbuck, daughter of Joseph and Ruth; removed from the Island 7th 5 mo. 1772.
ix **Elizabeth,** born 4th 6 mo. 1750; married (31st. 12 mo. 1767) Reuben Macy, son of Abraham and Anna; died 22d. 10 mo. 1770.
x **Rachel,** born 4th 10 mo. 1770: married (28th 12 mo. 1769) Tristram Swain, son of Tristram and Phebe; died 16th. 12 mo. 1831.
xi **Barnabas,** born 25th 9 mo. 1754; married (2d. 1 mo. 1777) Lydia Gardner, daughter of Peter and Deborah.

PAUL [4] (Jabez [3] William [2] George [1])
born 16th 8 mo. 1713; married (3d. 1 mo 1736-7) Hannah Gardner, daughter of Samuel and Patience; he died 20th 8 mo 1795; she died 15th. 11 mo 1788. Their children were—

i **Hezekiah,** born 23d 10 mo. 1737;
ii **Eunice,** born 5th 11 mo. 1743; died 23d 2 mo 1825; married (5th 4 mo. 1798) Jonathan Gorham Fitch, son of Beriah and Deborah.
iii **Seth,** born 28th 8 mo. 1745; died 1st 9 mo. 1800.
iv **Phebe,** born 4th 4 mo. 1753; died 8th 3 mo. 1815; married probably (December 27, 1772) Reuben Hussey.

v Hepzibah, born 1st 7 mo. 1757; removed from the Island 29th. 10 mo. 1792; married (28th 10 mo 1779) Joseph Harris, son of David and Martha.
vi Dinah, born 13th 10 mo. 1759; died 10th 7 mo. 1796; married (30th 5 mo. 1782) Silvanus Macy son of Daniel and Abigail.

BENJAMIN [4] (Jabez [3] William [2] George [1])
born 14th. 4 mo. 1721; married (9th 12 mo 1743-4) Abigail Bunker, widow of George and daughter of Joseph and Lydia Worth. He removed from the Island 29th 9 mo 1788. The record shows they had—

i Anna, who removed from the Island 19th 4 mo. 1776.
ii Barzillai, who married (2d 1 mo. 1777) Lydia Pinkham, daughter of Daniel and Eunice. He removed from the Island 26th 10 mo 1778.
iii Timothy, who removed from the Island 16th 8 mo 1798.
iv Elijah.

PETER [4] (Jabez [3] William [2] George [1])
born 8th. 1 mo. 1724-5; married (9th 1 mo. 1748-9) Judith Gardner, daughter of Jethro and Kezia; he was lost at see 1755. She died 30th 8 mo 1758. Their children were—

i Kezia, who died 29th 9 mo. 1770; married (7th. 1 mo. 1768) Peleg Bunker, son of Jonathan and Judith.
ii Peter, who died in 1777.

PELEG [4] (Jabez [3] William [2] George [1])
born 19th 4 mo. 1727; married (8th 12 mo. 1749) Lydia Worth, daughter of Joseph and Lydia. She died 17th 7 mo 1776 and he removed from the Island 27th 11 mo 1786. Their children were—

i Miriam, born 19th. 7 mo. 1752;
ii Latham, born 22d 10 mo. 1755; married (28th 8 mo. 1788) Susanna Barnard, daughter of Shubael and Susanna.

iii **Abial**, born 4th. 3 mo. 1760; married (1st 1 mo. 1778) Abishai Pinkham, son of Benjamin and Hephzibah; removed from the Island 26th. 10 mo. 1778.
iv **Anna**, born 27th 6 mo. 1762; removed from the Island 29th. 4 mo. 1776.
v **Paul**, born 12th. 11 mo. 1764; removed from the Island 28th. 1 mo. 1782.
vi **Rufus**, born 6th 2 mo 1766; removed from the Island 31st 1 mo. 1785.
vii **Way**, born 30th 4 mo 1768; removed from the Island, 27th 11 mo. 1786.
viii **Prince**, born 1st 8 mo. 1770; removed from the Island 27th. 11 mo. 1786.
ix **Lydia**, born 18th 7 mo. 1773; removed from the Island 27th, 11 mo. 1786.

OBED [4] (Benjamin [3] William [2] George [1]) born 14th. 2 mo. 1716; married (October 19. 1738) Mary Duanna. Their children were—

i. **Uriah**, born December 2, 1738; married (November 25, 1759) Susanna Giles.
ii **Obed**, born April 26, 1741; married (December 16, 1762) Hephzibah Giles.
iii **Job**, born June 8, 1745; married (November 25, 1767) Hephzibah Hussey.

DAVID [4] (Benjamin [3] William [2] George [1]) born 19th 1 mo. 1716; married (14th 6 mo. 1740) Elizabeth Gorham, daughter of Stephen and Elizabeth. He was lost at sea in 1755;* she died 23d. 6 mo. 1772. Their children were—

i **Lois**, born 10th 8 mo. 1741; married, first—(February 19, 1761) William Long; second-Benjamin Barney, son of Benjamin and Lydia.
ii **Eunice**, born 21st 7 mo 1744; removed from the Island 26th. 9 mo. 1785; married (April 2, 1769) Micajah Swain, son of Peleg and Mary.

---

*His widow married again (6th. 10mo. 1768) **William Russell**, son of Daniel and Deborah.

iii **David**, born 16th. 7 mo. 1748; removed from the Island 26th. 3 mo. 1781; probably married (October 11, 1770) Miriam Gardner.
iv **Solomon**, born 9 mo. 1750; removed from the Island 30th 11 mo. 1778; probably married (October 27. 1771) Abigail Coffin.
v **Alexander**, born 12 mo 1751;
vi **Elizabeth**, born 28th 6 mo. 1754; perhaps married (October 29. 1772) Benjamin Cartwright.

THOMAS [4] (Benjamin [3] William [2] George [1]) born 1st, 5 mo. 1719; married (23d, 12 mo. 1741) Anna Swain, daughter of Richard and Elizabeth. He died 13th, 5 mo. 1785; she died 3d, 11 mo. 1780. Their children were—

i **Richard**, born 27th, 11 mo. 1746; died 12th, 2 mo. 1788; married (15th, 12 mo. 1768) Eunice Mitchell, daughter of Richard and Mary.
ii **Bachelor**, appears to have been twice married; first, (February 11, 1759) to Bethiah Hussey;* second, (August 22, 1773) to Abigail Hussey.
iii **Thomas**, died young.
iv **Deborah**, born probably 1752; perhaps married (January 19, 1769) Eliphalet Smith.
v **Eliab**, born probably 1754.
vi **Isaiah**, born 15th, 7 mo. 1756.
vii **David**.
viii **Elizabeth**.
ix **Thomas**, married (July 29, 1788) Polly Chadwick.
x **Lawton**, born 24th, 12 mo. 1770.

JOSEPH [5] (Daniel [4] George [3] William [2] George [1]) born August 25, 1727; married (4th, 12 mo. 1747) Phebe Pinkham, daughter of Shubael and Abigail. He died 28th, 12 mo. 1792; she died 26th, 11 mo. 1804. Their children were—

i **Priscilla**, born 21st, 9 mo. 1749; probably married (November 8, 1772) Edward Lloyd Whittemore.

---

*Huldah, daughter of Bachelor and Bethiah and Daniel Coffin, son of Barnabas and Abigail, were married (2d. 9mo. 1784).

 ii **Ebenezer**, born 18th, 8 mo. 1751; probably married (September 7, 1775) Mary Maxey.
 iii **Daniel**, born 19th, 8 mo. 1753; killed by a whale 30th, 7 mo. 1770.
 iv **Ruth**, born 11th, 5 mo. 1755; probably married (March 5, 1775) Isaiah Macy Maxey.
 v **Abigail**, born 11th, 2 mo. 1757; died 3d, 5 mo. 1822.

SHUBAEL [5] (Zachariah [4] Jonathan [3] William [2] George[1])
born August 9, 1731; married (7th, 12 mo. 1750) Lydia Paddack, daughter of Daniel and Susanna. Their children were—

 i **Shubael**, born 6th, 2 mo. 1754; removed from the Island 26th, 9 mo. 1785.
 ii **Puella**, born 7th, 5 mo. 1756; removed from the Island 30th, 8 mo. 1779.
 iii **Francis**, born 31st, 7 mo. 1758; removed from the Island 28th, 9 mo. 1778.
 iv **Gilbert**, born 17th, 11 mo. 1762.
 v **Naomi**, born 17th, 6 mo. 1766.
 vi **Nathan**, born 8th, 11 mo. 1768.
 vii **Abiel**, born 29th, 9 mo. 1771.

Shubael, the father removed from the Island 27th, 3 mo. 1780, taking with him Gilbert, Naomi, Nathan and Abiel.

ABISHAI [5] (Samuel [4] Jabez [3] William [2] George [1]) born 21st, 5 mo. 1704; married—first (29th, 10 mo. 1753) Dinah Coffin, daughter of Zephaniah and Miriam; second, (8th, 12 mo. 1757) Hephzibah Allen, daughter of Daniel and Elizabeth. He died 17th, 6 mo. 1761; Dinah died 25th, 10 mo. 1756. Their children were—

By Dinah—

 i **Abishai**, born 4th, 2 mo. 1754; died 10th, 1 mo. 1836. Married (5th, 1 mo. 1775) Meriab Swain, daughter of David and Martha.
 ii **Miriam**, born 12th, 12 mo. 1755; removed from the Island 25th, 4 mo. 1774.

By Hephzibah—

iii **Thaddeus**, born 24th, 6 mo. 1758; removed from the Island 29th, 4 mo. 1776.

CHARLES [5] (Samuel [4] Jabez [3] William [2] George [1]) born 9th, 5 mo. 1740; married (11th, 12 mo. 1760) Mary Coffin, daughter of Zephaniah and Abigail; he died 25th, 5 mo. 1813; she died 6th, 2 mo. 1819. Their children were—

    i **Zephaniah**, born 1761.
   ii **Phebe**, born 1763.
  iii **Dinah**, born 1765.
  iv **Elizabeth**, born 1767.
   v **Rachel**, born 1770.
  vi **Charles** and vii **Mary**, (twins), born 1772.
 viii **Merab**, born 1775.
  ix **Barnabas**, born 1778.
   x **Thaddeus**, born 1780.

SILAS [5] (Samuel [4] Jabez [3] William [2] George [1]) born 28th, 9 mo. 1742; married (8th, 12 mo. 1763) Deborah Bunker, daughter of Jonathan and Judith; removed from the Island 28th, 12 mo. 1778. Their children were—

   i **Priscilla**.
  ii **Hepzibah**.
 iii **Bethuel**.
 iv **Elihu**.
  v **Phebe**.
 vi **Abraham**.

THE COFFIN FAMILY

Several theories are advanced regarding the origin of the family surname Coffin, or Coffyn as was the earlier spelling. Allen Coffin, Esq., says "Coffin is a word of Hebrew origin, signifying a small basket. Whether the Israelitish hosts were sufficiently enlightened to be in the enjoyment of baskets before the Egyptians, or whether the chosen people of God were especially favored with a knowledge of basketmaking while the rest of the world plodded on with less commodious means of transit, are matters which cannot at this remote period of time be satisfactorily answered.*

Further on Mr. Coffin writes—"From Arthur's 'Derivation of Family Names,' we find that Coffin is in Welsh Cyffin, which signifies a boundary, a limit, or a hill; Cefyn a ridge of a hill. This authority also says the name has its origin from Co, high, exalted, and fin, a head, extremity, boundary, but the family surname is probably not indebted to either of these last-named derivations. It is believed by many that, some time before the Norman Conquest of England by William, which took place in 1066, the family of Coffin lived in Normandy, a duchy of France, which the Norsemen had made peculiarly their own by invasion and conquest.†

Still further on Mr. Coffin writes—"Bardsley in his "English Surnames," says "It is to some dealer in earthenware we owe the name of 'Pots,' some worker in metals our "Hammers' some carpenter our 'Coffins,' once synonymous with 'Coffer.' "‡

Regarding the name, Lower, in Patronymica Britannica, says—

"This family possessed Alwington Manor, Co Devon, temp William Conqueror and they still (1860) reside at Portledge in that manor. Colvin or Colvinus held lands in chief (probably the same) under Edward the Confessor." There are some of the opinions—take your choice.

In "Nantucket Land and Land Owners," Mr. Worth says—"Tristram Coffin's house lot was a tract of the usual dimensions, bounded on the north by Cappaum Harbor. He called this region Northam or Cappamet. The spot where his house was placed is marked by a stone monument."**

TRISTRAM COFFIN

If any one man may be considered the patriarch of Nantucket, to whom more than to any other person, the descendants of the old Nantucket families may trace a common origin, that man is Tristram Coffin.

---

*Life of Tristram Coffyn, p. 3.
†Ibid, pp. 3-4.
‡Ibid, p. 5
**Ibid, p. 64.

Allen Coffin Esq. in his "Life of Tristram Coffyn"* traces the family origin in England back to the days of Norman Conquest, the ancient seat of the name in England, now called Portledge, in the Parish of Ilwington, near Bideford, County of Devon, having been granted to Sir Richard Coffyn, Knight, for valuable services rendered to William the Conqueror. Peter Coffyn, the father of Tristram was doubtless born about 1580 and died in 1627 or 1628. He married Joan Thember (or Thumber) and had two sons and four daughters. Tristram was the elder son; his brother, John, died in Plymouth Fort, England, after having been mortally wounded.†

Tristram was born at Brixton, in 1605, and married Dionis Stevens, daughter of Robert Stevens Esq. of Brixton, about 1630. They came to America about twelve years later. Their first settlement was at Salisbury and they subsequently removed to Haverhill. His name appears as a witness to an Indian deed in Pentucket (Haverhill) in November 1642. He removed to Newbury in 1648-9 and thence to Salisbury in 1654-5. In 1644, he was licensed to keep an ordinary, sell wine and keep a ferry on the Newbury side of Carr's Island. In 1653, his wife was presented to the General Court, charged with selling beer at three pence per quart, but as she proved by witnesses that she made it much stronger and gave quid pro quo, she was discharged.‡

Tristram returned to Salisbury and there made his plans to be one of the purchasers of Nantucket Island. He died in October 1681.**

The children of Tristram and Dionis†† were:

    i **Peter,** born in England in 1631; married Abigail Starbuck, daughter of Edward and Katharine. Had a brief residence on Nantucket.

   ii **Tristram,** born in England in 1632. Did not remove to Nantucket. Married widow of Henry Somerby.

  iii **Elizabeth,** born in England; married Capt. Stephen Greenleaf, son of Edmund and Sarah. Did not remove to Nantucket.

---

*P. 7. Ib. p. 18. The original Tristram always spelled his name Coffyn.

†Life of Tristram Coffyn, p. 20.

‡The law required four bushels of malt to the hogshead at a price not to exceed two-pence per ale quart. She proved that she used six bushels.

**Mr. Worth says (Lands and Land Owners, p. 64) "Tristram Coffin's house lot was of the usual dimensions, bounded on the north by Cappaum Harbor. He called this region Northam or Cappaumet. The spot where his house was placed is marked by a stone monument."

††Allen Coffin says in the Coffyn Family, page 24, concerning Dionis,—"It is quite remarkable that, while the name of Tristram has been perpetuated through all the generations, and in genealogical researches becomes a source of confusion it occurs so often, the name of Dionis is repeated but once in all the generations down to the present time.

iv James, born in England August 12, 1640; married (December 3, 1663) Mary Severance, daughter of John and Abigail.
v John, born in England; died in infancy.
vi Deborah, born in Haverhill, November 15, 1642, died December 8, of the same year.
vii Mary, born in Haverhill, February, 20, 1645; married (probably in 1662) Nathaniel Starbuck, son of Edward and Katharine.
viii John, born in Haverhill, October 30, 1647; married Deborah Austin, daughter of Joseph and Sarah.
ix Stephen, born in Newbury, May 11, 1652; married Mary Bunker, daughter of George, senior.

PETER [2] (Tristram [1])

Peter's residence on Nantucket began about the time of King Philip's War. He married Abigail Starbuck, daughter of Edward and Katharine. He is reputed to have been the wealthiest of the First Purchasers. He was chosen a magistrate at Nantucket and occupied an important position in the Town affairs, much to the disturbance of John Gardner, Peter Folger and their sympathizers. In Dover he was made a Freeman in 1666; in 1675 he was commissioned a Lieutenant in service in King Philip's War; he was a Representative in the General Court in 1672-73 and '79. He moved to Exeter in 1690, was a Justice and later Chief·Justice of the Supreme Court of New Hampshire and an owner of large mill property.* He died at Exeter, March 21, 1715.

The children of Peter and Abigail were:

i Abigail, born October 20, 1657; married (December 16, 1673) Daniel Davidson, of Ipswich, and Newbury.
ii Peter Jr. born August 20, 1660; married (August 15, 1682) Elizabeth Starbuck, daughter of Nathaniel and Mary.
iii Jethro, born September 16, 1663; married (   ) Mary Gardner, daughter of John and Priscilla.

---

*Allen Coffin says, p. 53, the lumber for his son Jethro's house (known as "the oldest house on Nantucket,") was the product of one of his mills. There is a tradition that Peter was to build the house on land which John Gardner, the bride's father was to furnish. When the time came for the marriage ceremony Peter inquired for a deed of the land He was informed that that little formality had been neglected. He said the ceremony could not be performed until that was done. Gardner was obliged to hustle and execute, sign and transfer the deed to the intended couple after which the marriage was performed. The building is now owned by the Nantucket Historical Association the recent owner Tristram Coffin Esq. of New York and Poughkeepsie, offering excellent terms and contributing liberally to the purchase price.

HISTORY OF NANTUCKET

    iv **Tristram,** born January 18, 1665; married Deborah Colcord.
    v **Robert,** born in 1667, married Joanna Dyer of Exeter. No children.
    vi **Edward,** born February 20, 1669; married Anna Gardner, daughter of John and Priscilla.
    vii **Judith,** born February 4, 1672.
    viii **Parnell,** died in infancy.
    ix **Elizabeth,** born January 27, 1680; married (June 5, 1698) Col. John Gilman, of Exeter, N. H.
    x **Eliphalet.** Never married.

JAMES [2] (Tristram [1])

born in England August 12, 1640; married (December 3, 1663) Mary Severance, daughter of John and Abigail of Salisbury. He died in Nantucket July 28, 1720.

Their children were—

    i **Mary,** born in 1665;* married—first, Richard Pinkham of Portsmouth, who died in Nantucket; and second, James Gardner, son of Richard and Sarah.
    ii **James,** born probably in Dover, N. H.; married, first, Love Gardner, daughter of Richard and Sarah, and second, (19th, 3 mo. 1692) Ruth Gardner, daughter of John and Priscilla.
    iii **Nathaniel,** born in Dover, 1691; married (August 17, 1692) Demaris Gayer, daughter of William.
    iv **John,** born in Nantucket; married Hope Gardner, daughter of Richard and Sarah.
    v **Dinah,** born in Nantucket; married (November 20, 1690) Nathaniel Starbuck Jr., son of Nathaniel and Mary.
    vi **Deborah,** born in Nantucket; married (October 10, 1695) George Bunker, son of William and Mary; died October 8, 1767.
    vii **Ebenezer,** born in Nantucket, March 30, 1678; married (December 12, 1700) Eleanor Barnard, daughter of Nathaniel and Mary.
    viii **Joseph,** born in Nantucket, February 4, 1679; married Bethiah Macy, daughter of John and Deborah.

---

*Sylvanus J. Macy in his Genealogy says some of the older children were probably born in Dover, where the father was made a freeman May 31, 1671. Allen Coffin says James filled several important offices in Nantucket, such as Judge of Probate. From him descended the loyalists Gen. John Coffin and Admiral Sir Isaac Coffin, also that eminent woman Lucretia (Coffin) Mott. (Page 55).

ix Elizabeth, born in Nantucket; married—first, Jonathan Bunker, son of William and Mary; second, Thomas Clark; died in Nantucket, March 30, 1769.

x Benjamin, born in Nantucket, August 28, 1683; lost overboard between Martha's Vineyard and Nantucket.

xi Ruth, born in Nantucket; married Joseph Gardner, son of Richard and Mary, died in Nantucket, May 28, 1748.

xii Abigail, born in Nantucket; married Nathaniel Gardner, son of Richard and Sarah; died in Nantucket, March 15, 1709.*

xiii Experience, born in Nantucket; died young.

xiv Jonathan, born in Nantucket, August 28, 1692; married (24th, 11 mo. 1711) Hephzibah Harker, daughter of Ebenezer.

JOHN [2] (Tristram [1])

born in Haverhill, October 30, 1647; married Deborah Austin, daughter of Joseph and Sarah.

John removed to Edgartown, soon after the death of his father, and from him the Martha's Vineyard Coffins descend. There he was commissioned Lieutenant of Militia. His wife died 4th, 2 mo. 1718. Their children, all of whom were born on Nantucket were—

i Lydia, born June 1, 1669; married—first, John Logan; second, John Draper; third, Thomas Phaxter of Hingham.

ii Peter, born August 5, 1671; married—first, Christian Condy; second, Hope Gardner, daughter of Joseph and Bethiah.

iii John Jr., born February 10, 1673.

iv Love, born April 23, 1676; never married.

v Enoch, born 1678; married Beulah Eddy about 1700; died in Edgartown.

vi Samuel, born ———; married (1705) Miriam Gardner, daughter of Richard and Mary.

vii Hannah, born ———; married Benjamin Gardner, son of Richard Jr. and Mary; died January 28, 1768.

viii Tristram, born ———; married (1714) Mary Bunker, daughter of William.

ix Deborah, born ———; married (June 18, 1708) Thomas Macy, son of John and Deborah; died September 23, 1760.

---

*Allen Coffin says, page 56, her interment was the first in Gardner's burial ground.

x **Elizabeth**, born ————; never married.
xi **Benjamin**, born 8 mo. 23d, 1683.

STEPHEN [2] (Tristram [1])

Stephen was about eight years old when his parents removed to Nantucket. He died in Nantucket November 14, 1734. Allen Coffin says.* "For him, to a considerable extent, Tristram reversed the English law of leaving to the oldest son his lands and estates and gave them to his youngest son. Stephen appears to have remained upon his father's estate, and succeeded to the management of the farm and general business cares, and by agreement was to be helpful to his father and mother in their age." He married (probably 1668) Mary Bunker, daughter of George and Jane. The children of Stephen and Mary were all born on Nantucket, and were—

    i **Daniel**, born ————; lost at sea 4 mo. 1724.
   ii **Dionis**, born September 21, 1671; married (   ) Jacob Norton.
  iii **Peter**, born November 14, 1673; married in Boston.
  iv **Stephen Jr.**, born February 20, 1675; married (21st, 9 mo. 1693) Experience Look.
   v **Judith**, born ————; married first, Peter Folger, son of Eleazer; second Nathaniel Barnard, son of Nathaniel; third, (31st, 6 mo. 1722) Stephen Wilcox. Died at Nantucket December 2, 1760.
  vi **Susanna**, born ————; married (January 9, 1700) Peleg Bunker, son of William and Mary; died June 11, 1740.
 vii **Mehitable**, born ————; married Armstrong Smith, son of George and Jane.
viii **Anna**, born ————; married Solomon Gardner, son of Richard 2d and Mary; died April 22, 1749.
  ix **Hephzibah**, born ————; married Samuel Gardner, son of James and Mary.
   x **Paul**, born April 15, 1695; married Mary Allen, daughter of Edward; lost at sea April, 1729.

PETER [3] (Peter [2] Tristram [1])

born August 20, 1660; married (August 15, 1682) Elizabeth Star-

*P. 58. Mr. Coffin's monograph contains much of interest regarding the Coffin family which could not be included in a general history.

buck, daughter of Nathaniel and Mary. He died in Nantucket in 1699; Their children were—
    i **Abigail,** born July 9, 1683; married at Newbury (1701) Jedidiah Fitch.
    ii **Tristram,** born April 26, 1685; died December 13, 1730; married Hannah Brown, daughter of John and Rachel. No children.
    iii **Nathaniel,** born March 26, 1687.
    iv **Samuel,** born February 26, 1689.
    v **Barnabas,** born February 11, 1690.
    vi **Eunice,** born September 23, 1693; married (29th, 10 mo. 1709) Ebenezer Gardner, son of Nathaniel and Abigail.
    vii **Jemima,** born 19th, 9 mo. 1695; married 29th, 1 mo. 1727) William Swain, son of John and Experience; died March 4, 1770.

JETHRO [3] (Peter [2] Tristram [1])

born September 16, 1663; married Mary Gardner, daughter of John and Priscilla. He died in 1726; she died October 27, 1767. Their children were all born in Nantucket and were—
    i **Margaret,** born June 10, 1689; married—first, Rev. Samuel Terry, of Barrington, Mass.; second, Rev. John Wilson.
    ii **Priscilla,** born December 26, 1691; married (————) John Gardner, son of John and Susanna; died November 23, 1772.
    iii **John,** born April 12, 1694.
    iv **Josiah,** born July 28, 1698; married (October 5, 1720) Elizabeth Coffin, daughter of James and Ruth.
    v **Abigail,** born February 12, 1700; married—first, Nathaniel Woodbury; second, Eliakim, son of John and Experience Swain. She died July 7, 1782.
    vi **Robert,** born April 21, 1704; married (August 30, 1728) Susanna Coffin, daughter of Jonathan and Hepsabeth.
    vii **Peter.**
    viii **Edward.**

JAMES [3] (James [2] Tristram [1])

married—first, Love Gardner, daughter of Richard; second, (May

19, 1692) Ruth, daughter of John and Priscilla Gardner; he died on Nantucket August 2, 1741. They had one son—

    i **Benoni.**

By his second wife, Ruth, he had—

    ii **George,** born April 22, 1693; died August 1727. Probably married (November 4, 1717) Ruth Swain.
   iii **Sarah,** born March 9, 1695; married (8th, 8 mo. 1711) Jeremiah Gardner, son of John and Susannah. She died December 1, 1739.
   iv **Nathan,** born November 13, 1696; died December 4, 1768.
    v **Elisha,** born Aug 10, 1699; died 1722; married (April 3, 1721) Dinah Bunker, daughter of Peleg and Susanna.
   vi **Joshua,** born September 16, 1701; died in 1722.
  vii **Elizabeth,** born October 27, 1703; married Josiah Coffin, son of Jethro and Mary; she died in 1774.
 viii **Priscilla,** born June 3, 1708; married (18th, 9 mo. 1723) Abel Gardner, son of Nathaniel and Abigail; died April 27, 1792.
   ix **Mary,** born July 29, 1710; married (February 13, 1725-6) John Bunker, son of George and Deborah; died July 19, 1785.
    x **James,** born June 10, 1713; died April 11, 1784.
   xi **Ruth,** born June 17, 1716; married Cromwell Coffin, son of Ebenezer and Eleanor; died September 30, 1801.
  xii **Benjamin,** born November 16, 1718; married—first, (March 22, 1738-9) Rebecca Coffin, daughter of —————————————— and second, (3d, 4 mo. 1766) Hannah Bunker, daughter of Jabez and Hannah.

NATHANIEL [3] (James [2] Tristram [1]
was born in _____ 1671 and died October 29, 1721. He married (October 17, 1692) Damaris Gayer, daughter of William and Damaris, who was born October 24, 1673, and died September 6, 1764. Their children were:

    i **Dorcas,** born July 22, 1693; married John Soley of Charlestown; died May 8, 1778.
   ii **Christian,** born April 8, 1695; married—first, John Edwards; second, Timothy Williamson.

iii **Lydia,** born May 16, 1697; married (16th, 7 mo. 1714) Joseph Chase, son of Isaac and Mary.
iv **William,** born December 1, 1699; married (September 3, 1722, Anne Holmes, of Boston.*
v **Charles,** born 1st 1 mo. 1702; married Mary Barrett.
vi **Benjamin,** born 3d, 4mo. 1705; married—first (5th, 2 mo., 1726) Jedidah Hussey, daughter of Batchelor and Abigail; second, (29th, 4 mo. 1762) Deborah Macy, daughter of Thomas and Deborah.
vii **Gayer,** born May 24, 1709; married Rebecca Parker.
viii **Nathaniel,** born July , 1711; married Mary Sheffield of Newport; died June 10, 1800.
ix **Catharine,** born June 15, 1715; married (January 8, 1735-6) Bethuel Gardner, son of Joseph and Ruth.

JOHN [3] (James [2] Tristram [1])

He died July 1, 1747; she died October 12, 1750. His wife was Hope the daughter of Richard and Sarah Gardner. Their children were:—

i **Richard,** born 12th 6 mo. 1694; married (———) Ruth Bunker, daughter of John and Hope.
ii **Peleg,** born Nov. 16, 1696.
iii **Judith,** born 8th 5 mo. 1700; married (28th 2 mo 1719-20) Ebenezer Gardner son of Nathaniel and Abigail; died December 24, 1788
iv **Elias,** born 18th 6 mo. 1702; married (January 15, 1728-9) Love Coffin, daughter of Ebenezer and Eleanor.†
v **Francis,** born Nov. 13, 1706; married (November 2, 1727) Theodate Gorham.
vi **Abigail,** born October 21. 1708, died 1770; married (November 20 1728) Zaccheus Folger, son of John and Mary.

EBENEZER [3](James [2] Tristram [1])

Ebenezer the fourth son of James senior married (December

---

*Nathaniel son of William was the father of Admiral Sir Isaac Coffin of the English Navy and of General John Coffin of the English Army. The line of descent was Tristram (1) James (2) Nathaniel (3) William (4) Nathaniel (5)

†One of a multitude of cases of intermarriage—their fathers were brothers.

12. 1700) Eleanor Barnard, daughter of Nathaniel and Mary; he died October 17, 1730; she died 1769, aged 90 years.
Their children were:

    i Oliver, born 30th 8 mo. 1701.
    ii Prince, born 19th 6 mo. 1703; married Mercy Skiffe.
    iii Love, born 17th 7 mo. 1705; married Elias Coffin, son of John and Hope.
    iv Cromwell,* born 1st 9 mo. 1709; married (November 25, 1731) Ruth Coffin, daughter of James Jr and Ruth. Died at Rhode Island April 5, 1783.
    v Jane, born 14th 4 mo. 1712; married—first William Bunker, son of Peleg and Susannah; second, Jonathan Ramsdell.
    vi Alexander, born 20th 12 mo. 1713; married (January 12 1737-38) Judith Bunker, daughter of Jonathan and Elizabeth; died in the West Indies April 1741.†
    vii Valentine, born December 21, 1716.
    viii Joseph, born November 19, 1719; married (January 8, 1740-41) Judith Coffin, daughter of Elisha and Dinah.
    Kimball, born   ; died in Virginia 1782.
    ix Benjamin, born January 27 1725-6; died young.

JOSEPH [3] (James, [2] Tristram [1])

Joseph was born February 4, 1680; he married Bethiah Macy, daughter of John and Deborah, born April 8, 1681. He died 14th 7 mo. 1719; she died June 6, 1738. Their children were:—

    i Micah, born July 6, 1705; married (September 23, 1726) Dorcas Coleman daughter of ‡
    ii Eunice, born 2d 9 mo. 1707; married (November 6 1726) Andrew Newel.
    iii Zaccheus, born 11th 1 mo. 1710; married (4th. 9 mo. 1731) Mary Pinkham, daughter of Shubael and Abigail.
    iv Hezekiah, born 4th. 8 mo. 1712; died November 15, 1768; married (3d 1mo. 1742) Lydia Folger daughter of Jethro and Mary.

---

*There was a daughter, Hannah, born 20th, 7 mo. 1707; died 2d 8 mo. 1708.
†The Friends' Records name a child of Alexander and Judith—Ebenezer, who married (1st. 3 mo. 1759) Mary Cartwright, daughter of Hazadiah and Abigail.
‡Micah and Dorcas had a son Thomas who married (29th 1 mo 1756) Abigail Russell, daughter of John and Ruth.

v Jedidah, born 4th 12 mo. 1715; married—first (4th 12 mo. 1733-4) John Hussey, son of Bachelor and Abigail; second (15th 2 mo. 1759) Robert Gardner, son of Benjamin and Hannah.
vi Miriam, born 2d 12 mo. 1717; married (26th 10 mo. 1737) Joseph Chase, son of Isaac and Mary.
vii Mary, born February 9, 1720; married (February 24. 1736-7) Isaac Chase.

JONATHAN [3] (James, [2] Tristram [1])

born August 28. 1692, married (24th 11mo. 1711) Hepzabeth Harker, daughter of Ebenezer and Patience. He died February 5, 1773; she died December 30, 1773. Their children were:

i Susanna, born December 30, 1712; married (August 30 1728) Robert Coffin son of Jethro and Mary.
ii Ephraim, born February 18, 1714;
iii Henry, born March 23, 1716; married Mary Woodbury.
iv Daniel, born February 22, 1718.
v Anna, born March 5, 1720; married (July 24. 1740) Paul son of Nathaniel and Ann Paddack; died July 10. 1802.
vi Jonathan, born May 24, 1723; married (June 2 1743) Priscilla Coffin daughter of Josiah and Elizabeth.
vii James, born ————; married Jemima Swain daughter of ————;
viii Joshua, born ————; married Beulah Gardner daughter of Peter; lost at sea 1780.
ix Hepzabeth, born ————; married (December 25, 1740) Peleg Coffin son of Bartlett and Judith; died May 28, 1785.*
x Mary born ————; married (August 11. 1743) Christopher Hussey son of Silvanus and Hepzabeth.

PETER [3] (John [2] Tristram [1])

born August 5, 1671; died August 27. 1749; married first Christian Conde, and second, Hope Gardner, daughter of Joseph and Bethiah. She died March 21, 1750. Their children were:

---

*The above is from Sylvanus J. Macy's Genealogy. The Probate Records recording the will of Jonathan in March 1773 mention his "deceased daughter Hephzabeth."

i **Bartlett,** born married (January 1, 1718-9) Judith Bunker, daughter of Peleg and Susanna.
ii **Lydia,** born November 23, 1697; died May 7. 1763; married (March 14, 1717) Samuel Long son of Robert and Sarah.
iii **Abner,** born ( ); married ( ) Phebe Butler,
iv **Tristram,** born ; married (8th 1 mo. 1743-44) Jemima Barnard daughter of Ebenezer and Mary.
v **Robert,** born ; died September 29, 1791; married (17th 11 mo. 1744) Jemima Gardner daughter of Samuel and Patience.
vi **Peter,** born November 3, 1729; married (13th 10 mo. 1750) Priscilla Coleman, daughter of Elihu and Jemima; died at New Garden, N. C. 1817.
vii **Margaret,** born ; married —first (November 18, 1725) John Davis; second, Daniel Bunker, son of George and Deborah.
viii **Jerusha,** born ; married (October 11, 1731) John Matthews.
ix **Hannah,** born ; died February 1797; married (15th 10 mo. 1743) Abishai Barnard, son of Benjamin and Judith.
x **Joseph** born probably about 1740. is not mentioned in the settlement of his father's estate and probably died young.

ENOCH [3] (John [2] Tristram [1])

was born in Nantucket in 1678. He married Beulah Eddy of Marthas Vineyard and removed there, where all their children were born. Their fourth child, **Abigail,** married Grafton Gardner, son of George and Eunice of Nantucket; and **Deborah,** the seventh, married, for her first husband, Tristram Gardner son of Ebenezer and Eunice.

SAMUEL [3] (John [2] Tristram [1])

married (1705) Miriam Gardner, daughter of Richard and Mary. He died February 22. 1764;* she died September 17. 1750. Their children were:—

*The Friends' Records say 1763.

HISTORY OF NANTUCKET 709

  i **Deborah*** born June 4, 1708; died 1789; married (10th 12 mo 1729) Tristram, Starbuck son of Nathaniel Jr and Dinah.
  ii **John†** born June 4, 1708; married (4th 10 mo. 1740) Kezia Folger, daughter of Daniel and Abigail.
    i **Libni,** born   ; died February 6. 1732.
    ii **Parnel** born   ; died October 26. 1727; married Robert Coffin, son of Jethro and Mary.
    iii **Sarah,** born   ; died 11th 4 mo 1750; married first, (14th 12 mo. 1733-34) Samuel Stanton, son of John and Elizabeth; second (31st 11mo 1744) James Pinkham son of Richard and Mary.
    iv **David,** born October 25, 1718; married (4th 12 mo. 1741) Ruth Coleman, daughter of Elihu and Jemima.† He died 7th 6 mo. 1804.
    v **William,** born   1720; married (4th 10 mo. 1740) Priscilla Paddock, daughter of Nathaniel and Anna. Removed from the Island in 1773.
    vi **Miriam,** born September 29, 1723; married (13th 11mo. 1742) Richard Pinkham, son of Shubael and Abigail. Removed from the Island June 1779.
    vii **Mary,** born   1724; died October 28, 1777; married (5th 11 mo. 1743) William Barnard, son of Ebenezer and Mary.
    viii **Priscilla,** born 21st 12 mo 1730) died 2d 2 mo 1801; married (February 9, 1748) Christopher Coleman son of Solomon and Deliverance.

TRISTRAM, [3] (**John** [2] **Tristram** [1])

married (29th 2 mo. 1714) Mary Bunker, daughter of William and Mary, who died January 29, 1763. Their children were——
    i **David,** born 1718; married (29th. 8 mo 1757) Abigail Folger, daughter of Jonathan and Margaret.
    ii **Samuel,** born 1720; married (6th 7 mo 1744) Elizabeth Gardner, daughter of Jonathan and Patience.
    iii **Tristram,** born 1722; married—first (7th 1 mo. 1744-45) Hephzibah Coffin, daughter of Zephaniah and Miriam; second (29th. 9 mo. 1750), Elizabeth Starbuck, daughter of Paul and Ann.

---

*According to Macy, Deborah and John were twins. The Friends' Records also name as the oldest child a daughter, Parnel.

†David seems to have married thrice times; the second time (3d. 1 mo. 1765) to Christian Allen, daughter of Edward and Catharine Heath, widow of Ebenezer Allen, the third time (5th. 1 mo. 1775) to Elizabeth Clasby, daughter of William and Abiel.

 iv **Jonathan,** born 1725; lost at sea 1755; married 4th. 11 mo. 1747) Eunice Barnard daughter of Robert and Hephzabah.*
 v **John,** born 1727; lost at sea 1755; married (12th. 8 mo. 1749) Anna Coleman, daughter of Elihu and Jemima.†
 vi **Richard,** born 1729.
 vii **Timothy,** born 1731.
 viii **Mary,** born 1733; died November 1805; married (8th 1 mo 1756) Jonathan Barnard, son of Robert and Hepzabeth, who died November 1805.
 ix **Matthew,** born 1735; lost at sea 1755.

PETER [3] (Stephen [2] Tristram [1])

born November 14, 1763; married a Boston woman.

They had but one child:—

 i **Daniel,** born ———————— married (28th 10 mo. 1737) Elizabeth Stratton daughter of William, born 14th 11 mo. 1712.‡

STEPHEN JR [3] (Stephen [1] Tristram [1])

was born February 20. 1675; married (November 21, 1693) Experience Look, daughter of Thomas and Elizabeth. Their children were:—

 i **Shubael,** born 2d 12 mo. 1694; married (December 6, 1717) Priscilla Starbuck, daughter of Nathaniel Jr. and Dinah.
 ii **Zephaniah,** born 28th 8mo 1699; married- first (November 10, 1725) Miriam Macy, daughter of John Judith; second, (October 6 1737) Abigail Coleman, daughter of Solomon and Mary.
 iii **Mary,** born 31st 3 mo. 1705.
 iv **Hepzabeth,** born 20th 10 mo. 1708; died 1782; married (August 1 1726) Robert Barnard, son of John and Sarah.

---

*Jonathan died prior to 1759 and Eunice, his widow, married (10th. 7 mo. 1760) Samuel Ray, son of Samuel and Mary.
†John's widow married (29th. 11 mo. 1764) Jonathan Gardner son of Barnabas and Mary.
‡Daniel died and Elizabeth married for her second husband (28th 8 mo. 1750) Paul Starbuck, son of Nathaniel and Dinah.

HISTORY OF NANTUCKET   711

  v **Dinah**, born 23d 5 mo. 1713; died September 1, 1793; married 31st 10 mo. 1730) Benjamin, son of Nathaniel and Dinah Starbuck; second, (at Hudson. N. Y.) Abishai Folger, son of Nathan and Sarah Folger.

PAUL [3] (Stephen [2] Tristram [1])
born April 15, 1695, married Mary, daughter of Edward and Ann Allen. He was lost at sea April 1729. Their children were:

  i **Peter**, born February 26 1718; married (10th 2 mo 1738) Deborah Hussey, daughter of George and Elizabeth.
  ii **Mary**, born December 28 1724; married (in Rhode Island 1741) John Thurston.
  iii **Isaiah** born August 28, 1728.

JOHN [4] (Jethro [3] Peter [2] Tristram [1])
born April 12 1694; died ————; married (————) Lydia Gardner, daughter of Richard and Mary. She died April 18, 1788. Their children were:—

  i **John** married Mary Davis.
  ii **Peter** married—first (December 3, 1747) Susanna Bunker. Second Judith Peckham; died April 12, 1799.
  iii **Parnal**, died in 1770; married—first, Joseph Paddock, son of Eliphalet and Naomi: and, second, John, son of Thomas and Patience Brook.
  iv **Richard**; married (————) Abigail Gardner.
  v **Lydia**, died February 25 1825; married Benjamin Fosdick.
  vi **Jethro**, married (December 11, 1746) Hannah Peckham; died December 29, 1806.
  vii **Kezia** died March 26, 1810; married (February 28 1745) John Gardner, son of Peleg and Hepzebeth.
  viii **Deborah**, born October 25, 1731; married, possibly, (November 2, 1753) Jonathan Myrick; died March 24 1816.

JOSIAH [4] (Jethro [3] Peter [2] Tristram [1])
was born July 28, 1698 and died January 15, 1780. He married

(probably in 1720) Elizabeth Coffin, daughter of James and Ruth. She died in 1774. Their children were:—

    i **Margaret**, born July 9 1721; married—first John Whitney; second Shubael Gardner, son of Joseph and Ruth.
    ii **Priscilla**, born October 19, 1723; died March 27 1796; married Jonathan Coffin son of Jonathan and Hepzabeth.
    iii **Ruth**, born November 4, 1725; died September 10, 1797; married Samuel Calder.
    iv **Mary**, born November 4, 1725; died August 1782; married John Gardner, son of John and Priscilla.
    v **Josiah**, born August 17, 1728; married—first (December 13, 1750) Judith Coffin son of Jethro and Mary; second Mary Woodbury; died August 31, 1811.
    vi **Elizabeth**, born November 8, 1731; died May 21 1792; married Nathaniel Woodbury Jr.
    vii **Edward**, born May 15, 1734; married Parnell Calef, of Boston.
    viii **Andrew**, born August 12, 1736.
    ix **Sarah**, born October 1, 1738; married Robert Calef son of Ebenezer and Elizabeth,
    x **Ann**, born April 11, 1741; died August 12, 1786; married Joseph Clark son of Thomas.
    xi **Abigail**, born June 1, 1743; died November 11, 1803; married Elias Coffin, son of Elias and Love.
    xii **Jennet**, born February 22, 1746; died August 25, 1838; married James Coffin, son of James and Priscilla.
    xiii, xiv, xv. Three other children died young.

ROBERT [4] (Jethro [3] Peter [2] Tristram [1])
born April 21, 1704; died August 8, 1757. He married—first, Parnell Coffin, daughter of Samuel and Miriam, who died October 26, 1727, leaving no children; and second (August 30, 1728) Susanna Coffin, daughter of Jonathan and Hepzabeth, who died April 9 1795. Their children were:

    i **Joanna**, born probably in 1729; married (September 12, 1743) Benjamin Stubs; died November 24, 1760.
    ii **Susanna**, born September 7, 1731; married (January 4, 1749) James Whippey, son of James and Patience.
    iii **Catharine**, born July 11, 1733; died September 5, 1882; married (February 8, 1749-50) Paul Folger son of Nathaniel and Priscilla.

HISTORY OF NANTUCKET 713

iv **Hepzabeth,** born November 18, 1736; married Joseph Allen.
v **Margaret,** born September 26, 1738; died October 7, 1805; married Jonathan Coffin son of Nathan and Lydia.
vi **Mary,** born November 18, 1740; married Coggeshall Rathbone.
vii **Ephraim,** born January 4, 1743; died July 5, 1810.
viii **Jethro,** born December 23, 1744; died July 4, 1776.
ix **Jonathan,** born December 22, 1746; died August 26, 1823.
x **Robert,** born December 4, 1755; died 1774.

GEORGE [4] (James [3] James [2] Tristram [1])
born April 22, 1693; died August 1727; married Ruth Swain, daughter of John and Experience: She died February 8, 1775. Their children were:

i **Abigail,** born July 12 1719; died June 27 1801; married (December 27 1737) Daniel Smith.
ii **Eunice,** born August 25, 1721; died January 2, 1776; married (March 6, 1740) Francis Brown, son of George and Sarah.
iii **Priscilla,** born May 24, 1724; died September 26; 1806; married (November 22, 1744) Jonathan Ramsdell.

NATHAN [4] (James [3] James [2] Tristram [1])
born November 13, 1696; died December 4, 1768; married Lydia Bunker, daughter of Jonathan and Elizabeth, who died December 4. 1785. Their children were:—

i **Jemima,** born October 1 1721; died April 3. 1805; married (8th 10 mo. 1743) Zaccheus Gardner, son of Barnabas and Mary.
ii **Elizabeth,*** born April 9, 1724; died May 12, 1805; married (November 6, 1740) Charles Swain son of Eliakim and Elizabeth.

---

*The Friend's Records give the marriage (9th. 11 mo. 1745) of Elihu Coffin, son of Nathan and Lydia, to Rachel Gardner, daughter of James and Susanna. It would appear that he was born in 1721 or 1722.

  iii **Elisha,** born February 9, 1726; married first (19th 1 mo 1747) Rachel Gardner, daughter James & Susanna; second (10th 1 mo 1747) Mary Gardner, daughter of Nathaniel and Mary.
  iv **George,** born May 23, 1728; married (February 19, 1750) Abigail Bunker, daughter of John and Mary.
  v **Simeon,** born July 11, 1730; married Jedidah Coffin.
  vi **Jonathan,** born September 3, 1732; married Margaret Coffin, daughter of Robert and Susanna.
  vii **Nathan,** born December 23, 1734; married Eunice Bunker; died at Easton, N. Y. February 1814.
  viii **Deborah,** born February 18, 1736; died November 13, 1804; married (November 19, 1764) Abner Briggs.
  ix **Lydia,** born March 20, 1739.
  x **Charles,** born October 8, 1742.

ELISHA [4] (James [3] James [2] Tristram [1])
born August 10, 1699; died 1722; married Dinah Bunker, daughter of Peleg and Susanna, who was born January 25, 1705 and died January 14, 1778. Their children were:

  i **Judith,** born March 23, 1722; died March 12, 1812; married (January 8 1740-41) Joseph Coffin son of Ebenezer and Eleanor.

JOSHUA [4] (James [3] James [2] Tristram [1])
born September 16, 1701; died 1722; married (3d 2 mo 1721) Priscilla Bunker, daughter of Peleg and Susannah, who died October 8, 1795. They had

  i **Susanna,** born August 1, 1721.

JAMES [4] (James [3] James [2] Tristram [1])
was born June 10. 1713; died April 11. 1784; married (January 16, 1734-5) Priscilla Rawson, who died April 30, 1791. Their children were:

  i **Joshua,** born October 10, 1737; married Catherine Coffin.

HISTORY OF NANTUCKET 715

ii **Margaret,** born probably 1739; died November 13, 17-92; married Jethro Hussey, son of George and Elizabeth.

iii **Susanna,** born December 14, 1740; died January 15, 1799; married John Pinkham, son of Solomon and Eunice.

iv **Abel,** born probably 1742; died 1777 a prisoner of war.

v **James,** born March 20. 1744; married Jennet Coffin, daughter of Josiah and Elizabeth.

BENJAMIN [4] (James [3] James [2] Tristram [1]) born November 16, 1718; married—first (March 22. 1738-9) Rebecca Coffin, daughter probably of Bartlett and Judith; Second Hannah Bunker daughter of Jabez and Hannah. Their children were:—

i **Elisha,** born March 21, 1740.
ii **Rebekah,** born February 21, 1741.
iii **Benjamin,** born September 1, 1744; married (4th 2 mo 1773) Judith Macy, daughter of Francis and Judith.
iv **Lurana,** born September 1, 1746.
v **Susanna,** born August 25, 1748.
vi **Seth,** born June 25, 1753.

BENJAMIN [4] (Nathaniel [3] James [2] Tristram [1]) born 3d 4 mo. 1705; married—first (5th 2 mo. 1726) Jedidah Hussey, daughter of Bachelor and Abigail; second (29th 4 mo. 1762) Deborah Macy, daughter of Thomas and Deborah. Their children were——

By Jedidah—

i **Reuben,** born 21st. 1 mo. 1726-7; died 23d 9 mo. 1804; married (10th 1 mo. 1747) Mary Joy, daughter of David and Mary.
ii **Nathaniel,** born 27th 1 mo. 1729; married (6th 1 mo. 1757) Rebekah Coleman, daughter of Barnabas and Rachel.
iii **William,** born 13th. 11 mo. 1730; removed from the Island 21st. 7 mo. 1775; married (7th 2 mo. 1754) Hephzibah Barney daughter of Benjamin and Lydia.

HISTORY OF NANTUCKET

    iv **Benjamin,** born 26th 9 mo. 1732; removed from the Island 23d 9 mo. 1773; married (7th 2 mo. 1754) Elizabeth Hussey, daughter of Daniel and Sarah.
    v **Micajah,** born 18th. 8 mo. 1734; died 25th. 5 mo. 1827; married (6th 1 mo. 1757) Abigail Coleman, daughter of Elihu and Jemima.
    vi **Abigail,** born 24th 10 mo. 1736; died 31st. 8 mo. 1758; married (27th 2 mo. 1755) Matthew Macy, son of Jabez and Sarah.
    vii **Joseph,** born 25th 12 mo. 1738; died 14th 1 mo. 1740.
    viii **Anna,** born 28th 6 mo. 1740; removed from the Island 25th 10 mo. 1773; married (6th 1 mo 1763) Charles Clasby son of William and Abiel.
    ix **Seth,** born 31st 5 mo. 1742; removed from the Island 23d 9 mo. 1773; married (3d 12 mo. 1767) Lydia Barnard, daughter of William and Lydia.
    x **Paul,** born 25th 11 mo. 1744; married (1st. 2 mo. 1770) Ruth Pinkham, daughter of Shubael and Eunice.
    xi **Elihu,** born 4th 10 mo. 1746.
    xii **Isaiah,** born 8th 12 mo. 1748; died 8th 5 mo. 1749.
    xiii **Abraham,** born 5th 9 mo. 1750.
    xiv **Abner,** born 20th 3 mo. 1753.

By Deborah—

    xv **Isaac,** born 1st 9 mo. 1764.
    xvi **Thomas,** born 5th 9 mo. 1766.
    xvii **Deborah,** born 25th. 8 mo. 1768.

Benjamin died 3d. 11 mo. 1780; Jedidah, his first wife, died 6th 8 mo. 1759; Deborah, his second wife, died 28th 11 mo. 1803.

NATHANIEL [4] (Nathaniel [3] James [2] Tristram [1]) born July 1711; married Mary Sheffield of Newport; died June 10 1800. Their children were:—

    i **Katharine,** born 30th 7 mo. 1737.
    ii **Nathaniel** born 29th 9 mo 1739; married (10th 2 mo. 1763) Phebe Coffin, daughter of Tristram and Jemima. He married for his second wife (10th 10 mo. 1771) Priscilla Gardner daughter of Thomas and Hannah.
    iii **Sheffield,** born 24th 2 mo. 1741; removed from the Island 31st. 10 mo. 1785; married (10th 1st mo. 1765) Elizabeth Barnard, daughter of Matthew and Mary.

HISTORY OF NANTUCKET 717

iv James, born 13th 9 mo. 1743.
v Walter, born 20th 10 mo. 1748.
vi Matthew, born 20th 5 mo. 1751.
vii Elihu, born 13th 4 mo. 1754.
viii Obediah, born 31st. 10 mo. 1757.
ix Lettice, born 18th 11 mo. 1760; married (30. 1 mo. 1783) Reuben Ray, son of Alexander and Elizabeth.

RICHARD, [4] (John, [3] James [2] Tristram [1]) born 12th 6 mo. 1694; married (November 20 1718) Ruth Bunker, daughter of John and Elizabeth. He died 4th 3 mo. 1768; she died 14th. 1 mo. 1779. Their children were—

i Judith, born 2d 7 mo. 1719; died 15th 5 mo. 1799; married (30th 5 mo. 1738) Francis Macy, son of Thomas and Deborah.
ii Christopher, born 30th 4 mo. 1721; lost at sea 1756.
iii Phebe, born 20th 11 mo. 1723; died 9 th 4 mo. 1756; married (6th 8 mo. 1743) Tristram Swain son of John and Mary.
iv Daniel, born 21st 7 mo. 1725; died 9 th 9 mo. 1745.
v Barnabas, born 11th 8 mo. 1727; died 28th. 5 mo. 1777; married (1st. 1 mo. 1749-50) Abigail Folger, daughter of Daniel and Abigail.
vi Abigail, born 22d. 6 mo. 1729; married (8th 9 mo. 1750) Seth Swain, son of John and Mary.
vii Richard, born 31st, 5 mo. 1731; married (8th 11 mo. 1753) Mary Starbuck, daughter of Paul and Ann.
viii Ruth, born 9th. 2 mo. 1733; married (7th 10 mo. 1749) William Folger, son of Abishai and Sarah.
ix Lydia, born 22d 7 mo. 1735; removed from the Island 7th 5 mo. 1772.*
x Margaret, born 25th 6 mo. 1738; died 6 th 9 mo. 1744.
xi Francis, born 11th 1 mo. 1743; died 14th 5 mo. 1768.
xii Silvanus, born 21st 1 mo. 1745; married (31st 12 mo. 1767) Elizabeth Hussey, daughter of William and Abigail.

ELIAS [4] (John, [3] James, [2] Tristram [1]) born 18th 6 mo. 1702; married (January 15, 1728-9) Love Coffin, daughter of Ebenezer and Eleanor. Their children were:—

---

*Quite a number of the Coffin families removed to New Garden, North Carolina about the time of the Revolution and after. Like other Nantucket people some of them eventually continued through East Tennessee into Indiana, where they became prominent citizens. From the Coffins have sprung quite a group of professional men. Among them is the well-known emancipationist Levi Coffin and Lucretia (Coffin) Mott.

> i **Jane**, born January 5, 1730-1.
> ii **Dinah**, born April 6, 1733.
> iii **Anna**, born August 11, 1735.
> iv **Merab**, born September 3, 1737; married; probably, (November 20, 1755) John Woodbury.
> v **Love** born October 27, 1739; probably married (October 12, 1759) Jeremiah Prior.
> vi **Elias**, born August 8, 1741; married (March 4 1762) Abigail Coffin.

FRANCIS [4] (John, [3] James, [2] Tristram [1]) born November 13. 1706; married (November 2. 1727) Theodate Gorham.* Their children were:—

> i **Peleg** born November 8, 1728; married (6th 2 mo 1749) Elizabeth Hussey, daughter of George and Elizabeth.
> ii **William**, born August 5, 1730; married (28th 2 mo. 1754 Jedidah Folger, daughter of John and Rebekah.
> iii **Judith**, born August 13, 1732; married (6th 10 mo. 1750) Nathaniel Hussey, son of Silvanus and Hephzibah.

PRINCE [4] (**Ebenezer**, [3] James, [2] Tristram [1]) born 19th 6 mo. 1703; married Mercy Skiffe. They had a daughter—

> i **Mary**, who married (10th 11 mo. 1750) Tristram Folger son of Jethro and Mary.

ZACCHEUS [4] (**Joseph** [3] James [2] Tristram [1]) born 11th, 1 mo. 1710; married (4th, 9 mo. 1731) Mary Pinkham, daughter of Shubael and Abigail. He died 2d, 10 mo. 1797; she died 24th, 12 mo. 1788. Their children were—

> i **Eunice**, born 17th, 8 mo. 1732; removed from the Island 27th, 6 mo. 1785; probably married (October 31, 1751) Stephen Paddack.

*After the death of Francis his widow married (4th. 10 mo. 1735) Reuben Gardner son of Solomon and Anna.

HISTORY OF NANTUCKET

ii Joseph, born 5th, 12 mo. 1733; died 13th, 7 mo. 1786; married (5th, 2 mo. 1756) Eunice Paddock, daughter of Daniel and Susanna.
iii Anna, born 22d, 1 mo. 1736; died 9th, 12 mo. 1780; married (20th, 1 mo. 1757) Silvanus Russell, son of Jonathan and Patience.
iv Shubael, born 29th, 3 mo. 1739; married (6th, 1 mo. 1763) Mary Mitchell, daughter of Richard and Mary.
v Hezekiah, born 20th, 8 mo. 1741; died 8 mo. 1779; married (4th, 2 mo. 1762) Abigail Coleman daughter of Daniel and Elizabeth.
vi Bethiah, born 14th, 11 mo. 1743; died 5th, 6 mo. 1806; married (5th, 1 mo. 1764) Matthew Bunker, son of James and Bethiah.
vii Zaccheus, born 19th, 3 mo. 1751; probably married (March 22, 1770) Thankful Joy.
viii Mary, born 14th, 4 mo. 1754.

HEZEKIAH [4] (Joseph [3] James [2] Tristram [1]) born 4th, 8 mo. 1712; died 15th, 11 mo. 1768;* married (3d, 1 mo. 1742) Lydia Folger, daughter of Jethro and Mary. She died 7th, 9 mo. 1807. Their children were—

i Mary, born 28th, 9 mo. 1743.
ii Andrew, born 22d, 6 mo. 1745; died 30th, 9 mo. 1752.
iii Elijah, born 21st, 6 mo. 1747; probably married, (June 10, 1770) Abigail Folger.
iv Elizabeth, born 12th, 10 mo. 1749; died 12th, 9 mo. 1788; married (2d, 2 mo. 1769) William Ray, son of William and Mary.
v Uriah, born 8th, 10 mo. 1751; removed from the Island 29th, 4 mo. 1776.
vi Lydia, born 4th, 11 mo. 1753; died 14th, 12 mo. 1753.
vii Lydia, born 7th, 7 mo. 1755; died 16th, 5 mo. 1759.
viii Abihu, born 24th, 9 mo. 1757; probably married (March 15, 1783) Elizabeth Wolton.
ix Eliel, born 31st, 12 mo. 1759; married (December 29, 1769) Lydia Fosdick.
x Libbeus, born 22d, 1 mo. 1762; died 23d, 1 mo. 1820.
xi Laban, born 16th, 10 mo. 1764; died 19th, 11 mo. 1853; married (9th, 2 mo. 1797) Jemima Folger, daughter of Benjamin and Judith.

---

*The Friends Records give the date as 15th, 1 mo. 1768, which is doubtless correct.

HENRY [4] (Jonathan [3] James [2] Tristram [1])
born March 23, 1716; married (February 15, 1738-9) Mary Woodbury. Their children were—

    i **Elizabeth**, born May 21, 1744.
    ii **Henry**, born March 25, 1848. Married (November 30, 1769) Lydia Fosdick.

DANIEL [4] (Jonathan [3] James [2] Tristram [1])
born February 22, 1718; married (December 28, 1737) Elizabeth Stretton. Their children were—

    i **Judith**, born September 8, 1739. Married (28th, 11 mo. 1765) George Lawrence son of George and Mehitable.
    ii **Elizabeth**, born March 3, 1741; married (4th, 2 mo. 1762) Jonathan Gorham Fitch, son of Beriah and Deborah.

JONATHAN [4] (Jonathan [3[James [2] Tristram [1])
born March 24, 1723; married (June 2, 1743) Priscilla Coffin, daughter of Josiah and Elizabeth. Their children were—

    i **Joshua**, born August 7, 1745.
    ii **Daniel**, born November 28, 1749.

BARTLETT [4] (Peter [3] John [2] Tristram [1])
married (January 1, 1718-9) Judith Bunker, daughter of Jonathan and Elizabeth. Their children were—

    i **Peleg**, born December 5, 1719. Married (December 25, 1740) Hephzibah Coffin.
    ii **Rebecca**, born December 7, 1721. Married (March 22, 1738-9) Benjamin Coffin.
    iii **Enoch**, born July 5, 1727. Probably married (May 10, 1745) Love Gardner, daughter of Peter and Elizabeth.
    iv **Christian**, born June 18, 1730.
    v **Judith**, born March 4, 1733.

vi **Bartlett,** born January 17, 1737.
vii **Uriah,** born January 2, 1739.

ABNER [4] (Peter [3] John [2] Tristram [1])
married Phebe Butler. Their children were—

  i **Timothy,** born May 14, 1734.
  ii **Joseph,** born March 23, 1738.
  iii **Elizabeth,** born May 2, 1740.

TRISTRAM [4] (Peter [3] John [2] Tristram [1])
married (8th, 1 mo. 1743-4) Jemima Barnard, daughter of Ebenezer and Mary. He died 19th, 1 mo. 1763; she died 19th, 7 mo. 1757. Their children were—

  i **Phebe,** born probably in 1744; died 22d, 3 mo. 1770; married (10th, 2 mo. 1763) Nathaniel Coffin, son of Nathaniel and Mary.
  ii **Abishai,** removed from the Island 29th, 8 mo. 1774.
  iii **Lydia.**
  iv **Jemima.**
  v **Miriam.**
  vi **Huldah.**

ROBERT [4] (Peter [3] John [2] Tristram [1])
married (17th, 11 mo. 1744) Jemima Gardner, daughter of Samuel and Patience; died September 29, 1791. Their children were—

  i **Hepzibah,** born 11th, 11 mo. 1744-5; died 14th, 1 mo. 1801.
  ii **Patience,** born 4th, 8 mo. 1749; died 5th, 9 mo. 1827.
  iii **Robert,** born 23d, 10 mo. 1760.
  iv **Jerusha,** born 1st, 4 mo. 1765.

PETER [4] (Peter [3] John [2] Tristram [1])
born November 3, 1729; married (13th, 10 mo. 1750) Priscilla

Coleman, daughter of Elihu and Jemima. His wife died 4th, 10 mo. 1770. He removed to New Gardner, N. C., with the rest of his family excepting Elizabeth who removed the following year, 30th, 8 mo. 1784, where he died. Their children were—

    i **Christopher.**
   ii **Joseph.**
  iii **Peter.**
  iv **Sarah.**
   v **Ann.**
  vi **Elizabeth.**

JOHN [4] (Samuel [3] John [2] Tristram [1]) born June 4, 1708; married (4th, 10 mo. 1740) Kezia Folger, daughter of Daniel and Abigail. They had but one child, a daughter—

    i **Kezia**, who married (April 5, 1777) Phineas Fanning.

DAVID [4] (Samuel [3] John [2] Tristram [1]) born October 25, 1718; married (4th, 12 mo. 1741) Ruth Coleman, daughter of Elihu and Jemima. He died 7th, 6 mo. 1804; his wife died 25th, 5 mo. 1763. Their children were—

    i **Phebe,** born 29th, 12 mo. 1743; died 25th, 1 mo. 1782; married (31st, 12 mo. 1761) David Joy, son of David and Sarah.
   ii **Seth,** born 17th, 7 mo. 1746; died 31st, 5 mo. 1801; married (3d, 12 mo. 1767) Susanna Barnard, daughter of Timothy and Mary.
  iii **Elihu,** born 8th, 11 mo. 1748.
  iv **David,** born 6th, 9 mo. 1750; lost at sea 1783; married (9th, 1 mo. 1772) Elizabeth Swain, daughter of Charles and Elizabeth.
   v **Miriam,** born 29th, 5 mo. 1752; removed from the Island 25th, 3 mo. 1776.
  vi **Obediah,** born 12th, 9 mo. 1757; died at sea.
 vii **Jemima,** born 2d, 2 mo. 1759; died 17th, 8 mo. 1842; married—first————— Morton; second, (4th, 9 mo. 1806) Prince Gardner, son of Robert and Jedidah.
viii **Gideon,** born 7th, 5 mo. 1761.
  ix **Ruth,** born 19th, 5 mo. 1763; died 2d, 2 mo. 1841.

WILLIAM [4] (Samuel [3] John [2] Tristram [1])
born 1720; married (4th, 10 mo. 1740) Priscilla Paddock, daughter of Nathaniel and Ann. They removed from the Island 8th, 4 mo. 1773, taking all their family with them who had not previously gone. Their children were—

  i **Deborah**, born 31st, 1 mo. 1743; married (2d, 1 mo. 1766) Mathew Barnard, son of Robert and Hephzibah.*
  ii **Libni**, born 7th, 8 mo. 1745; removed from the Island 25th, 4 mo. 1771; married (29th, 1 mo. 1767) Hephzibah Starbuck, daughter of Joseph and Ruth.
  iii **William**, born 25th, 7 mo. 1747; removed from the Island 30th, 10 mo. 1772; married (29th, 12 mo. 1768) Lydia Coleman, daughter of Jethro and Lydia.†
  iv **Samuel**, born 8th, 10 mo. 1749; married (29th, 11 mo. 1770) Mary Carr, son of Thomas and Mary.
  v **Barnabas**, born 25th, 10 mo. 1751; married (7th, 1 mo. 1773) Phebe Marshall, daughter of Joseph and Phebe.
  vi **Matthew**, born 13th, 2 mo. 1754.
  vii **Bethuel**, born 9th, 2 mo. 1756.
  viii **Abijah**, born 22d, 5 mo. 1760.
  ix **Priscilla**.

SAMUEL [4] (Tristram [3] John [2] Tristram [1])
born 1720; married (6th, 7 mo. 1744) Elizabeth Gardner, daughter of Jonathan and Patience. Their children were*—

  i **Elihu**, born 9th, 7 mo. 1745.
  ii **Thomas**, born 7th, 11 mo. 1747.
  iii **Simeon**, born 5th, 4 mo. 1750.
  iv **Samuel**, born 7th, 9 mo. 1752; died at sea 12 mo. 1771.
  v **Tristram**, born 5th, 4 mo. 1755.
  vi **Obed**, born 14th, 9 mo. 1757. Married (3d, 1 mo. 1781) Deborah Coleman, daughter of Jethro and Lydia.
  vii **Phebe**, born 10th, 11 mo. 1760.
  viii **Barnabas**, born 7th, 3 mo. 1763; died 1802.
  ix **Miriam**, born 14th, 9 mo. 1765.
  x **Rebecca**, born 29th, 5, 1770.

*In the list of marriages in the Friend's Records the parents of Deborah and William are given as David and Ruth which is clearly a clerical error as David had no children of those names while his brother William did have.
†A note on the Friend's Records says the children were "all born at Martha's Vineyard."

TRISTRAM [4] (Tristram [3] John [2] Tristram [1])
born in 1722; was twice married—first (7th, 1 mo. 1744-5) to Hephzibah Coffin, daughter of Zephaniah and Mary, who died 30th, 10 mo. 1746; second (29th, 9 mo. 1750) Elizabeth Starbuck, daughter of Paul and Ann, who died 12th, 4 mo. 1819. Their children were—

By Hephzibah—

    i Tristram, born 18th, 6 mo. 1746; married (3d, 3 mo. 1768) Mary Pinkham, daughter of Richard and Miriam.

By Elizabeth—

    ii Hephzibah, born 7th, 3 mo. 1752; died 6th, 4 mo. 1819; probably married (October 13, 1774) Nathaniel Barnard.
    iii Reuben, born 6th, 7 mo. 1754; married (3d, 2 mo. 1774) Pernal Gardner, daughter of Daniel and Provided.
    iv Jonathan, born 25th, 6 mo. 1756; married (2d, 10 mo. 1777) Abigail Austin, daughter of Benjamin and Susanna.
    v Frederick, born 2d, 10 mo. 1761; died 17th, 6 mo. 1773.

JONATHAN [4] (Tristram [3] John [2] Tristram [1])
born in 1725; lost at sea 1755; married (4th, 11 mo. 1747) Eunice Barnard, daughter of Robert and Hepzibah. Their children were—

    i Hepzibah, born October 14, 1748.
    ii Mary, born August 17, 1750; removed from the Island 28th, 12 mo. 1772; married (4th, 2 mo. 1768) Paul Starbuck, son of Edward and Damaris.
    iii William, born 1752.
    iv Eunice, born 3 mo. 1755; removed from the Island 30th, 11 mo. 1778; married (13th, 1 mo. 1774) Stephen Coffin, son of Stephen and Mary.

JOHN [4] (Tristram [3] John [2] Tristram [1])
born 1727; lost at sea 1755; married (12th, 8 mo. 1749) Anna

Coleman, daughter of Elihu and Jemima. She died 3d, 6 mo. 1768. Their children were—

    i **Phebe**, born 9th, 6 mo. 1751; married (30th, 11 mo. 1769) Benjamin Worth, son of Benjamin and Mary.
    ii **John**, born 12th, 4 mo. 1753.
    iii **Anna**, born 9th, 6 mo. 1755.

ZEPHANIAH [4] (Stephen [3] Stephen [2] Tristram [1]) born 28th, 8 mo. 1699: married—first (November 10, 1725) Miriam Macy, daughter of John and Judith; second, (October 6, 1737) Abigail Coleman, daughter of Solomon and Mary. Miriam died 2d, 8 mo. 1736; Abigail, who was born 15th, 8 mo. 1713; died 4th, 8 mo. 1787. The children were—

By Miriam—

    i **Hepzibah**, born 15th, 4 mo. 1726; died 30th, 10 mo. 1746; married (7th, 1 mo. 1744-5) Tristram Coffin, son of Tristram and Mary.
    ii **Stephen**, born 30th, 1 mo. 1730-31; married (30th, 11 mo. 1751-2) Mary Bunker, daughter of Samuel and Priscilla.
    iii **Shubael**, born probably in 1734; removed from the Island 31st, 5 mo. 1779; married first, (9th, 1 mo. 1755) Abigail Paddack, daughter of Eliphalet and Naomi; second, (8th, 11 mo. 1764) Mary Swain, daughter of Caleb and Margaret.
    iv **Dinah**, born 1736; died 25th, 10 mo. 1756; married (29th, 10 mo. 1753) Abisha Bunker, son of Samuel and Priscilla.

By Abigail—

    v **Mary**, born 27th, 6 mo. 1738; died 6th, 2 mo. 1819; married (11th, 12 mo. 1760) Charles Bunker, son of Samuel and Priscilla.
    vi **Miriam**, born 19th, 2 mo. 1740; died 12th, 2 mo. 1813; married (4th, 10 mo. 1759) Richard Macy, son of Zaccheus and Hephzibah.
    vii **Paul**, born 1 mo. 1742; removed from the Island 14th, 3 mo. 1776; married (8th, 12 mo. 1763) Susanna Bunker, daughter of Jonathan and Judith.
    viii **Zephaniah**, born 1 mo. 1747; removed from the Island 30th, 11 mo. 1778; married (7th, 1 mo. 1768) Hephzibah Bunker, daughter of Jonathan and Judith.

ix Solomon, born 1 mo. 1750; married probably (October 18, 1784) Phebe Gardner.
x Abigail, born 7 mo. 1752; removed from the Island 20th 11 mo. 1780. Married ——————— Bunker.

PETER [4] (Paul [3] Stephen [2] Tristram [1])
born February 26, 1718; married (10th, 2 mo. 1738) Deborah Hussey, daughter of George and Elizabeth, who died 9th, 2 mo. 1785. Their children were—

    i Mary, born 23d, 4 mo. 1741; died 14th, 10 mo. 1763.
    ii Elizabeth, born 25th, 6 mo. 1745; died 27th, 4 mo. 1788.

ELISHA [5] (Nathan [4] James [3] James [2] Tristram [1])
born February 9, 1726; married (10th, 1 mo. 1747) Mary Gardner, daughter of Nathaniel and Mary. Their children were—

    i Rachel, born 9th, 6 mo. 1749.
    ii Judith, born 9th, 10 mo. 1751; probably married, (February 28, 1771) Thomas Brock.
    iii Elisha, born 9th, 8 mo. 1758.
    iv Joshua, born 9th, 8 mo. 1758; died 1781.
    v Nathaniel, born 11th, 9 mo. 1761; lost at sea.

NATHANIEL [5] (Benjamin [4] Nathaniel [3] James [2] Tristram [1])
born 27th, 1 mo. 1729; married (6th, 1 mo. 1757) Rebekah Coleman, daughter of Barnabas and Rachel, who died 20th, 3 mo. 1777. Their children were—

    i Gilbert, born 11th, 6 mo. 1757; died 7th, 10 mo. 1758.
    ii Abial, born 25th, 10 mo. 1759; died 10th, 2 mo. 1832.
    iii Moses, born 1st, 7 mo. 1762.
    iv Albert, born 2d, 6 mo. 1764; died 22d, 6 mo. 1765.
    v Clement, born 20th, 2 mo. 1767.
    vi Rachel, born 9th, 4 mo. 1769.
    vii Ralph, born 17th, 1 mo. 1771.
    viii Arnold, born 14th, 9 mo. 1773; died 11th, 9 mo. 1774.

MICAJAH [5] (Benjamin [4] Nathaniel [3] James [2] Tristram [1])
born 18th, 8 mo. 1734; died 25th, 5 mo. 1827; married (6th, 1 mo. 1757) Abigail Coleman, daughter of Elihu and Jemima. Their children were—

    i Isaiah, born 11th, 9 mo. 1757; died 17th, 4 mo. 1813; married (2d, 3 mo. 1780) Sarah Folger, daughter of Christopher and Abigail.
    ii Gilbert, born 1st, 8 mo. 1759; married (30th, 11 mo. 1780) Phebe Barnard, daughter of William and Mary.
    iii Jedidah, born 5th, 7 mo. 1761; died 11th, 11 mo. 1792: married (29th, 1 mo. 1784) Francis Joy, son of Francis and Phebe.
    iv Zenas, born 3d, 6 mo. 1764; died 8th, 7 mo. 1822.

BARNABAS [5] (Richard [4] John [3] James [2] Tristram[1])
born 11th, 8 mo. 1727; died 28th, 5 mo. 1777; married (1st, 1 mo. 1749-50) Abigail Folger, daughter of Daniel and Abigail. Their children were—

    i Margaret, born 30th, 1 mo. 1751.
    ii Daniel, born 22d, 3 mo. 1754; married (2d, 9 mo. 1784) Huldah Bunker, daughter of Bachelor and Bethiah.
    iii Abial, born 7th, 12 mo. 1758; married (1st, 3 mo. 1781) Jonathan Barney, son of Benjamin and Huldah.
    iv Rebecca, born 22d 4 mo. 1764.
    v Eunice, born 31st, 7 mo. 1766.
    vi Benjamin, born 5th, 1 mo. 1768.

RICHARD [5] (Richard [4] John [3] James [2] Tristram [1])
born 31st, 5 mo. 1731; married (8th, 11 mo. 1753) Mary Starbuck, daughter of Paul and Ann. Their children were—

    i Phebe, born 9th, 7 mo. 1754; died 5th, 3 mo. 1807; married (20th 12 mo. 1770) Jonathan Coffin, son of David and Mary.
    ii Barzillai, born 8th, 9 mo. 1756; died 1st, 7 mo. 1777.
    iii Christopher, born 24th, 7 mo. 1758; probably married (October 16, 1784) Abigail Coleman.

    iv **Sarah,** borr 25th, 11 mo. 1761; died 12th, 6 mo. 1788; married (1st, 11 mo. 1781) Bartlett Coffin, son of Benjamin and Rebecca.
    v **Laban,** born 15th, 11 mo. 1764; removed from the Island 30th, 9 mo. 1802; married (27th, 4 mo. 1786) Phebe Bunker, daughter of Charles and Mary.
    vi **Lydia,** born 21st, 10 mo. 1767; married (1st, 12 mo. 1785) Daniel Barney, son of Benjamin and Jemima.
    vii **Charles,** born 17th, 2 mo. 1769; married (29th, 11 mo. 1792) Miriam Parker. widow of Timothy and daughter of Francis and Naomi Chase.

WILLIAM [5] (Francis [4] John [3] James [2] Tristram [1]) born August 5, 1730; married (February 28, 1754) Jedidah Folger, daughter of John and Rebekah. They had—

    i **William,** born 16th, 12 mo. 1756.

PELEG [5] (Francis [4] John [3] James [2] Tristram [1]) born November 8, 1728; married (6th, 2 mo. 1749) Elizabeth Hussey, daughter of George and Elizabeth. Their children were—

    i **Matilda,** born 4th, 12 mo. 1750; died 4th, 9 mo. 1752.
    ii **Francis,** born 28th, 10 mo. 1752; removed from the Island 27th, 1 mo. 1820 and died 6th, 6 mo. 1820; married (6th, 8 mo. 1807) Lydia Bunker, daughter of Uriah and Judith.
    iii **Jared,** born 29th, 3 mo. 1754; married (30th, 4 mo. 1778) Eunice Barnard, daughter of Joseph and Mary.
    iv **Peleg,** born 3d, 11 mo. 1756; married (28th, 5 mo. 1778) Eunice Barker, daughter of Josiah and Elizabeth.

THOMAS [5] (Micah [4] Joseph [3] James [2] Tristram [1]) born ——————— married (29th, 1 mo. 1756) Abigail Russell, daughter of John and Ruth. Their children were—

    i **Prince,** born 25th, 11 mo. 1756.

ii Deborah, born 25th, 9 mo. 1765; died 17th, 12 mo. 1788.
iii Bartlett, born 14th, 6 mo. 1767; married (29th, 11 mo. 1787) Elizabeth Bunker, daughter of Charles and Mary.
iv Francis, born 22d, 8 mo. 1771.

JOSEPH [5] (Zaccheus [4] Joseph [3] James [2] Tristram [1]) born 5th 12 mo. 1733; died 13th 7 mo 1786; married (5th, 2 mo. 1756) Eunice Paddock, daughter of Daniel and Susanna. They had one child—

i Susanna, born 16th, 12 mo. 1756; married (4th, 8 mo. 1774) Abishai Swain, son of Tristram and Phebe.

STEPHEN [5] (Zephaniah [4] Stephen [3] Stephen [2] Tristram [1])
born 30th, 1 mo. 1730-31; married (30th, 11 mo. 1751-2) Mary Bunker, daughter of Samuel and Priscilla, who died 11th, 10 mo. 1822. Their children were—

i Stephen, born 22d, 11 mo. 1752; removed from the Island 30th, 11 mo. 1778; married (13th, 1 mo. 1774) Eunice Coffin, daughter of Jonathan and Eunice.
ii Job, born 29th, 10 mo. 1755; probably married (August 1, 1785) Mary Ray.
iii Miriam, born 21st, 1 mo. 1760; died 1787; married 7th, 11 mo. 1782) Joseph Clasby, son of John and Ruth.
iv Noah, born 25th, 2 mo. 1762; removed from the Island 28th, 4 mo. 1777.
v Eber, born 20th, 2 mo. 1765; married (3d, 2 mo. 1791) Hepsibah Fitch, daughter of Jonathan G. and Elizabeth.
vi Alpheus, born 19th, 3 mo. 1767; probably married August 7, 1787) Lovey Pitts.
vii Elizabeth, born 7th, 1 mo. 1771; married (1st, 9 mo. 1791) Lot Clasby, son of John and Ruth.
viii Phebe, born 23d, 1 mo. 1775; married (30th, 7 mo. 1794) Isaiah Ray, son of Alexander and Elizabeth.

SHUBAEL [5] (Zephaniah [4] Stephen [3] Stephen [2] Tristram [1])

born probably in 1734; married—first (9th, 1 mo. 1755) Abigail Paddack, daughter of Eliphalet and Naomi; second, (8th, 11 mo. 1764) Mary Swain, daughter of Caleb and Margaret. He removed from the Island 31st, 5 mo. 1779. Abigail died 25th, 11 mo. 1761. Their children were—

By Abigail—

    i **Eliab**, born probably in 1756.
    ii **Dinah**, born ———.

By Mary—

    iii **Ammiel**, born 30th, 9 mo. 1765.
    iv **Judith**, born 27th, 8 mo. 1767.
    v **Hepzibah**, born ——— 9 mo. 1769.
    vi **Solomon**, born ——— 11 mo. 1771.
    vii **Shubael**, born ——— 7 mo. 1774.
    viii **Caleb**, born 3d, 7 mo. 1778.

The father and his second wife and all the children removed from the Island 31st, 5 mo. 1779.

Prof. Maria Mitchell, one of the greatest of American astronomers was a lineal descendant of Thomas Macy, Peter Folger, Tristram Coffin, Edward Starbuck, and Richard Gardner.

COLEMAN

Thomas Coleman* was the original man of the name to be connected with affairs in Nantucket. Coffin's History of Newbury states that he came from Wittshire, England, in 1635. He first settled in Newbury. According to the Records of the Town of Newbury he was engaged by Richard Saltonstall and others in England and America in November, 1635, "for the keeping of horses and sheep in a general place for the space of three years." His work proved unsatisfactory, and each of the contractors was authorized to provide for his own. In the original purchase of the Island, Thomas Coleman was chosen by John Swain as his partner. At what time he removed to the Island is not clear but evidently it was very early. At a meeting of the Town, March 4, 1663, it was voted that "John Coleman shall have land Lay out on the North side of the lots of Robert Barnard for the use of the said John Coleman, his father Thomas Coleman having given half of his accommodation on the Island half the house lot to be Layd out in the place before mentioned for John Coleman, the aforesaid Thomas Coleman doth Lay down one half of his Lot already Layd out." In October, 1664, the Town chose Richard Swain and Thomas Coleman Surveyors of Highways. It may be assumed then that he was a resident as early at least as 1664. His first wife's name was Susanna ———— and she died November 17, 1650. He married (July 11, 1651) Mary, widow of Edmund Johnson. She died at Hampton, January 30, 1663. He married a third time—to Margery—(Ashbourne according to some authorities).† His children were—by Susanna: **Benjamin**, born May 1, 1640; **Joseph**, born December 2, 1642; **John**, born ———— 1644; **Isaac**, born February 20, 1647;‡ (probably by Mary) **Joanna**, (by the third wife) **Tobias**. Thomas died in 1685, aged 83 years.

Joseph married Ann Bunker, daughter of George, Senior; Isaac was drowned with John Barnard and his wife, June 6, 1669, while coming from the Vineyard in a canoe; John married (probably in 1666) Joanna Folger, daughter of Peter, Senior; Tobias married Lydia Osborne, daughter of Thomas's wife. He had one

---

*Patronymica Britannica says of the name "An ancient Anglo Saxon personal name, mentioned by Bode, Coleman and Colemannus in Domesday. Probably derived from the occupation of charcoal burning and synonymous with Collier."

†"Early Settlers of Nantucket," p. 61. This would seem to be an error as a letter from (Rev.) Thomas Osborne dated Nantucket 25th, 8 mo. 1682, written to George Little (Rev) and quoted by Joshua Coffin in the Historic Genealogical Register for Jan. 1862, in which Osborne, who is a Baptist minister, mentions his own marriage to Margery Coleman, widow of Thomas. Margery, whose maiden name is not given, married—first—Osgood; second, Thomas Rowell; third, Thomas Coleman; fourth, Thomas Osborne—certainly showing a marked preference for Thomas as a name to cling to.

‡Probably the lad who accompanied Tristram Coffin and Edward Starbuck on their first trip to the Island for observation. Savage makes Tobias the oldest son; Nantucket authorities do not agree with him.

daughter **Deborah,** born in Nantucket, May 25, 1676, and removed with his family at an early period to Martha's Vineyard.

Joseph had but one son, who was born November 17, 1673 and was drowned in his boyhood. A daughter **Ann,** born November 10, 1675, who married Edward Allen was his only other child.

The family in Nantucket then may properly be said to have descended from John and Joanna.

Mr. Worth says,* Thomas' house lot "was 1,000 feet square, bounded on the north by the lot of Christopher Hussey, on the east by the Long Woods and on the South by the lot of Capt. Pyke." It was about half a mile southwest from the north head of the Hummock Pond. On his decease the house and lot descended to Tobias. Joseph's lot was located at High Cliff, which Mr. Worth thinks locates it in the section west of the estate of the late Charles O' Connor Esq. John's house lot was a little west of the Elihu Coleman house, comprised ten acres and extended southeast to Robert Barnard's lot.

JOHN [1]

married (probably in 1666) Joanna Folger, daughter of Peter, Senior. The Probate Court Records show that in the settling of John's estate, December 7, 1715, there were eight children:

    i **John,** born August 2, 1667; married (1694) Priscilla Starbuck, daughter of Nathaniel and Mary.

    ii **Jeremiah,** born probably in 1668; married (20th, 11 mo. 1714-15) Sarah Pratt.

    iii **Thomas,** born October 17, 1669; married Jane Challenge.

    iv **Isaac,** born February 6, 1671; married

    v **Phebe,** born June 15, 1674; married ———— Cathcart.

    vi **Abigail,** married James Tisdale.

    vii **Benjamin,** born January 17, 1676.

    viii **Solomon;** married—first, (1st, 9 mo. 1711) Mary Macy, daughter of John and Deborah, who died 27th, 6 mo. 1715; second, (1718) Deliverance Swett.

JOHN [2] (John [1])

born August 2, 1667; married Priscilla Starbuck, daughter of

*Nantucket Land and Land Owners, p. 66.

Nathaniel and Mary. He died 19th, 1 mo. 1762; she died 14th, 3 mo. of the same year. Their children were—

   i **Persis**, born December 7, 1695, who died young.
   ii **Nathaniel**, born December 20, 1697; married (4th, 10 mo. 1729) Mary Gardner, widow of Nathaniel and daughter of Peter and Judith Folger.
   iii **Elihu**, born February 12, 1699; married (6th, 10 mo. 1720) Jemima Barnard, daughter of John.
   iv **Barnabas**, born April 24, 1704; died in infancy.
   v **Jethro**, born 8th, 7 mo. 1706; married—first, (6th, 11 mo. 1731) Lydia Paddack, daughter of Nathaniel and Ann; second, (31st, 1 mo. 1748) Lydia Macy, daughter of Thomas and Deborah.
   vi **Barnabas**, born 14th, 9 mo. 1708; married—first, (March 3, 1728) Elizabeth Barnard, daughter of Nathaniel and Judith; second, (8th, 9 mo. 1733) Rachel Hussey, daughter of Silvanus and Abial.
   vii **Phebe**, born 10th, 4 mo. 1711; married (3d, 10 mo. 1730) Barzillai Folger, son of Nathan and Sarah.
   viii **Priscilla**, born 28th, 9 mo. 1713; married (7th, 11 mo. 1731-2) Samuel Bunker, son of Jabez and Hannah.
   ix **John**, born 20th, 11 mo. 1715; married (9th, 9 mo. 1738) Ruth Pinkham, daughter of Shubael and Abigail.
   x **Mary**, born 30th, 3 mo. 1718; married (2d, 10 mo. 1741) William Russell, son of Daniel and Deborah; died 11th, 1 mo. 1767.

JEREMIAH [2] (John [1])
born probably in 1668; married (20th, 11 mo. 1714-15) Sarah Pratt Their children were—

   i **Peter**, born 6th, 2 mo. 1716; probably married (December 20, 1750) Susanna Upham.
   ii **Lydia**, born February 17, 1717-18; married—first, (28th, 8 mo. 1751) William Starbuck, son of Jethro and Dorcas; second (29th, 10 mo. 1761) Theophilus Pinkham, son of Richard and Mary.
   iii **Silvanus**, born June 2, 1720.
   iv **Johanna**, born September 19, 1722; probably married (March 9, 1750) Eleazer Clark.
   v **Enoch**, born March 24, 1724-5; married (5th, 11 mo. 1748) Mary Myrick, daughter of Andrew and Jedidah.
   vi **Jeremiah**, born October 19, 1729; probably married (February 12, 1756) Anna Russell.

SOLOMON [2] (John [1])

was twice married—first, (1st, 9 mo. 1711) to Mary Macy, daughter of John and Deborah, who died 27th, 6 mo. 1715; second, (20th, 8 mo. 1718) to Deliverance Swett. Their children were—*

By Mary—

    i Abigail, born probably in 1712; died 4th, 8 mo. 1787; married (6th, 8 mo. 1737) Zephaniah Coffin, son of Stephen and Experience.

By Deliverence—

    ii Daniel, born 12th, 7 mo. 1719; married (December 9, 1741) Elizabeth Mooers.
    iii Elizabeth, born 3d, 5 mo. 1722; married (9th 8 mo. 1746) Jonathan Gwinn, son of David and Alice.
    iv Christopher, born 30th, 6 mo. 1723; died 4th, 5 mo. 1795; married (9th, 12 mo. 1748) Priscilla Coffin, daughter of Samuel and Miriam.
    v Peleg, born 12th, 8 mo. 1725; died 31st, 5 mo. 1808; married (12th, 10 mo. 1751) Mary Worth, widow of Benjamin and daughter of Shubael and Jerusha Folger.
    vi Hepzibah, born 20th, 11 mo. 1727; died 2d, 5 mo. 1820.
    vii George, born 14th, 3 mo. 1730; married (10th, 11 mo. 1750) Eunice Folger, daughter of Jethro and Mary.
    viii Francis, born 25th, 6 mo. 1732; married (7th, 2 mo. 1760) Abigail Bunker, daughter of Samuel and Priscilla.
    ix Solomon, born 3d, 1 mo. 1735; married (14th, 12 mo. 1755) Mehitable Gardner, daughter of James and Susanna.

NATHANIEL [3] (John [2] John [1])

born December 20, 1697; married (4th, 10 mo. 1728) Mary Gardner, widow of Nathaniel and daughter of Peter and Judith Folger. He died 19th, 3 mo. 1783; she died 3d, 12 mo. 1763. Their children were—

    i Elizabeth, born 30th, 6 mo. 1730; married (16th, 9 mo. 1749) Samuel Ray, son of Samuel and Mary.
    ii John, born 15th, 8 mo. 1732; married (7th, 2 mo. 1754) Anna Davis, daughter of John and Margaret.
    iii Benjamin, born 8th, 1 mo. 1735; lost at sea 1756.

---

*A clause in Solomon's will (probated in Feb. 1772) provided that none of his heirs "shall ever sell or dispose of my Dwelling House and the Land it stands upon except one to another among themselves."

HISTORY OF NANTUCKET 735

ELIHU [3] (John [2] John [1])*
born February 12, 1699; married (6th, 10 mo. 1720) Jemima Barnard, daughter of John and Sarah. He died 24th, 1 mo. 1789; she died 25th, 12 mo. 1779. Their children were—

    i Ruth, born 9th, 9 mo. 1721; married (4th, 12 mo. 1741) David Coffin, son of Samuel and Miriam.
   ii William, born 3d, 6 mo. 1723; married (26th, 2 mo. 1756) Eunice Swain, daughter of John and Mary.
  iii Eunice, born 18th, 10 mo. 1724; married (13th, 8 mo. 1743) John Macy, son of John and Judith.
  iv Phebe, born 10th, 6 mo. 1726; married (14th, 9 mo. 1745) Seth Folger, son of Shubael and Jerusha.
   v Anna, born 24th, 12 mo 1728; married (12th, 8 mo. 1749) John Coffin, son of Tristram and Mary, who died 1755; and, second, (1764) Jonathan Gardner, son of Barnabas and Mary.
  vi Priscilla, born 15th, 8 mo. 1731; married (13th, 10 mo. 1750) Peter Coffin, son of Peter and Hope.
 vii Mary, born 25th, 7 mo. 1733; married (3d, 1 mo. 1760) Shubael Pinkham, son of Shubael and Abigail.
viii Abigail, born 21st, 9 mo. 1735; married (6th, 1 mo. 1757) Micajah Coffin, son of Benjamin and Jedidah.

JETHRO [3] (John [2] John [1])
was born 8th 7 mo. 1706; married—first (6th 11 mo. 1731) Lydia Paddack, daughter of Nathaniel and Ann; he removed from the Island in 1779; she died 21st, 1 mo. 1747; married second, (31st, 1 mo. 1748) Lydia Macy, daughter of Thomas and Deborah. Their children were—

By Lydia Paddack—

   i Jethro, born 28th, 8 mo. 1734; lost at sea 1755.
  ii Paul, —— —— —— ——; lost at sea 1755.
 iii Barnabas, —— —— —— ——; lost at sea 1756.
 iv Elihu, —— —— —— ——; married (30th, 12 mo. 1762) Elizabeth Macy, daughter of Jonathan and Lois.
  v Lydia, † ————————; married (29th, 12 mo. 1768) William Coffin, son of David and Mary.

---

*Reference to the Chapter on the subject of Slavery will show that Elihu Coleman while yet a young man was one of the earliest avocates of emancipation in America. The home which Elihu built and in which he lived is still standing, an evidence of the thoroughness of its construction and the excellence of the Nantucket timber of which it was built.
†Removed from the Island with her husband in 1779.

By Lydia Macy, his second wife—

>   vi **Eunice,** born — 5 mo. 1749; married (31st, 12 mo. 1767) Christopher Gardner, son of Robert and Jedidah.
>   vii **Charles,** born 16th, 10 mo. 1750; married (7th, 1 mo. 1773) Katherine Hussey, daughter of William and Abigail.
>   viii **Simeon,** born 22d, 9 mo. 1752; probably married (October 27, 1771) Rebekah Swain.
>   ix **Jethro,** born 1st, 1 mo. 1755.
>   x **Deborah,** born 6th, 1 mo. 1757; married (3d, 1 mo. 1781) Obed Coffin, son of Samuel and Elizabeth.
>   xi **Anna,** born 12th, 4 mo. 1759.

Eunice died 26th, 10 mo. 1772. Lydia and Simeon remained on the Island. With those exceptions the surviving children seem to have removed from the Island in 1779.

BARNABAS [3] (John [2] John [1])

born 14th, 9 mo. 1708; married—first, (3d, 11 mo. 1728) Elizabeth Barnard, daughter of Nathaniel and Judith; second, (8th, 9 mo. 1733) Rachel Hussey, daughter of Silvanus and Abial. He died 23d, 6 mo. 1781; she died 15th, 11 mo. 1729. Their children were—

By Elizabeth Barnard—

>   i **Nathaniel,** born 11th, 8 mo. 1729; married (28th, 10 mo. 1749) Hephzibah Hussey, daughter of Silvanus and Hephzibah.

By his second wife Rachel Hussey—

>   ii **Sarah,** born 25th, 7 mo. 1734; married (7th, 12 mo. 1753) Timothy Folger, son of Abishai and Sarah.
>   iii **Abiel,** born 16th, 9 mo. 1736; married (6th, 12 mo. 1753) Timothy Folger, son of Abishai and Sarah.
>   iv **Rebecca,** born 10th, 10 mo. 1738; died in infancy.
>   v **Rebecca,** born 28th, 12 mo. 1740; married (6th, 1 mo. 1757) Nathaniel Coffin, son of Benjamin and Jedidah.
>   vi **Judith,** born 28th, 4 mo. 1742; married (9th, 2 mo. 1763) Andrew Worth, son of Christopher and Dinah.
>   vii **Seth,** born 1st, 5 mo. 1744; married (29th, 12 mo. 1768) Deborah Swain, daughter of Reuben and Elizabeth.
>   viii **Silvanus,** born 12th, 5 mo. 1746; married (2d, 6 mo. 1768) Mary Swift, daughter of Benjamin and Wait.

ix **William,** born 19th, 6 mo. 1748; married (31st, 5 mo. 1770) Abigail Barnard, daughter of Joseph and Mary.

x **Barnabas,** born 23d, 4 mo. 1751; married (September 7, 1776) Abial Clark.

xi **Elizabeth,** born 29th, 3 mo. 1755; married (7th, 1 mo. 1773) Abishai Folger, son of Abishai and Dinah.

xii **Obed,** born 1st, 9 mo. 1757; married (30th, 11 mo. 1780) Elizabeth Swain, daughter of Joseph and Elizabeth.

xiii **Hepzibah,** born 15th, 10 mo. 1759; married (30th, 10 mo. 1777) John Russell, son of John and Ruth.

JOHN [3] (John [2] John [1])

born 20th, 11 mo. 1715; married (9th, 9 mo. 1738) Ruth Pinkham, daughter of Shubael and Abigail. No children seem to be recorded.

ENOCH [3] (Jeremiah [2] John [1])

born March 24, 1724-5; married (5th, 11 mo. 1748) Mary Myrick, daughter of Andrew and Jedidah; she died 23d, 11 mo. 1845. Their children were —

i **Eunice,** born 20th, 9 mo. 1749; probably married (November 8, 1770) Benjamin Whippey.

ii **Silvanus,** born 15th, 9 mo. 1751; probably married (July 31, 1774) Huldah Gwin.

iii **Abiel,** born 4th, 9 mo. 1755; died 11th, 11 mo. 1759.

iv **Lydia,** born 4th, 11 mo. 1755.

v **Abigail,** born 3d, 9 mo. 1761.

vi **Andrew,** born 30th, 11 mo. 1763; married (3d, 11 mo. 1791) Lydia Folger, daughter of Jonathan and Lydia.

vii **Elizabeth,** born 30th, 11 mo. 1763.

viii **Job,** born 8th, 6 mo. 1768; married (October 28, 1790) Elizabeth Fosdick.

CHRISTOPHER [3] (Solomon [2] John [1])

born 30th, 6 mo. 1723; married (9th, 12 mo. 1748) Priscilla Coffin, daughter of Samuel and Miriam. He died 4th, 5 mo. 1795; she died 2d, 2 mo. 1801. Their children were—

i Miriam, born 30th, 8 mo. 1751; probably married April 7, 1771) David Rand.
  ii Stephen, born 11th, 9 mo. 1754.
  iii David, born 22d, 5 mo. 1758; married (29th, 5 mo. 1781) Elizabeth Russell, daughter of Reuben and Ruth.
  iv Phebe, born 10th, 10 mo. 1760; married (30th, 4 mo. 1782) Peter Joy, son of Reuben and Anna.
  v Obadiah, born 26th, 2 mo. 1763.
  vi Christopher, born 11th, 6 mo. 1765.
  vii Thaddeus, born 2d, 11 mo. 1767.
  viii Bethuel, born 29th, 4 mo. 1770.
  ix Libni, born 15th, 2 mo. 1773.

PELEG [3] (Solomon [2] John [1])

born 12th, 8 mo. 1725; married (12th, 10 mo. 1751) Mary Worth, widow of Benjamin and daughter of Shubael and Jerusha Folger. He died 31st, 5 mo. 1808; she died 15th, 6 mo. 1815. Their children were—

  i Lydia, born 17th, 9 mo. 1753.
  ii Anna, born 20th, 6 mo. 1755. Removed from the Island in 1776.

GEORGE [3] (Solomon [2] John [1])

born 14th, 3 mo. 1730; married (10th, 11 mo. 1750) Eunice Folger, daughter of Jethro and Mary. Their children were—

  i Paul, who died in 1772. Probably born in 1751.
  ii Hepzibah, born 19th, 6 mo. 1753.
  iii George, born 28th, 10 mo. 1755.
  iv Eunice.
  v Nathaniel. Eunice and Nathaniel both died in 1781.
  vi Thaddeus, died in infancy.
  vii Eunice, died in infancy.
  viii Judith, born 8th, 3 mo. 1769.

FRANCIS [3] (Solomon [2] John [1])

born 25th, 6 mo. 1732; married (7th, 2 mo. 1760) Abigail Bunker, daughter of Samuel and Priscilla. He died 6th, 10 mo. 1821; she died 1st, 6 mo. 1812. Their children were—

    i **Priscilla,** born 9th, 11 mo. 1760.
   ii **Abishai,** born ――― (probably in 1762).
  iii **Phebe,** born 11th, 10 mo. 1764. Married (October 18, 1783) David Swain.
  iv **Silas,** born 17th, 3 mo. 1767.
   v **Elizabeth,** born 3d, 10 mo. 1770.
  vi **Moses,** born 12th, 11 mo. 1776.
 vii **Aaron,** born (probably in 1778).
viii **Miriam,** born 1st, 7 mo. 1779.

SOLOMON [3] (Solomon [2] John [1])

born 3d, 1 mo. 1735; married (14th, 12 mo. 1755) Mehitable Gardner, daughter of James and Susanna. Their children were—

    i **Deborah,** born 13th, 9 mo. 1758.
   ii **Susanna,** born 15th, 9 mo. 1760. Probably married (February 18, 1781) Joseph Brown.
  iii **Solomon,** born 28th, 7 mo. 1766; married (August 27, 1790) Hepzibeth Wyer.
  iv **Gardner,** born 6th, 7 mo. 1768. Married (November 9, 1790) Hepzibeth Ray.
   v **Sylvia,** born 15th, 1 mo. 1771. Married (August 3, 1790) William Ramsdale, Jr.
  vi **Lydia,** born 6th, 3 mo. 1775. Married (July 21, 1795) John Marshall.
 vii **Janet,** born 28th, 6 mo. 1776.

DANIEL [3] (Solomon [2] John [1])

born 12th, 7 mo. 1719; married (December 9, 1741) Elizabeth Moores. The Friends Records record the marriage of two daughters—

    i **Abigail,** who married (4th, 2 mo. 1762) Hezekiah Coffin, son of Zaccheus and Mary.
   ii **Elizabeth,** who married (22d, 12 mo. 1768) Ebenezer Pinkham, son of Richard and Miriam.

FOLGER

Savage in his Genealogical Dictionary in describing Peter Folger, the first of the name to be connected with Nantucket, says that he came from Norwich, County Norfolk, England in 1635, went early from Watertown to Martha's Vineyard, probably with Thomas Mayhew. He bestowed great pains in teaching the Indians, as successor to Mayhew, and removed about 1663 to the island, where his name has ever since been in high regard.

Nathaniel Barney says of him* "Peter Folger of whom Cotton Mather speaks "as a pious and learned Englishman" has been named as the interpreter for Tristram Coffin Senior when he first visited Nantucket. He was the only child of John Folger, whose wife was Meribah Gibbs, and came from Norwich, England, a widower, in 1636, having his residence at some time thereafter at Martha's Vineyard. Peter married Mary Morrill in 1644, having bought her of Hugh Peters, to whom she owed service, and paid the sum of £20, which he very gallantly declared was the best appropriation of money he had ever made. Their children were two sons and seven daughters, the last of whom, Abiah, was born at Nantucket the 15th of August, 1669. She was the mother of Doct'r Franklin, and her visits to her relatives here were very frequent, even in her old age. During one of her visits particularly she was desirous of a bunch of mint from the garden of her deceased father. The young man whom she enlisted for the service was Thomas Arthur, and on receiving the parcel from his hands she said to the youth—"I saw that mint placed by my father, in that garden, three score years ago."

Peter Folger's houselot was on the road extending from Main street west, and about two miles from the Upper Square. It may be readily identified by a monument erected on the site by the Daughters of the American Revolution, in honor of his daughter, Abiah, the mother of Franklin.

Patronymica Britannica says of the name, giving preference to Foulger as the form, that it signifies "A follower (Anglo Saxon folgere), an attendant, a servant, a free-man who had not a house of his own, but who was the retainer of some "heorth-faest" or house-keeper."

PETER AND MARY

The children of Peter and Mary were—

    i **Joanna**, who married John Coleman, son of Thomas Sr. and Johanna.
    ii **Bethiah**, who married (February 26, 1668) John Barnard, son of Robert Sr. and Joanna.
    iii **Dorcas**, who married Joseph, Pratt of Charlestown, (February 12, 1675).

---

*Unpublished M. S.

HISTORY OF NANTUCKET 741

    iv **Eleazer**, born 1648, who married (1671) Sarah Gardner, daughter of Richard Sr. and Sarah.
    v **Bethsheba**, who married John* Pope, of Boston.
    vi **Patience**, who married—first, Ebenezer Harker; second, James Gardner, son of Richard and Mary.
    vii **John**, born in 1659, who married Mary Barnard, daughter of Nathaniel and Mary.
    viii **Experience**, who married John Swain Jr., son of John and Mary.
    ix **Abiah**, born August 15, 1667;† married probably in 1690, Josiah Franklin, father of Benjamin Franklin.

ELEAZER [2] (Peter [1])

born in 1648 in Edgartown; was married to Sarah Gardner, daughter of Richard Sr. in 1671 and died in 1716. He was a man of marked ability and satisfactorily filled the important positions to which he was called. At the time of his death he was one of the Representatives of the Town in the General Court. The children of Eleazer and Sarah were—

    i **Eleazer**, born July 2, 1672; married—first Bethiah Gardner, daughter of Joseph and Bethiah; second, Mary Marshall, daughter of Joseph.
    ii **Peter**, born August 28, 1674; married Judith Coffin, daughter of Stephen and Mary; died in 1707.
    iii **Sarah**, born August 24, 1676; married (March 10, 1702-3)‡ Anthony Odar, son of Nicholas Odar of Newport, Isle of Wight, England.
    iv **Mary**, born February 14, 1684; married (27th, 12 mo. 1704-5) John Arthur.
    v **Nathan**, born 1678; married (December 29, 1699) Sarah Church, ** daughter of John and Abigail of Dover.
    vi **Daniel** and vii **Elisha** died young.

JOHN [2] (Peter [1])

was born 1659; died 1732; married Mary Barnard, daughter of Nathaniel and Mary. Their children were—††

---

*William C. Folger gives this name as Joseph.
†The only child of Peter and Mary who was born in Nantucket.
‡As recorded by the Town Clerk.
**She was a sister of Col. Benj. Church, the conqueror of King Philip of Mount Hope.
††William C. Folger (N. E. Hist. General Register vol. 16, p. 272) gives Bethiah as the second child born 24th, 11 mo. 1692; married (9 mo. 1718) Samuel Barker of Falmouth.

 i **Jethro,** born October 17, 1689; married (1st, 12 mo. 1710-11) Mary Starbuck, daughter of Nathaniel Jr. and Dinah.
 ii **Nathaniel,** born 18th, 12 mo. 1694; married (November 18, 1718) Priscilla Chase, daughter of Lieut. Isaac Chase of Marthas Vineyard.
 iii **Jonathan,** born 10th, 2 mo. 1696; married—first (6th, 1 mo. 1717) Margaret Gardner, daughter of Nathaniel; second, Deborah Bunker, widow of Benjamin; third, Susanna Paddack, widow of Daniel.
 iv **Richard,** born 14th, 5 mo. 1698; married (March 11, 1722) Sarah Pease, daughter of Joseph of Martha s Vineyard; died September 1782.
 v **Shubael,** born 25th, 8 mo. 1700; married (10th, 12 mo. 1720) Jerusha Clark, daughter of Thomas and Mary; he died August 21, 1776.
 vi **Abigail,** born 8th, 4 mo. 1703; married—first (31st, 6 mo. 1721) Daniel Folger, son of Peter; second, (20th, 8 mo. 1748) Daniel Pinkham, son of Richard.
 vii **Zaccheus,** born 14th, 6 mo. 1706; married (November 20, 1728) Abigail Coffin, daughter of John and Hope. He died 20th, 7 mo. 1779.
 viii **Hannah,** born 20th, 7 mo. 1708; never married.

ELEAZER [3] (Eleazer [2] Peter [1])
died probably in September, 1753, as his will was probated October 1 of that year. He was twice married; first (September 27, 1706) to Bethiah Gardner, who died June 20, 1716; second, (September 25, 1717) to Mary Marshall, daughter of Joseph. The latter survived him. The children were, by Bethiah—

 i **Gideon,** born May 5, 1709; never married.
 ii **Urian,** born November 11, 1711; married Jedidah Pitts, widow of Jonathan. He had no children.
 iii **Eliphaz,** born June 26, 1713; married (7 mo. 1735 o s) Priscilla Gorman, daughter of Thomas; he died January 1, 1794.

Bethiah died June 20, 1716. The children by Mary, who died December 11, 1765, aged 70 years, were—

 iv **Charles,** born June 20, 1718; never married; died February 28, 1784.
 v **Deborah,** born August 5, 1719; married Benjamin Frost, son of John.

vi **Ruth**, born March 3, 1720-1; died September 16, 1729.
vii **Bethiah**, born November 8, 1722; married (30th, 10 mo. 1755) James Pinkham, son of Richard and Mary. No children.
viii **Frederick**, born February 17, 1724-5; married Mary Trott, daughter of Benjamin.*
ix **Stephen**, born September 19, 1727; married Jane Cook. Died on an English prison-ship in New York in 1782, without children.
x **Margaret**, born December 2, 1729; married (4th, 10 mo. 1753) Jonathan Swain, son of Richard 3d and died February 2, 1822.
xi **Sophia**, born August 21, 1731; married (4th, 4 mo. 1765) Matthew Worth, son of William and Mary and died January 31, 1789.
xii **Mary**, born January 1, 1735-6; married (29th, 1 mo. 1761) William Black, son of Dugal and Persis.
xiii **Peleg**, born October 13, 1733, is named in the will. He was an Elder among the Friends; did not marry.

PETER [3] (Eleazer [2] Peter [1])
born August 28, 1674, married Judith Coffin, daughter of Stephen Jr. and Experience. He died probably early in June 1707 as his will was probated June 19, of that year.

i **Keziah**, born February 23, 1699-1700; married first, (November 29, 1716) Jethro Gardner, son of James; second, (1737) Paul Starbuck, son of Nathaniel and Dinah.
ii **Daniel**, born January 13, 1701-2; married (31st, 6 mo. 1721) Abigail Folger, daughter of John and Mary. Lost at sea 1744.
iii **Anna**, born May 25, 1703; married (9th, 10 mo. 1720) William Starbuck, son of Jethro and Dorcas.
iv **Mary**, born August 10, 1705; married first (15th, 7 mo. 1725) Nathaniel Gardner, son of Nathaniel and Abigail; second, (7 mo. 1729) Nathaniel Coleman, son of John and Priscilla.

NATHAN [3] (**Eleazer [2] Peter [1]**)
born in ———— 1678; married (December 29, 1699) Sarah

---

*Frederick was a schoolmaster. Register of Probate 47 years. Clerk of the Courts and a Justice of the peace.

Church. His will was probated September 5, 1747; his wife died prior to that. Their children were—

    i **Abishai,** born September 27, 1700; married first (November 6 1727) Sarah Mayhew of Martha's Vineyard; second (7 mo. 1735), Dinah Starbuck, widow of Benjamin.

    ii **Leah,** born December 14, 1701; married first (May 26. 1724) Richard Gardner 3d; second, Seth Paddack, son of Joseph.

    iii **Esther,** born November 3, 1704; never married.

    iv **Timothy,** born September 24, 1706; married (December 5, 1733) Anna Chase.

    v **Peter,** born June 24, 1708; married (April 23, 1731) Christian Swain, daughter of John. He died in 1762.*

    vi **Barzillai,** born January 4, 1710-11; married (December 3, 1730) Phebe Coleman, daughter of John and Priscilla.

    vii **Judith,** born December 18, 1712; married (January 22, 1728-9) Thomas Jenkins, son of Matthew. (They were the parents of Seth and Thomas Jenkins, founders of Hudson, N. Y.)

JETHRO [3] (John [2] Peter [1])

born 17th 8 mo 1689; married (1st 12 mo. 1710-11) Mary Starbuck daughter of Nathaniel Jr. He died, April 19, 1772; She died July 22, 1763. Their children were—

    i **Jedidah,** born 22d 5 mo 1711; married (16th 1 mo. 1730) Robert Gardner son of Benjamin and Hannah; she died 2d 10 mo 1757.

    ii **John,** born 1714; married (13th 10 mo. 1733) Rebecca Baker daughter of John and Hannah of Barnstable. Died abroad.†

    iii **Anna,** born 1720; married (2d 1 mo. 1738) James Mitchell of Rhode Island.

---

*In his will, probated in March 1763 and dated November 15, 1762. he mentions his wife Christian, sons, Owen, Peter and Reuben, and daughters Anna, Mary, Ruth, Lydia, Rachel and Eunice. Anna married (6th, 10 mo. 1750) Eliphalet Gardner, son of James and Susanna. Peter's widow married (28th, 2 mo. 1770) Peter Jenkins, son of Matthew and Mary.

The Friends Records note the marriages of two children of Timothy and Anna—Anna, who married (2d, 2 mo. 1738) Peleg Coggeshall, son of Calef and Mercy; and Benjamin who married (3d 12th mo. 1761) Phebe Worth, daughter of Christopher and Dinah.

†Jedidah, daughter of John and Rebecca, married (28th 2nd mo. 1754) William Coffin, son of Francis and Theodate.

iv Lydia, born 1722; married (3d 1 mo. 1742) Hezekiah Coffin. son of Joseph and Bethiah; she died 4th 9 mo 1807.
v Eunice, born 1724; married (10th 11 mo. 1750) George Coleman, son of Solomon and Deliverance; died 9th. 4 mo. 1782.
vi Tristram, born 1727; married (10th. 11mo. 1750) Mary Coffin daughter of Prince and Mercy who died in 1776; Second Mary Folger, widow of Nathaniel, daughter of Timothy Wyer; he died 2d 2 mo. 1785.
vii Hepzibah born 1729; married (3d 1 mo. 1747) Jonathan Swain son of Richard and Elizabeth; died 18th 1 mo. 1750.
viii Jethro, born 1731; married (4th 12 mo. 1753) Mary Barnard daughter of Thomas and Sarah who died July 1, 1767; second (1st 12 mo 1768) Anna Swain daughter of John 3d and Mary; he died May 22, 1796; she died Feb 14, 1801.

NATHANIEL [3] (John [2] Peter [1])
born February 18, 1694, married (November 18, 1718) Priscilla Chase, daughter of Isaac of Tisbury. He died 15th, 4 mo. 1775; she died 30th 12 mo 1753.
Their children were:

i Elizabeth, born 1719; married Paul Pease (August 8, 1737). died November 1795.
ii Rebecca, born September 10, 1721; married Benjamin Marchant. She died 5th 10 mo. 1778.
iii Judith, born June 3, 1726; married (10th 11 mo. 17- Marchant. She died 5th, 10 mo 1778.
44) Edmund Heath, son of Edmund and Katherine. She died February 8, 1775.
iv Paul, born November 5, 1729; married (February 8 1749-50) Catherine Coffin, daughter of Robert and Susanna. He died June 11, 1799; she died September 4, 1822.

JONATHAN [3] (John [2] Peter [1])
born April 10, 1696, married (March 6, 1717) Margaret Gardner,

daughter of Nathaniel.* He died 6th 3 mo 1777; she died 16th 5 mo. 1727. Their children were;

    i **Ruth**, born 10th 4 mo. 1718; never married; died 14th 12 mo. 1733.
    ii **Dinah**, born 24th 4 mo. 1720; married (January 3, 1744) Stephen Chase; died 18th 2 mo. 1786.
    iii **Reuben**, born 10th 6 mo. 1722; died 28th 8 mo. 1808; married first (22d, 1 mo. 1743-4) Dinah Hussey, daughter of George and Elizabeth; second (31st, 1 mo. 1765) Mary Pinkham, daughter of Jonathan and Anna Ramsdel. She died October 9, 1807.
    iv **Abigail**, born 27th 5 mo. 1724; married (29th 8 mo 1757) David Coffin son of Tristram and Mary; died 8th 8 mo. 1792.
    v **Jonathan**, born 7th 5 mo. 1727; died 28th 4 mo. 1812; married (20th 10 mo. 1750) Lydia Barnard, daughter of Ebenezer and Mary. She died June 7, 1800.

RICHARD [3] (John [2] Peter [1])
born July 14, 1698; married (October 11, 1722) Sarah Pease, daughter of Joseph, of Marthas Vineyard. Their children were:

    i **Susanna**, born 18th 5 mo. 1724; married Ebenezer Cleaveland.
    ii **Rachel**, born 13th, 4 mo. 1726; married John Ellis, son of Humphrey. She was struck by lightning and killed 14th 6 mo. 1756.†
    iii **Sylvanus**, born 11th, 4 mo. 1728.
    iv **David**, born 3d 7 mo. 1730; married first Anna Pitts daughter of Jonathan; second (September 9, 1784) Susanna Foy, daughter of John Ellis.
    v **Ruth**, born 30th 9 mo. 1732; married Christopher Pinkham son of John.
    vi **Solomon**, born 13th 1 mo. 1735; married Lydia Russell, daughter of Benjamin. He died August 7, 1813; she died July 7, 1809.
    vii **Martha**, born 25th 3 mo. 1737; married Obadiah Gardner son of Logan.
    viii **Hepzibah**, born December 24, 1743; married first (February 6, 1766) William Mooers. son of Thomas; second John Hall. She died June 6, 1812.

---

*Jonathan also married—second (5 mo. 1728) Deborah Bunker widow of Benjamin and daughter of Zachariah Paddack of Yarmouth, who died 27th 4 mo. 1750; third Susanna Paddack, widow of Daniel, daughter of Stephen Gorham, who died 13th 7 mo. 1777.
†W. C. Folger, N. E. Hist. & Geneal Reg.

ix Elisha, born September 16, 1746; married Deborah Swain, daughter of Caleb and Margaret. He died January 25, 1836; she died April 1825.

SHUBAEL [3] (John [2] Peter [1])
born August 25, 1700; married (10th 12 mo. 1720) Jerusha Clark, daughter of Thomas. He died 22d 8 mo. 1776; she died 20th 8 mo. 1778. Their children were;

- i Phebe, born 2d 11 mo. 1724; died 25th 2 mo. 1802; married (8th. 11 mo. 1740) Joseph Marshall son of Joseph and Abigail.
- ii Seth, born 8th, 8 mo. 1726; married (14th, 9 mo. 1745) Phebe Coleman, daughter of Elihu and Jemima. He died November 17, 1807; she died December 1797.
- iii Mary, born 20th 10 mo. 1728; married first (7th 9 mo. 1745) Benjamin Worth, son of Richard and Lydia; second (8 mo 1751) Peleg Coleman son of Solomon and Deliverance.
- iv Benjamin, born 8th 8 mo. 1731; married (5th 12 mo. 1754) Judith Barnard daughter of Timothy and Mary.
- v Jemima, born 9th 11 mo. 1734; married (8th 3 mo. 1753) Solomon Gardner son of Andrew and Mary.
- vi Shubael, born 24th, 5 mo. 1737; lost at sea, 1774; married (5th 1 mo. 1757) Lydia Bunker, daughter of George and Abigail.
- vii Abigail, born 2d 8 mo. 1739; married (6th 1 mo. 1757) Benjamin Gardner son of James and Susanna. He died on a prison ship in New York in December 1777.

ZACCHEUS [3] (John [2] Peter [1])
born August 14, 1706; married (November 20, 1728) Abigail Coffin, daughter of John and Hope. Their children were—

- i Mary, born June 3, 1730; did not marry.
- ii James, born June 13, 1731; married Mary Aldrich, who died February 15, 1802.
- iii John, born July 30, 1733; married—first Love Gabriel, daughter of Manuel, who died 3d 9 mo. 1768; second Lydia Gardner, daughter of Robert and Jedidah.

    iv **Nathaniel,** married (1759) Mary Wyer, daughter of Timothy.
    v **Anna,** born 4th, 7 mo. 1744; married (April 11, 1779) Christopher Swain, son of Richard; she died February 15, 1819.
    vi **Abigail,** married Elijah Coffin, son of Hezekiah.
    vii **Andrew,** never married.
    viii **Reuben.**
    ix **Zaccheus.**

ELIPHAZ [4] (Eleazer, [3] Eleazer [2] Peter [1])
born June 26. 1713; died 1st 1 mo 1794; married (probably in 1738) Priscilla Gorham daughter of Thomas. Their children were:

    i **Eunice,** born 6th 5 mo. 1739.
    ii **Paul,** born 20th 5 mo. 1741.
    iii **Elisha,** born 2d 11 mo 1743; died 10 mo. 1783.
    iv **Rachel,** born 25th 7 mo. 1746; died 11th 9 mo. 1830.
    v **Stephen,** born 18th 12 mo. 1748.
    vi **Gorham,** born 25th 12 mo. 1753.

DANIEL [4] (Peter [3] Eleazer [2] Peter [1])
born January 13, 1701-2; married (August 31, 1721) Abigail Folger, daughter of John and Mary; he died 30th 8 mo. 1744; she died 21st 11 mo 1787. Their children were;

    i **Elisha,** born 3d 12 mo. 1721-2; lost at sea 1740.
    ii **Kezia,** born 9th 10 mo. 1723; married (4th 10 mo. 1740) John Coffin, son of Samuel and Miriam.*
    iii **Peter,** born 17th 2 mo. 1726; died 30th 8 mo. 1744.†
    iv **Judith,** born 15th 1 mo. 1728-9; married James Gardner, son of Jethro and Kezia.‡
    v **Abigail,** born 25th 4 mo. 1731; married (1st 1 mo. 1749-50) Barnabas Coffin, son of Richard and Ruth.

---

*Kezia Folger was in many respects a remarkable woman. She was the original Miriam Coffin pictured in Mr. Hart's novel. She was a pronounced royalist during the Revolution. Many of the stories of smuggling, etc., told concerning her are unquestionably pure fiction. She was a thorough business woman and made no secret of the purchase of goods. During the latter part of her life she was much involved in litigation. She died March 25, 1798, being killed by a fall down the stairs in her home.
  †Lost at sea with his father.
  ‡Judith subsequently married (3d 12 mo. 1749) Caleb Macy son of Richard.

vi **Mary**, born 6th, 7 mo. 1733; married (10th, 5 mo. 1753) William Starbuck, son of Thomas and Rachel.
vii **Daniel**, born 14th, 1 mo. 1735-6; married (2d, 2 mo. 1758) Judith Worth, daughter of Christopher and Dinah; removed from the Island 1775.

ABISHAI [4] (Nathan, [3] Eleazer [2] Peter [1]) born September 27 1700. appears to have been twice married—first to Sarah Mayhew. Sarah, his first wife died July 11, 1734; second to Dinah Starbuck; he died 22d, 1 mo. 1778.
Their children were:

By Sarah Mayhew—

1 **William**, born ———; married (7th 10 mo. 1749) Ruth Coffin, daughter of Richard and Ruth.
ii **George**, born ———; married — first (7th 12 mo. 1752) Sarah Coleman, daughter of Barnabas and Rachel; second to Sarah Shove daughter of Barnabas.
iii **Timothy**, born ———; married (6th, 12 mo. 1753) Abiel Coleman, daughter of Barnabas and Rachel.

By his second wife, Dinah—

iv **Sarah**, born 16th 8 mo. 1739; married (9th 2 mo. 1758) Hezekiah Gardner, son of David and Mary.
v **Abishai**, married (7th 1 mo. 1773) Elizabeth Coleman daughter of Barnabas and Rachel.
vi **Hephzibah**, married (4th 12 mo. 1760) Daniel Hussey son of Daniel and Sarah.
vii **Dinah**. Married Seth Jenkins.
viii **John**, born 1746.
ix **Robert**, born 1748.
x **Reuben** born 1755.

TIMOTHY [4] (Nathan [3] Eleazer [2] Peter [1]) married (6th 12 mo. 1753) Abiel Coleman, daughter of Barnabas and Rachel. They removed from the Island in 1793. Their children were:

i **Silvanus**, born 28th 10 mo. 1754.
ii **Abial**, born 4th 1 mo. 1757.

  iii **Sarah,** born 27th 4 mo. 1760; married Peter Macy, (28th, 11 mo. 1780).
  iv **Lucretia,** born 28th 4 mo. 1762; married Samuel Starbuck (27th 11 mo. 1783.)
  v **Margaret,** born 4th 6 mo. 1764.
  vi **Timothy,** born 2d 12 mo. 1768.
  vii **Benjamin Franklin,** born 25th 2 mo. 1769*; married Mary Lawrence (9th 12 mo. 1790).

BARZILLAI [4] (Nathan, [3] Eleazer, [2] Peter [1]) born January 4, 1710-11, married (December 3, 1730) Phebe Coleman, daughter of John and Priscilla. He died April 11, 1790; she died February 17. 1791. Their children were:

  i **Judith,** born 15th 3 mo 1731; married (2d 12 mo. 1748) Benjamin Barnard, son of Matthew and Mary.
  ii **Christopher,** born 28th 12 mo. 1732; died 21st 4 mo. 1774; married (3d 1 mo 1765) Anna Joy, daughter of David and Sarah—and, second, (6th. 12 mo. 1770) Susanna Gardner, daughter of Christopher and Mary Hussey.†
  iii **Walter,** born 18th, 1 mo. 1735; married (13th, 1 mo. 1757) Elizabeth Starbuck, daughter of Thomas and Rachel.
  iv **Nathan,** born 26th 3 mo. 1737; married (10th 2 mo. 1763) Elizabeth Worth, daughter of Christopher and Dinah, removed from the island 1779.
  v **Phebe,** born 26th 11 mo. 1739; married (10th 1 mo 1760) Francis Joy, son of David and Sarah.
  vi **Barzillai,** born 9th 5 mo. 1742; married (30th 1 mo. 1766) Miriam Gardner, daughter of Stephen and Jemima.
  vii **Gilbert,** born 5th 12 mo. 1744; married (12th 12 mo. 1771) Anna Gardner, daughter of Charles and Anna.
  viii **Charles,** born 13th 4 mo. 1747; died 25th 5 mo. 1748.
  ix **Elizabeth,** born 3d 7 mo. 1749;
  x **Tristram,** born 8th, 8 mo. 1751; married first, (4th, 1 mo. 1776) Rhoda Hussey daughter of George and Deborah and second, Mary Joy, daughter of Reuben and Anna.

---

*This is among the earliest instances of the use of middle names.
†The Town Records show that a Christopher Folger and Abigail Barnard were married June 6, 1753. Doubtless it was this same Christopher.

HISTORY OF NANTUCKET 751

TRISTRAM [4](Jethro [3] John [2] Peter [1])
born 10th 8 mo. 1727; married (10th 11 mo. 1750) Mary Coffin, daughter of Prince and Mary; she died 2d 9 mo. 1776. Their children were

    i Tristram, born 18th 4 mo. 1752.
    ii Hephzibah, born 16th, 10 mo. 1754.
    iii Lebbeus, born 22d 11 mo. 1756.
    iv Abraham, born 11th 6 mo. 1759.
    v Joseph, born 7th 9 mo. 1761.
    vi Amy, born 15th 7 mo. 1764.
    vii Jared, born 13th, 10 mo. 1766; died 7th, 7 mo. 1793.
    viii Elijah, born 9th 8 mo. 1769; died 14th 8 mo. 1788.
    ix Tristram, born 25th 10 mo. 1772.

JETHRO [4] (Jethro [3] John [2] Peter [1])
was born 29th 9 mo. 1721; died 22d 5 mo. 1796; married (4th 12 mo. 1753) Mary Barnard, daughter of Thomas and Sarah, who died 1st 7 mo. 1767. Their children were:

    i Sarah, born 17th 9 mo. 1754.
    ii Anna, born 6th 9 mo. 1756.
    iii Jedidah, born 29th 1 mo. 1759.
    iv Lydia, born 21st 6 mo. 1761.
    v Elihu, born 2d. 10 mo. 1763.
    vi Mary, born 4th 1 mo. 1766.

Jethro married a second time. (1st 12 mo. 1768) to Anna Swain, daughter of John and Mary, but there is no record of any children by the second wife.

REUBEN [4] (Jonathan [3] John [2] Peter [1])
was twice married—first (22d. 1 mo. 1743-4) to Dinah Hussey, daughter of George and Elizabeth; and second (31st 1 mo. 1765) to Mary Pinkham, widow, daughter of Jonathan and Anna Ramsdel. He died 28th 8 mo. 1808; Dinah died 20th 9 mo. 1763; Mary died 11th 10 mo. 1807. Their children were—

By Dinah:

    i Margaret, born 27th, 4 mo. 1747; married (2d 1 mo. 1766) Tristram Barnard son of William and Mary and removed from the Island in 1773.

        ii **Latham**, born 5th 10 mo. 1749; removed from the Island in 1777.
       iii **Rhoda**, born—2 mo 1754; died the same year.
       iv **Matilda**, born 20th, 4 mo. 1756; removed from the Island in 1784.
       v **Rebecca**, born 3d 6 mo. 1758.
      vi **Asa**, born 30th 8 mo. 1760.

By Mary—

      vii **Dinah**, born 18th 11 mo. 1765; died 10th 10 mo. 1766.
     viii **Franklin**, born 14th 2 mo. 1767; died 5th 12 mo. 1768.
      ix **Mary**, born 25th 1 mo. 1769; died 25th. 6 mo. 1769.
       x **Mary**, born 18th 11 mo. 1771; died 11th 11 mo. 1842.
      xi **Abigail**, born 17th, 4 mo. 1778.
     xii **Obadiah**, born 10th 12 mo. 1755; married (November 18, 1780) Ruth Macy, daughter of Francis and Judith.

JONATHAN [4] (Jonathan [3] John [2] Peter [1]) married (December 20, 1750) Lydia Barnard, daughter of Ebenezer and Mary. Their children were:

        i **Peregrine**, born 21st 6 mo. 1754: died 24th 12 mo. 1831. married (30th 9 mo. 1779) Rachel Hussey, daughter of Nathaniel and Judith.
       ii **Obed**, born 21st 2 mo. 1756.
      iii **Merab**, born 30th 7 mo. 1758. died in infancy.
       iv **Ebenezer**, born 21st 6 mo. 1760; died 4th 7 mo. 1781
       v **Lydia**, born 14th 10 mo. 1764.
      vi **Hezekiah**, born 30th. 10 mo. 1766.
      vii **Barnard**, born 16th. 4 mo. 1770; died 20th, 8 mo. 1795.
     viii **Mary**, born 10th 5 mo. 1772; removed from the Island 1792.
      ix **Elizabeth**, born 21st 9 mo. 1774; died 17th 1 mo. 1800.

SETH [4] (Shubael, [3] John [2] Peter [1]) born 8th 8 mo. 1728: died 17th 11 mo. 1807; married (14th 9 mo. 1745) Phebe Coleman, daughter of Elihu and Jemima, who died 8th 12 mo. 1797. Their children were:

        i **Thomas**, born 24th 10 mo. 1746.
       ii **Seth**, born 1st 1 mo. 1749.

HISTORY OF NANTUCKET 753

 iii **Benjamin,** born 18th 8 mo. 1750; died 5th 10 mo. 1755.
 iv **Phebe,** born 8th 7 mo. 1753.
 v **Benjamin,** born 29th 3 mo. 1756.
 vi **Timothy,** born 12th 12 mo. 1757; died 18th 4 mo. 1759.
 vii **Jemima,** born 31st 3 mo. 1762.
 viii **Shubael,** born 11th, 11 mo. 1763.

BENJAMIN [4] (Shubael [3] John [2] Peter [1])
born October 8, 1731; married (5th December 1754) Judith Barnard, daughter of Timothy and Mary. Their children were:

 i **Hepzibah,** born 23d, 9 mo. 1755; died 26th, 6 mo. 1759.
 ii **Eunice,** born 14th, 11 mo. 1756.
 iii **Jemima,** born 16th, 9 mo. 1758.
 iv **Job,** born 3d, 10 mo. 1760.
 v **Susannah,** born 13th, 9 mo. 1762.
 vi **Mary,** born 11th 9 mo. 1765.
 vii **Timothy,** born 9th 7 mo 1767.

SHUBAEL [4] (Shubael [3] John [2] Peter [1])
born 24th 5 mo. 1737; married (5th 1 mo. 1757) Lydia Bunker daughter of George and Abigail; he was lost at sea in 1774. Their children were:

 i **Lydia,** born 9th 5 mo. 1758; died 2d 5 mo. 1759.
 ii **Hepzibah,** born 30th, 6 mo. 1760; removed from the Island 27th, 7 mo. 1815; probably married (February 6, 1766) William Moors.
  27th 7 mo. 1815; probably married (February 6, 1766) William Moors.
 iii **Simeon,** born 23d 7 mo. 1762; probably married (June 26, 1787) Phebe Wyer.
 iv **Isaiah,** born 29th, 5 mo. 1765; probably married (August 28, 1788) Rachel Worth.
 v **George,** born, 31st 5 mo. 1767; died 17th 8 mo. 1769.
 vi **Lydia,** born 27th 12 mo. 1768; removed from the Island 29th. 4 mo. 1802; married (31st 1 mo 1788) Benjamin Austin, son of Benjamin and Susanna.
 vii **Sally,** born 9th 11 mo. 1771.

DANIEL [5] (Daniel [4] Peter [3] Eleazer [2] Peter [1]) born 14th 1 mo. 1735-6; married (2d 2 mo. 1758) Judith Worth, daughter of Christopher and Dinah; they removed from the Island 27th, 2 mo. 1775. Their children, born in Nantucket, all of whom accompanied their parents, were:—

 i **Elisha**, born 14th. 8 mo. 1760.
 ii **Clarinda**, born 20th. 8 mo. 1762.
 iii **Abigail**, born 5th, 9 mo. 1766.
 iv **Judith**, born 26th. 11 mo. 1768.
 v **Moses**, born 14th 9 mo. 1772.
 vi **Aaron**, born 13th 11 mo. 1774.

WALTER [5] (Barzillai [4] Nathan [3] Eleazer [2] Peter[1]) born 18th, 1 mo. 1735; married (13th 1 mo. 1757) Elizabeth Starbuck, daughter of Thomas and Rachel. Their children were:—

 i **Elizabeth**, born 31st, 5 mo. 1758; married (3d 4 mo. 1777) Richard Worth, son of Richard and Anna. Removed from the Island 27th 6 mo. 1799.
 ii **Hepzibah**, born 28th 8 mo. 1760; died 21st 9 mo. 1821.
 iii **Phebe**, born 11th. 11mo. 1762; died 2d 10 mo. 1765.
 iv **Walter,*** born 12th 6 mo. 1765; married (29th 12 mo. 1785) Anna Ray, daughter of Alexander & Elizabeth.
 v **Lydia**, born 12th 4 mo. 1767; married (29th 6 mo. 1786) Samuel Macy, son of Jonathan and Lois.
 vi **Ezekiel**, born 20th 3 mo. 1769; died 29th 9 1770.
 vii **Phebe**, born 10th. 11 mo. 1771; married (6th 12 mo. 1798) Samuel Coleman, son of Elisha and Elizabeth.
 viii **Cleona**, born 10th, 1 mo. 1773; died 1 mo. 1775.
 ix **Aaron**, born 27th 2, 1776; married (1798-9) Polly Thompson.
 x **Rebecca**, born 23d, 3 mo. 1778; married (8th, 5 mo. 1800) Alexander Folger, son of George and Sarah; died 23d, 7 mo. 1823.

---

*Walter Folger Jr., was in many respects a remarkable man. Prof. Silliman classed him as a very talented scientist. He studied medicine and law and was a Counsellor at Law. Chief Justice of the Court of Sessions, member of both branches of the General Court and Representative in Congress four years. In science he made many astronomical calculations and won more than local fame in his scientific work, especially in its astronomical phase.

Note.—Another distinguished member of the Folger family was Hon. Charles James Folger, born in Nantucket in 1818 who was successively Judge of the Ontario, N. Y., Court of Common Pleas; four years County Judge of Ontario; member of the New York Senate for five terms. Sub-Treasurer of the United States at New York, Chief Justice of the New York Court of Appeals and Secretary of the United States Treasury.

HISTORY OF NANTUCKET

xi Gideon, born 20th 4 mo. 1781; married (10th 1 mo. 1805) Eunice Macy daughter of Silvanus and Anna.

WILLIAM [5] (Abishai, [4] Nathan [3] Eleazer [2] Peter [1]) married (7th 10 mo. 1749) Ruth Coffin daughter of Richard and Ruth; he died 5th 6 mo 1815; she died 11th 3 mo. 1814.
Their children were:—

    i **Judith**, born 16th, 7 mo. 1750. Married (1767) Zaccheus Bunker.
    ii **Lydia**, born 30th 6 mo. 1753; died 30th 12 mo. 1753.
    iii **William**, born 10th 11 mo. 1754. Married Susan Swain.
    iv **Sarah**, born 24th 3 mo. 1757. Married (1777) Tristram Hussey.
    v **Lydia**, born 20th 4 mo. 1759. Married Zaccheus Hussey.
    vi **Richard**, born 12th 6 mo. 1760; died 23d 12 mo. 1775.
    vii **Francis**, born 12th 7 mo. 1762; died 10th 12 mo. 1784.
    viii **Elizabeth**, born 8th 9 mo. 1766. Married (1786) Josiah Barker.
    ix **Phebe**, born 21st 9 mo. 1768. Married Uriel Hussey.
    x **Anna**, born 25th. 3 mo. 1771. Married Thomas Coffin.
    xi **Mayhew**, born 9th 3 mo. 1774.* Married (1789) Mary Joy.

George [5] (Abishai, [4] Nathan [3] Eleazer [2] Peter[1]) born————; married (7th 12 mo. 1752) Sarah Coleman, daughter of Barnabas and Rachel; she died 8th 3 mo. 1778. Their children were: ——

    i **Mayhew**, born 9th 10 mo. 1753; died 2d 2 mo 1760.
    ii **George**, born 16th 6 mo 1756.
    iii **Rebecca**, born 25th. 8 mo. 1758.
    iv **Mayhew**, born 9th 9 mo. 1760.
    v **Hephzibah**, born 28th 7 mo. 1762.
    vi **Susannah**, born 6th 8 mo. 1764; died 21st 4 mo 1777.
    vii **Dinah**, born 22d 6 mo. 1766.
    viii **Barnabas**, born 4th, 9 mo. 1768.
    ix **Clement**, born 26th 1 mo. 1770.
    x **Alexander**, born 22d 12 mo. 1773.
    xi **Arnold**, born 2d. 3 mo. 1778; died 3 months later.

---

*Capt. Mayhew Folger, commanding the ship Topaz discovered in 1809 on Pitcairn's Island the lost mutineers of the English ship Bounty.

GARDNER

The two brothers, Richard and John Gardner, sons of Thomas, were residents of Salem, before coming to Nantucket. They were probably both born in England, coming to America about 1640. Richard was the first to remove to Nantucket, where he was granted a half share March 22, 1666-7, to exercise his trade as a "Seaman." His oldest son, Joseph, was also granted a half share February 15, 1667, to exercise his trade as a "Shoe Maker." Joseph's contract, under vote of the Town February 15, 1667, grants him "half a share of accommatition answarable to the other Tradesmen on conditions that he supply the occasions of the Island in way of a Shoemaker, and likewise that he shall not leve the Island in point of Dwelling for the Space of four years or if it so fall out that he shall remove off from the Island within the aforesaid Terme that he shall leave the said accomadation aforementioned to his brother Richard on the terms aforesaid that he supply the occasions of the Island as a Shoemaker." It is very probable that father and son removed in 1667 or 1668.* The Records show that at this time John Bishop, sold to Richard Gardner a tract of land at Wesco Pond.

About the same time a grant of land was made to John Gardner. There seems, however, to be no evidence that John removed to the Island until 1672 or 1673.†

Mr. Worth says "His" (Richard's) "house lot was around Wesco now called Lily Pond, so irregular in form as to be called the "Crooked Record." His house was on the west end of Sunset Hill, where is now." (1901) "the residence of Eben W. Francis. He was Chief Magistrate in 1673 and held other Town offices. None of the old records are in his handwriting, from which it may be inferred that he was not educated. * * * His house was probably the easternmost of that day. * * * Joseph Gardner was constable, assessor and selectman each once. * * * He probably lived within the limits of the "Crooked Record."

"John Gardner, called Capt. Gardner, married Priscilla Grafton. He died in 1706, 82 years old, and left a widow and 12 children. His house lot was on the north side of the road which is now called North street, and included 30 acres, and extended from the road to the Cliff. It was west of the Hamblin house."‡

Richard Gardner Senior married Sarah Shattuck, daughter of Samuel. Their children were: i, **Joseph**; ii, **Sarah**** iii, **Richard** (born October 23, 1653); iv, **Deborah**, (born December 12, 1658);

---

*Mr. Worth says in 1665 (Land and Land Owners p. 68).

†S. Baring Gould in "Family Names and Their Story" says "The name (Gardner) is French; we may conclude, therefore, that the Anglo-Saxons had no gardens, only orchards. The surname is often spelled Gardiner and Gardner, also Jardine." (p 108). Patronymica Britannica says of the name—"Its principal modern forms are Gardiner, which according to Camden's joke denotes the gentleman, and the more plebeian Gardner. Gardener itself is rare."

‡"Land and Land Owners" pp. 68-9.

**Gardner makes Sarah the third and Richard the second child. (Thomas Gardner, Planter, pp. 49-50).

v, **Damaris** (born November 21, 1662); vi, **James** (born May 19, 1664); vii, **Miriam**; viii, **Nathaniel** (born November 16, 1669); ix, **Hope** (born November 16 1669); x, **Love** (born May 2, 1672). Sarah married Eleazer Folger son of Peter; Deborah married first John Macy, son of Thomas, and second, Stephen Pease; Miriam married (September 22, 1684) John Worth, son of William; Hope married John Coffin, son of James and Mary. Richard Senior died January 23, 1688; his widow died 1724, aged about 92 years.

John Gardner married (February 20, 1654*) Priscilla Grafton, daughter of Joseph. Their children were—i, **John**; born February 20, 1654; ii, **Joseph** born July 8, 1655; iii, **Priscilla** born November 6, 1656; who Savage thinks had married John Arthur in Salem, but her husband having died she followed her father to Nantucket; iv, **Benjamin**, born February 3, 1658 (died young); v, **Rachel**, born August 3, 1661, who married first John Brown and second James Gardner her cousin; vi, **George**, born———; died 17th, 2d mo. 1750, married Eunice Starbuck, daughter of Nathaniel and Mary; vii, **Benjamin**, born May 17, 1664; viii, **Ann**, born February 20, 1667, who married Edward Coffin, son of Peter Jr. and Abigail; ix, **Nathaniel**, born September 24, 1668; and x, **Mary**, born May 27, 1670, who married (1686) Jethro Coffin, son of Peter.† About 1672 he removed to Nantucket and there had xi, **Mehitable**, born November 24, 1674, who married (August 14, 1704) Ambrose Dawes; and xii, **Ruth**, born January 26, 1676, who married (19th, 3 mo. 1692) James Coffin, son of James and Mary. In his will, probated October 2, 1706, he mentions his wife, one son only—xiii, **George**— and six daughters, so it is likely his other sons did not come to the Island.

JOSEPH [2] (Richard [1])

married (March 30, 1670) Bethiah Macy, daughter of Thomas Senior and Sarah. Their children were—

    i **Sarah**, born October 23, 1672, who married Joseph Paddack (March 5, 1696).
    ii **Damaris**, born February, 16, 1674, who married Stephen Barnard, son of Nathaniel.

---

*Savage thinks this date erroneous.
†In his will, probated in 1706, dated December 2, 1705, John Gardner mentions a son George and grandsons Jeremiah and Nathaniel Gardner. Also a grandson John Gardner to whom he devises land and his ⅛ of a watermill in Salem. He mentions land, stock, cattle, etc., on Nantucket and Martha's Vineyard.

  iii **Bethiah**, born August 13, 1676, who married Eleazer Folger Jr., son of Eleazer and Sarah (September 27, 1706).
  iv **Deborah**, born March 30, 1681.
  v **Hope Macy**, born January 7, 1683, who married Peter Coffin, son of John and Deborah.
  vi **Mary**, born 26th, 12 mo. 1686, who married Matthew Jenkins, (9th, 8 mo. 1706).
  vii **Abiel**, born 1st, 12 mo. 1691-2, who married William Clasby, Senior of England (20th, 8 mo. 1719)

Nathaniel Barney says* "One daughter did not marry and an only son was drowned in his youth. This daughter must have been iv, Deborah, who was born March 30, 1681.

RICHARD [2] (Richard [1])

born October 23, 1653; married (May 17, 1674) Mary Austin, daughter of Joseph and Dover;† died 8th, 3d mo. 1728; his will, which was probated July 17, 1728, makes no mention of his wife so doubtless she died first. Their children were—

  i **Patience**, born June 29, 1675.
  ii **Joseph**, born May 8, 1677; died 29th, 7 mo. 1747; married Ruth Coffin, daughter of James Senior.† By the terms of his father's will after some minor bequests, the residue of the estate was left to the sons. Joseph to receive a double share.
  iii **Solomon**, born July 1, 1680; died 17th, 6 mo. 1760; married Anna Coffin, daughter of Stephen and Mary.†
  iv **Benjamin**, born July 20, 1683; died 22d, 1 mo. 1764; married Hannah Coffin, daughter of John and Deborah.†
  v **Miriam**, born July 14, 1685; died 17th, 9 mo. 1750; married Samuel Coffin, son of Lieut. John and Deborah.†
  vi **Peter**, died 28th, 5 mo. 1767; married Elizabeth Coffin, daughter of Enoch and Beulah.†
  vii **Lydia**, born June 16, 1687; died February 8, 1688.
  viii **Lydia**, (2d) died April, 1788; married John Coffin. son of Jethro and Mary.
  ix **Richard**, died February 27, 1724-5; married (May 26, 1724) Leah Folger, daughter of Nathan and Sarah.
  x **William**, died 1739; married (February 20, 1719) Hepzibah Gardner, widow of Peleg Gardner and daughter of George and Eunice Gardner.

---

*Unpublished M. S.
†Thomas Gardner, Planter, pp. 49, 50.

JAMES [2] (Richard [1])

born May 19, 1662, at Salem; married—first Mary Starbuck, daughter of Nathaniel and Mary, and the first child born of English parents on Nantucket; second, Rachel, widow of John Brown, of Salem and daughter of John Gardner; third— Patience Harker, widow of Ebenezer and daughter of Peter and Mary Folger; fourth Mary Pinkham, widow of Richard and daughter of James and Mary Coffin.* His children were—

i Samuel,† died 28th, 10 mo. 1757; married—first (September 4, 1707) Hepzibah Coffin, daughter of Stephen and Mary; second (27th, 10 mo. 1710) Patience Swain, daughter of John and Mary; third, Mary Swain, widow of John 3d, daughter of Moses and Mary Swett, of Hampton.

ii Jethro,† died 7th, 3 mo. 1734; married (1 mo. 1716) Keziah Folger, daughter of Peter and Judith.

iii Barnabas, born 12th, 2 mo. 1695; died 14th, 9 mo. 1768; married (December 11, 1718) Mary Wheeler, of Boston.

iv Jonathan, born 12th, 7 mo. 1696; died 3d, 7 mo. 1777; married (14th, 8 mo. 1723) Patience Bunker, daughter of Jonathan and Elizabeth.

v Elizabeth,† died 22d, 7 mo. 1763; married (December 25, 1703) Stephen Gorham, son of John of Barnstable.

vi Mehitable,† died 28th, 2 mo. 1777; married (1724) Philip Pollard, son of George and Mary.

vii James,† died 10th 4 mo. 1776; married (September 1, 1724) Susannah Gardner, daughter of Nathaniel and Abigail. She died in 1781.

NATHANIEL [2] (Richard [1])
born 16th, 9 mo. 1669; died in England 1713; married Abigail Coffin, daughter of James and Mary, who died 15th, 3 mo. 1709. Their children were—

---

*Thomas Gardner, Planter, p. 51.
†Gardner Genealogy—"Thomas Gardner, Planter."

i **Hannah,** born 6th, 5 mo. 1686; died 25th, 3 mo. 1773; married (November 19, 1706) Jabez Bunker, son of William and Mary.
ii **Ebenezer,** born 27th, 8 mo. 1688; died 16th, 4 mo. 1763; married first (September 1, 1709) Eunice Coffin, daughter of Peter and Elizabeth; second, Judith Coffin, daughter of John and Hope.
iii **Peleg,** born 22d, 5 mo. 1691; died 19th, 1 mo. 1771-2; married (23d, 7 mo. 1714) Hepzabeth Gardner, daughter of George and Eunice.
iv **Judith,** born 28th, 8 mo. 1693; died 17th, 9 mo. 1765; married (3d, 11 mo. 1711) Benjamin Barnard, son of Nathaniel and Judith.
v **Margaret,** born 28th, 11 mo. 1695; died 16th, 5 mo. 1727; married (11 mo. 1716) Jonathan Folger, son of John and Mary.
vi **Nathaniel,** born 14th, 10 mo. 1697; died 5 mo. 1727) married (15th, 7 mo. 1725) Mary Folger, daughter of Peter and Judith.*
vii **Andrew,** born 26th, 10 mo. 1699; died 2d, 3 mo. 1782; married (1st, 7 mo. 1721) Mary Gorham, daughter of Stephen and Elizabeth.
viii **Abel,** born 6th, 6 mo. 1702; died 11th, 9 mo. 1771; married (18th, 9 mo. 1723) Priscilla Coffin, daughter of James and Ruth.
ix **Susannah,** born 4th, 6 mo. 1706; died 6 mo. 1781; married (September 1, 1724) James Gardner, son of James and Rachel.

JOSEPH [3] (Richard [2] Richard [1])
born May 8, 1677; married Ruth Coffin, daughter of James and Mary. Under the terms of his will, drawn April 19, 1743, and probated October 23, 1747, the estate was left to his sons (i) **Bethuel,** (ii) **Charles,** (iii) **Shubael** and (iv) **Caleb;** his daughters (v) **Patience** (Brock) and (vi) **Margaret;** his wife Ruth; and grandchildren Timothy Gardner, Mary Gardner and Obed Gardner. When the division was made, in 1748, it was stated that Shubael had died at sea.

SOLOMON [3] (Richard [2] Richard [1])
was born July 1, 1680; married Anna Coffin, daughter of Stephen and Mary. His will, which was dated August 13, 1753, was probated July 21, 1760, so that it is reasonable to presume that he died

*Mary, widow of Nathaniel, married (4th, 10 mo. 1729) Nathaniel Coleman, son of John and Priscilla.

HISTORY OF NANTUCKET 761

in June or July of that year. As his wife's name is not mentioned in it, it is also reasonable to assume that she died prior to its execution. In his will he names ten children:—*

 i **Reuben**, who married (4th, 10 mo. 1735) Theodate Coffin, widow of Francis and daughter of Shubael and Puella Gorham.
 ii **David**, who married (15th, 9 mo. 1733) Mary Gardner, daughter of Samuel and Patience.
 iii **Stephen**, who married (7th, 8 mo. 1742) Jemima Worth, daughter of William and Mary.
 iv **Richard**, who married (5th, 12 mo. 1746) Sarah Macy, daughter of John and Judith.
 v **Solomon**, who married (1st, 9 mo. 1750) Mary Pollard, daughter of Philip and Mehitable.
 vi **Paul**, who married (7th, 2 mo. 1754) Rachel Starbuck, daughter of Thomas and Rachel.
 vii **Elizabeth**, who married (October 12, 1722) Richard Swain.
 viii **Sarah**, who married (20th, 10 mo. 1733) David Joy, son of Samuel and Lydia.
 ix **Mary**, who married (6th, 12 mo. 1734-5) John Worth, son of Jonathan and Mary.
 x **Dinah**, who married (6th, 1 mo. 1739-40) David Macy, son of John and Judith.

BENJAMIN [3] (Richard [2] Richard [1])
was born July 20, 1683. In his will, executed December 7, 1763, and probated February 3, 1764, he names his wife Hannah (Coffin, daughter of John and Deborah) his sons i **Robert** and ii **Benjamin**; his daughter iii **Rebekah** (Russell, wife of Benjamin); his grandsons **Silvanus, Abishai** and **Obadiah** Gardner, and grandson **Solomon** Folger. Robert married first (16th, 1 mo. 1730) Jedidah Folger, daughter of Jethro and Mary and second Jedidah Hussey, widow of John and daughter of Joseph and Bethiah Coffin.

PETER [3] (Richard [2] Richard [1])
 The will of Peter Gardner, drawn May 19, 1767, and probated July 3 of the same year, names his wife, Elizabeth, a son i, **Enoch**, and daughters ii, **Love** Coffin, iii, **Deborah** Gardner, iv, **Lydia** Hammond v, **Elizabeth** Gardner and vi, **Beulah** Coffin.

*There seems by the Town Records to have been a daughter Naomy who died 1st, 2 mo. 1718.

WILLIAM [3] (Richard [2] Richard [1])

The probate Records contain the will of William Gardner, cooper, executed April 19, 1739, and probated September 7 of the same year. His widow, Hephzibah Gardner, to whom he was married February 20, 1719, three sons and two daughters, (not named), survived him.

SAMUEL [3] (James [2] Richard [1])

married (27th 10 mo. 1710) Patience Swaine, daughter of John. He died 28th 10 mo. 1757; she died 23d 8 mo. 1746. Their children were:—

i **Mary**, born 26th 8 mo. 1713; died 22d 11 mo. 1797; married (15th 9 mo 1733) David Gardner, son of Solomon and Anna.

ii **Hepzibah**, born 5th 1 mo. 1718; died 7th 6 mo. 1775; married (5th 10 mo. 1734) Zaccheus Macy son of Richard and Deborah.

iii **Hannah**, born 21st 2 mo. 1720; died 15th 11 mo. 1788; married (3d 1 mo. 1736) Paul Bunker, son of Jabez and Hannah.

iv **Jemima**, born ; died 10th 3 mo. 1792; married (17th 11 mo. 1744) Robert Coffin, son of Peter and Hope.

v **Daniel**, born 17th 11 mo. 1727; died 1780; married (17th 1 mo. 1747) Provided Allen, daughter of Nathaniel and Provided.*

JETHRO [3] (James [2] Richard [1])

married (29th, 9 mo. 1716) Kezia Folger, daughter of Peter.† Their children were—

i **Peleg**, born 8th, 1 mo. 1718-19.

ii **Hezekiah**, born 19th, 10 mo. 1720; died 24th, 2 mo. 1788; married 12th, 11 mo. 1743) Priscilla Swain, daughter of John and Mary.

iii **James**, born 2d, 10 mo. 1723; died 13th, 2 mo. 1748; married Judith Folger, daughter of Daniel and Abigail.

iv **Judith**, born 9th, 12 mo. 1726-7; died 30th, 8 mo. 1758; married (9th, 1 mo. 1748-9) Peter Bunker, son of Jabez and Hannah.

v **Peter**, born 14th, 1 mo. 1728-9; died 13th, 11 mo. 1764.

vi **Matthew**, born 1st, 12 mo. 1730-31; died 31st, 10 mo.

---

*The Town Records give also (VI) Seth born 29th, 5 mo. 1722.

†In the Friends Records is recorded the marriage 29th, 10 mo. 1737) of Kezia Gardner, widow of Jethro, to Paul Starbuck, son of Nathaniel and Dinah.

1759; married (7th, 12 mo. 1752) Susanna Paddack, daughter of Daniel and Susanna.

vii Jethro, born ———————; died 1st, 6 mo. 1759.

BARNABAS [3] (James [2] Richard [1])

born 11th, 2 mo. 1695, married (December 11, 1718) Mary Wheeler. He died 14th, 9 mo. 1768; she died 18th, 1 mo. 1788. Their children were—

- i Susannah, born 30th, 8 mo. 1719; married (25th, 1 mo. 1751) Caleb Russell, son of Joseph and Mary. Left Nantucket.
- ii Zaccheus, born 10th, 8 mo. 1721; married (8th, 10 mo. 1743) Jemima Coffin, daughter of Nathan and Lydia.
- iii Jedidah, born 10th, 9 mo. 1724; died 15th, 2 mo. 1798; married (29th, 10 mo. 1757) Benjamin Marshall, son of Joseph and Mary.
- iv Priscilla, born 8th, 9 mo. 1726; died 11th, 3 mo. 1756.
- v Jonathan, born 19th, 12 mo. 1728; died 20th, 1 mo. 1807; married first (5th, 10 mo. 1751) Miriam Worth, daughter of Joseph and Lydia; second (29th, 11 mo. 1764) Anna Coffin, widow of John and daughter of Elihu and Jemima Coleman; third (6th, 7 mo. 1769; Eunice Barnard, daughter of Robert and Hepzibah.
- vi Abigail, born 26th, 1 mo. 1731; married (26th, 2 mo. 1761; Matthew Macy, son of Jabez and Sarah. Removed from the Island 1773.
- vii Hannah, born 12th, 3 mo. 1733; married (9th, 2 mo. 1758) Benjamin Taber, son of Benjamin and Susanna; moved from the Island in 1761.
- viii Jethro, born 6th, 3 mo. 1735; married (31st, 1 mo. 1760; Abigail Chase, daughter of Stephen and Patience; lost at sea 1764.
- ix Mary, born 7th, 1 mo. 1737; married (5th, 2 mo. 1756) Francis Worth, son of Richard and Sarah; removed from the Island 1771.
- x Hepzibah, born 11th, 11 mo. 1739; married (26th, 2 mo. 1761) Thomas Clark, son of David and Ruth.

JONATHAN [3] (James [2] Richard [1])

born 12th, 7 mo. 1696, married Patience Bunker (14th, 8 mo. 1723) he died 3d, 7 mo. 1777; she died 11th, 1 mo. 1794. Their children were—

i **Elizabeth,** born 12th, 8 mo. 1724; married (6th, 7 mo. 1744) Samuel Coffin, son of Tristram and Mary.

ii **Seth,** born 12th, 8 mo. 1726; married (14th, 10 mo. 1749) Sarah Ray, daughter of Samuel and Mary; removed from the Island 1777.

iii **Simeon,** born 17th, 9 mo. 1728; married (22d, 9 mo. 1750) Sarah Long, daughter of Samuel and Lydia.

iv **Elihu,** born 9th, 4 mo. 1731; died 12th, 10 mo. 1807.

v **Kezia,** born 18th, 4 mo. 1733; died 23d, 6 mo. 1809; married (7th, 12 mo. 1750) Jonathan Paddack, son of Eliphalet and Naomi.

vi **Ruth,** born 5th, 6 mo. 1735; died 23d, 6 mo. 1809; married (6th, 12 mo. 1753) John Clasby, son of William and Abiel.

vii **Eunice,** born 12th, 4 mo. 1737; married (5th, 2 mo. 1756) David Ray, son of Samuel and Mary.

viii **Barnabas,** born 7th, 7 mo. 1740.

ix **Miriam,** born 26th, 1 mo. 1743.

x **Dinah,** born 23d, 12 mo. 1745.

xi **Mary,** born 29th, 6 mo. 1749; married (30th, 11 mo. 1769) Francis Clark, son of Peter and Ruth.

JAMES [3] (James [2] Richard [1])

born_____; married (September 1, 1724) Susannah Gardner, daughter of Nathaniel and Abigail. His children were—

i **Rachel,** born May 29, 1725; married (9th, 11 mo. 1745) Elihu Coffin, son of Nathan and Lydia.

ii **Eliphalet,** born October 17, 1726; **married** first, (6th, 10 mo. 1750) Anna Folger, daughter of Peter and Christian; second, (6th, 8 mo. 1772) widow Lydia Clasby, daughter of Tristram Starbuck.

iii **Deborah,** born August 16, 1728.

iv **Benjamin,** born September 25, 1732; married (6th, 1 mo. 1757) Abigail Folger, daughter of Shubael and Jerusha.

v Mehitable, born April 1, 1738; married (14th, 12 mo. 1755) Solomon Coleman, son of Solomon and Deliverance.

vi James, born February 17, 1744-5.*

EBENEZER [3] (Nathaniel, [2] Richard [1])
born October 27, 1688, married, first, (29th 10 mo. 1709) Eunice Coffin, daughter of Peter Jr and Elizabeth, and second (probably in 1724) Judith Coffin, daughter of John and Hope. He died 16th 4 mo 1763. The children were—

By Eunice:—

i **Tristram**, born 1st 5 mo. 1712; lost at sea 1743 or 1744.

ii **Abigail**, born 11th 12 mo. 1714-15; married (10th 10 mo 1730) Peter Jenkins, son of Matthew and Mary; died 28th 1 mo. 1769.

iii **Uriah**, born 2d 12 mo. 1716-17; married (April 27, 1738) Ruth Bunker daughter of Daniel and Priscilla

iv **Eunice**, born 29th 1 mo. 1718; died 1st 2 mo. 1787.

By Judith:—

v **Anne**, born 16th 11 mo. 1720-21;

vi **Peleg**, born 31st 11 mo. 1722-3

vii **Margaret**, born February 16, 1724-5

viii **Joseph**, born January 17, 1726-7; married (16th 9 mo. 1749) Eunice Worth, daughter of Richard and Lydia.

ix **Lydia**, born February 9, 1728-9; married (29th 11 mo 1746) Zaccheus Howes, son of Thomas and Abigail

x **Susanna**, born December 16, 1730; married (2d 1 mo. 1748-9) Shubael Barnard son of Matthew and Mary.

xi **Ebenezer**, born December 2, 1732

xii **Judith**, born March 31, 1735.†

---

*The will of James, Senior, dated May 1766 and probated June, 1778 mentions also a daughter vii **Susanna**.

†The Friends Records state the marriage (1st, 3 mo. 1749) of **Samuel**, son of Ebenezer and Judith, to Sarah Jenkins, daughter of Thomas and Judith.

NATHANIEL [3] (Nathaniel [2] Richard [1])
born 14th 10 mo. 1697, married (15th 7 mo. 1725) Mary Folger, daughter of Peter and Judith. According to the record she died in 1727 leaving two children, a daughter Mary and a son.

 i Nathaniel, who married (5th 12 mo. 1746) Ruth Hussey, daughter of George and Elizabeth.
 ii Mary, married (10th 1 mo. 1747) Elisha Coffin, son of Nathan and Lydia.

ANDREW [3] (Nathaniel [2] Richard [1])
was born 26th 10 mo. 1699; married (1st 7 mo. 1721) Mary Gorham daughter of Stephen. He died 2d 3 mo. 1782; she died 18th 2 mo. 1780. Their children were:—

 i Christopher, born 14th 12 mo. 1722; died 1762.
 ii Nathaniel, born 3d 3 mo. 1724; married (7th 9 mo. 1751) Anna Beard, daughter of John and Deborah.
 iii Thomas, born 13th 6 mo. 1727; died 31st 8 mo. 1768;
 iv Andrew, born 2d 7 mo. 1729; lost at sea.
 v Solomon, born 27th 2 mo. 1731; married (8th 3 mo. 1753) Jemima Folger, daughter of Shubael and Jerusha.
 vi Mary, born 28th 8 mo. 1734;
 vii Abigail, born 2d 4 mo. 1737;
 viii Elizabeth, born 20th 1 mo. 1741;
 ix Stephen, born 5 mo. 1743.
 x Josiah
 xi Zacchary

ABEL [3] (Nathaniel [2] Richard [1])
was born 6th 6mo. 1722. He married (18th 9 mo. 1723) Priscilla Coffin daughter of James Jr. and Ruth. His will, which was drawn May 23, 1768, and probated October 4, 1771, mentions his wife Priscilla, sons James, Abel, Joshua (deceased), Nathan, Ephraim and Shubael and children of daughter Abigail Gardner (deceased) and daughters Priscilla Russell, Sarah Gardner, Phebe Rawson, Elizabeth Aldridge and Eunice Bunker. The record of their births is—

 i Abigail, born November 7, 1726.

HISTORY OF NANTUCKET 767

ii James, born December 9, 1728, married (February 13, 1752)Abigail Coffin.
iii Phebe, born September 9, 1730; married Paul Rawson (January 24, 1750).
iv Joshua, born July 12, 1732, married (January 9, 1756) Elizabeth Gardner.
v Elizabeth, born July 7, 1734, married (December 13, 1753) Ichabod Aldridge.
vi Sarah, born August 15, 1736.
vii Eunice, born May 7, 1738, married (December 18, 17 55) Caleb Bunker.
viii Abel, born April 29, 1741.
ix Nathan, born July 24, 1743.
x Priscilla, born October 27, 1745, married (December 20, 1764) Simeon Russell.
xi Shubael, born April 14, 1748, married (October 20, 17-71)Hephzibah Gardner.
xii Ephraim, born October 27, 1751.

BETHUEL [4] (Joseph [3] Richard [2] Richard [1]) married (January 8 1735-6) Katharine Coffin, daughter of Nathaniel and Damaris. Their children were—

i Katharine, born October 7, 1747.
ii Gayer, born March 16, 1750.
iii Ruth, born May 28, 1752.
iv Charles, born June 14, 1755.

CHARLES [4] (Joseph [3] Richard [2] Richard [1] married (December 27, 1738) Anna Pinkham, daughter of Shubael and Abigail. Their children were:—

i Joseph, born 9th 11 mo. 1739-40; died 30th 7 mo. 1798; married (1st 3 mo. 1759) Abigail Clark, daughter of Josiah.
ii Love, born 7th 3 mo. 1742; removed from Island 1779.
iii Abigail, born 5th 3 mo. 1744; died 20th 6 mo. 1823; married (6th 12 mo. 1764) Barnabas Paddack, son of Daniel.
iv Anna, born 18th 4 mo. 1751; died 4th 1 mo. 1828. Married (12th 12 mo. 1771) Gilbert Folger, son of Barzillai and Phebe.

    v **Hephzibah,** born 15th 10 mo. 1753; married (4th 6 mo. 1772) William Barnard son of Timothy and Mary.
   vi **Walter,** born 21st 8 mo. 1758.
  vii **Rebecca,** born 17th 6 mo. 1761; removed from Island 1778.
 viii **Isaiah,** born 20th 7 mo. 1763.
   ix **Susannah,** born 25th 2 mo. 1765.

SHUBAEL [4] (Joseph [3] Richard [2] Richard [1]) probably died at sea. unmarried. By his father's will filed December 20, 1748, Shubael was left part of his estate, but it was subsequently found he was not living.

ROBERT, [4] (Benjamin [3] Richard [2] Richard [1]) married (16th 1 mo. 1730) Jedidah Folger, daughter of Jethro and Mary. He died 13th 7 mo. 1797; she died 2d 10 mo. 1757. Their children were:

    i **Abishai,** born 25th 5 mo. 1731; died 17th 9 mo. 1770; married first (27th 12 mo. 1752) Lydia Macy daughter of Robert and Abigail; second (26th 2 mo. 1767) Mary Macy, widow of Thomas, daughter of Tristram and Deborah Starbuck.
   ii **Lydia,** born 6th 8 mo. 1732; died 1st 1 mo. 1811; married John Folger, son of Zaccheus and Abigail.
  iii **Anna,** born 25th 7 mo. 1734; married (8th 3 mo. 1753) Richard Swain, son of Richard and Elizabeth.
  iv **Rebecca,** born 7th 6 mo. 1736; died 28th 6 mo. 1806; married (10th 1 mo. 1760) Richard Chadwick, son of Richard and Deborah.
   v **Robert,** born 9th 6 mo. 1738; married (28th 1 mo. 1762) Miriam Macy, daughter of David and Dinah.
   vi **Jethro,** born 19th. 7 mo. 1740; married (28th 1 mo. 1762) Love Gardner, daughter of Charles and Anna; removed from the Island 1779.
  vii **Prince,** born 21st 9 mo. 1742; died 19th 4 mo. 1816; married (11th 6 mo. 1767) Deborah Barnard, daughter of Francis and Elizabeth, who died 9 mo 1806 Jemima Morton (widow) daughter of David and Ruth Gardner.
 viii **Eunice,** born 11th 8 mo. 1744; died 23d 2 mo. 1809; married (4th 2 mo. 1762) Shubael Macy son of Nathaniel and Abigail.

ix Christopher, born 24th 6 mo. 1746; married first (31st 12 mo. 1767) Eunice Coleman, daughter of Jethro and Lydia; second (9th 11 mo. 1775) Anna Barnard,* daughter of Francis and Elizabeth; removed from the Island 1799.
x Jedidah, born 27th, 10 mo. 1748; died young.
xi Miriam, born 25th 8 mo. 1750; removed from the Island 1779.
xii Jedidah, born 10th 2 mo. 1753.
xiii Elizabeth, born 10th 1 mo. 1756; died 17th 4 mo. 1784.

REUBEN [4] (Solomon [3], Richard [2] Richard [1])
The will of Reuben Gardner, executed October 13, 1783 and probated January 7, 1785, names his wife, Theodate; his son Shubael ("if he" should return home"); daughter Naomi Chase; grandsons Reuben and Thaddeus Gardner; three grand daughters, children of deceased son Reuben; grandson Reuben; grand daughter Lydia Gardner. Reuben married (4th 10 mo 1735) Theodate Coffin, widow of Francis and daughter of Shubael and Puella Gorham. She died 7th 4 mo. 1787. The Friends' Records show the following:—

i Reuben, born 10th 9 mo. 1736.
ii Thaddeus, born 22d 6 mo. 1739: lost at sea 1767. Married (28th 1 mo. 1762) Susanna Hussey, daughter of Christopher and Mary.
iii Shubael, born 7th 1 mo. 1742; died abroad. Married (4th 2 mo. 1762) Judith Barker, daughter of Robert and Jedidah.
iv Naomi, born 29th 8 mo. 1746; died 15th 11 mo. 1827. Married (5th 1 mo. 1764) Francis Chase son of Joseph and Miriam. By the Town Records he appears to have first married Love—by whom he had a son (v) Obed, born November 17, 1732.

DAVID [4] (Solomon [3] Richard [2] Richard [1])
married (15th 9 mo. 1733) Mary Gardner, daughter of Samuel and Patience. She died 22d 11 mo. 1797. Their children were:

*Widow of ——— Bunker.

i **Dinah,** born 8 mo. 1736; died—10 mo. 1736.
ii **Hephzibah,** born 18th 4 mo. 1734
iii **Hezekiah,** born 24th 9 mo. 1737; died 3d 1 mo. 1760; married (9th 2 mo. 1758) Sarah Folger daughter of Abishai and Dinah.
iv **Anna,** born 5th 10 mo. 1740; married (3d 2 mo. 1763) Silvanus Gardner, son of Logan and Hannah; removed from the Island 1778.
v **Dinah,** born 28th 10 mo. 1742; died 11th 4 mo. 1818.
vi **Hannah,** born 12th 6 mo. 1745; removed from the Island 1780.
vii **Paul,** born 4th 1 mo. 1747-8; died the following year.
viii **David,** born 9th 6 mo. 1750.
ix **Elijah,** born 8th 12 mo. 1752.
x **Mary,** born 7th 12 mo. 1756; married (6th 1 mo. 1774) Nathaniel Ray, son of William and Mary.
xi **Ruth,** born 25th 8 mo. 1760; died 15th 3 mo. 1846.

STEPHEN [4] (Solomon [3] Richard [2] Richard [1]) married (7th 8 mo. 1742) Jemima Worth, daughter of William and Mary. They removed from the Island with others of the family in 1772 and 1774. Their children were;

i **William,** born 9 mo 1743; removed from the Island 1772. He married (27th 11 mo. 1766) Susanna Gardner, daughter of James and Susanna.
ii **Miriam,** born 19th 4 mo. 1745; married (30th 1 mo. 1766) Barzillai Folger, son of Barzillai and Phebe.
iii **Stephen,** born 10 mo. 1746; removed from the Island 1174; married (27th 11 mo. 1766) Abigail Pinkham, daughter of Shubael and Eunice.
iv **Jemima,** born 1 mo. 1748; died 24th 11 mo. 1768; married (7th 1 mo 1768) Howland Swain son of Reuben and Elizabeth.
v **Mary,** born 1751; married (7th 1 mo. 1768) John Sweet, son of John and Anna.
vi **Barzillai,** born 12th 1 mo. 1753; removed from the Island 1774.
vii **Judith,** born 1756; removed from the Island 1772.
viii **Rhoda,** born 1757.
ix **Isaac,** born 1761.

RICHARD [4] (Solomon [3] Richard [2] Richard [1]) married (5th, 12 mo. 1746) Sarah Macy, daughter of John and Judith. Their children were—

    i **Richard.**
   ii **Silvanus.**
  iii **Eliab.**
  iv **Hezekiah.**
   v **Sarah.**
  vi **Merab.**
 vii **Jonathan.**

Richard was probably born in 1747. The entire family removed from the Island 28th, 11 mo. 1771.

SOLOMON [4] (Solomon [3] Richard [2] Richard [1]) married (1st 9 mo. 1750) Mary Pollard, daughter of Philip and Mehitable. He was lost at sea in 1764; she removed from the Island in 1775. Their children were:—

    i **Solomon,** born probably in 1751.
   ii **Elizabeth,** born 8 mo. 1759; removed from the Island 1778.
  iii **Pernal,** born 2d 2 mo. 1761; removed from the Island 1800.

PAUL [4] (Solomon [3] Richard [2] Richard [1]) married (7th, 2 mo. 1754) Rachel Starbuck, daughter of Thomas and Rachel. He died 17th, 3 mo. 1813; she died 29th, 8 mo. 1775. Their children were—

    i **Paul,** born 4th, 12 mo. 1755; married (30th, 3 mo. 1786) Sarah Mitchell, daughter of Jethro and Rachel.
   ii **Libni,** born 8th. 9 mo. 1758; married (1st, 4 mo. 1784) Elizabeth Worth, daughter of Reuben and Mary.
  iii **George,** born 30th, 6 mo. 1760; probably married (August 20, 1783) Judith Smith.
  iv **Lydia,** born 11th, 7 mo. 1763; married (28th, 10 mo. 1784) Obed Mitchell, son of Jethro and Rachel.
   v **Rachel,** born 17th, 7 mo. 1765; died 6th, 1 mo. 1783.
  vi **Dorcas,** born 8th, 6 mo. 1767; removed from the Island 25th, 7 mo. 1816; married (26th, 4 mo. 1816) William Peckham, son of Benjamin and Mary.
 vii **Zenas,** born 11th, 2 mo. 1769; married (30th, 9 mo. 1790) Susanna Hussey, daughter of George and Deborah.

ZACCHEUS [4] (Barnabas [3] James [2] Richard [1])
born 10th 8 mo. 1721; married (8th 10 mo. 1743) Jemima Coffin, daughter of Nathan and Lydia. Their children were—

    i **Lydia**, born 30th 9 mo. (September) 1744; removed from the Island 1775
    ii **Zaccheus**, born 10th 12 mo. (December) 1746.
    iii **Elizabeth**, born 8th 12 mo. (December) 1749.
    iv **Nathan**, born 5th 10 mo. 1754.
    v **Susannah**, born 15th 12 mo. 1756.
    vi **Thaddeus**, born 6th 11 mo. 1759
    vii **Barnabas**, born 5th 5 mo. 1763.
    viii **Jethro**, born 3d 5 mo. 1767;

JONATHAN [4] (Barnabas [3] James [2] Richard [1])
born 19th, 12 mo. 1728; married—first (5th, 10 mo. 1751) Miriam Worth, daughter of Joseph and Lydia; second (1764) Anna Coffin, widow of John and daughter of Elihu and Jemima; third (1769) Eunice Barnard, daughter of Robert and Hepzibah. He died 20th, 1 mo. 1807; Miriam died 15th, 11 mo. 1763; Anna died   and Eunice died 29th, 10 mo. 1800. Their children were—

By Miriam:

    i **Phebe**, born 25th, 8 mo. 1753; married (8th, 9 mo. 1774) Elisha Macy, son of Caleb and Judith.
    ii **Miriam**, born 26th, 11 mo. 1755; died 21st, 5 mo. 1756.
    iii **Huldah**, born 11th, 10 mo. 1758; died 28th, 11 mo. 1848.
    iv **Naomi**, born 18th, 4 mo. 1761; died 2d, 11 mo. 1762.
    v **Miriam**, born 4th, 11 mo. 1763; died 12th, 7 mo. 1865.

By Eunice:

    vi **Zaccheus**, born 9th, 6 mo. 1772; died 9th, 6 mo. 1772.
    vii **Freeman**, born 25th, 4 mo. 1774; married (July 3, 1796) Anna Gardner.

SETH [4] (Jonathan [3] James [2] Richard [1])
born 12th, 8 mo. 1726; married (14th, 10 mo. 1749) Sarah Ray, daughter of Samuel and Mary. His children were—

 i **Miriam,** born 6th, 9 mo. 1750; probably married (October 11, 1770) David Bunker.
 ii **Alexander,** born 8th, 7 mo. 1752; married (7th, 9 mo. 1775) Hannah Paddock, daughter of Eliphalet and Naomi.
 iii **Anna,** born 10th, 11 mo. 1754.
 iv **Noah,** born 22d, 11 mo. 1756.
 v **Aaron,** born 19th, 1 mo. 1759; married (July 5, 1783) Naomi Gardner.
 vi **Moses,** born 5th, 9 mo. 1761.
 vii **Rosanna,** born 13th, 9 mo. 1763.
 viii **Hannah,** born 2d, 12 mo. 1765.
 ix **Archelus,** born 25th, 3 mo. 1768.
 x **Ruth,** born 19th, 7 mo. 1770.

Moses removed from the Island 29th, 4 mo. 1776; Miriam in 29th, 12 mo. 1777; and the other members of the family, including Anna, probably, and excepting Alexander, removed 26th, 7 mo. 1779.

PELEG [4] (Jethro [3] James [2] Richard [1])
married, probably (November 1, 1744) Eunice Gardner. Their children were—

 i **Kezia,** born November 11, 1745.
 ii **Rachel,** born May 13, 1747; married (4th, 12 mo. 1766) Philip Chase, son of Philip and Hannah.
 iii **Sarah,** born March 1, 1749.
 iv **Elizabeth,** born February 16, 1751.
 v **Barzillai,** born April 18, 1753.

HEZEKIAH [4] (Jethro [3] James [2] Richard [1])
born 19th, 10 mo. 1720, died 24th, 2 mo. 1788; married (12th, 11 mo. 1743) Priscilla Swain, daughter of John and Mary. She died 11th 8 mo. 1795. They appear to have had but one child:

 i **Phebe,** born 11th, 8 mo. 1746.

MATTHEW [4] (Jethro [3] James [2] Richard [1])
born 1st, 12 mo. 1720-21; died 31st, 10 mo. 1759; married (7th,

12 mo. 1752) Susanna Paddack, daughter of Daniel and Susanna. They had but one child, a daughter—

    i **Judith**, born 1st, 11 mo. 1753; died 24th, 4 mo. 1833.

DANIEL [4] (Samuel [3] James [2] Richard [1])
born 17th, 11 mo. 1727; died 9th, 7 mo. 1780; married (17th, 1 mo. 1747) Privided Allen, daughter of Nathaniel and Provided, who died 3d, 12 mo. 1799. Their children were—

    i **Phebe**, born 17th, 5 mo. 1749; removed from the Island 2d, 4 mo. 1801; married (11th, 12 mo. 1766) Silas Parker, son of Thomas and Experience.
   ii **Rachel**, born 1st, 11 mo. 1752; married (31st, 10 mo. 1782) George Russell, son of John and Ruth.
  iii **Edmund**, born 2d, 8 mo. 1754; died 11th, 3 mo. 1777; married (28th, 11 mo. 1776) Phebe Hussey, daughter of Nathaniel and Judith.
  iv **Parnel**, born 24th, 6 mo. 1756; married (3d, 2 mo. 1774) Reuben Coffin, son of Tristram and Elizabeth.
   v **Elizabeth**, born 8th, 6 mo. 1760; died 1760.
  vi **Silas**, born 27th, 7 mo. 1762; married (March 13, 1781) Susanna Folger.
 vii **Abial**, born 7th, 9 mo. 1764; married (28th, 9 mo. 1786) Zenas Coffin, son of Micajah and Abigail.

ELIPHALET [4] (James [3] James [2] Richard [1])
born October 17, 1726; married (6th, 10 mo. 1750) Anna Folger, daughter of Peter and Christian. Their children were—

    i **Freeman**, born 7th, 6 mo. 1752; died 3d, 6 mo. 1753.
   ii **Rachel**, born 4th, 8 mo. 1753; died 25th, 8 mo. 1753.
  iii **Owen**, born 28th, 3 mo. 1755; died 25th, 12 mo. 1831.
  iv **Walter**, born 22d, 2 mo. 1757; died 24th, 3 mo. 1757.

Eliphalet's wife Anna died 27th, 6 mo. 1771 and he married (6th, 8 mo. 1772) Lydia Clasby (widow) of Joseph, daughter of Tristram and Deborah Starbuck, who died 30th, 1 mo. 1809. They had but one child—

    v **Mary**, born 30th, 9 mo. 1773.

Eliphalet died 1st, 4 mo. 1799.

HISTORY OF NANTUCKET 775

BENJAMIN [4] (James [3] James [2] Richard [1]) born September 25, 1732; married (6th 1 mo. 1757) Abigail Folger, daughter of Shubael and Jerusha. He died abroad 11 mo. 1777. Their children were—

    i Rachel, born 4th, 11 mo. 1758; died 11th, 9 mo. 1830.
   ii Francis, born 27th 3 mo. 1760; died abroad in 1817.
  iii Eunice, born 29th, 8 mo. 1763.
  iv Tristram, born 30th, 7 mo. 1766; died 8 mo. 1766.
   v Gideon, born 9th, 10 mo. 1767.
  vi Susannah, born 29th, 2 mo. 1769
 vii James, born 8th, 7 mo. 1772.
viii William, born 7th, 3 mo. 1774.
  ix Lydia, born 9th, 8 mo. 1776.

JOSEPH [4] (Ebenezer [3] Nathaniel [2] Richard [1]) born January 17, 1726-7; married (16th, 9 mo. 1749) Eunice Worth, daughter of Richard and Lydia. He died at sea 1757; she removed from the Island 28th, 9 mo. 1767. The names of their children, the dates of whose birth are not recorded, are

   i, Shubael; ii, Margaret; iii, Reuben and iv, Lydia.

NATHANIEL [4] (Nathaniel [3] Nathaniel [2] Richard [1]) was born March 29, 1727; married (17th 12 mo. 1746) Ruth Hussey, daughter of George and Elizabeth. Their children were:—

    i Mary, born 29th 12 mo. 1748-9; married (2d 1 mo 1766) John Swain son of Reuben and Elizabeth.
   ii Nathaniel, born 16th 10 mo. 1754;
  iii Elizabeth, born 13th 10 mo. 1758; removed from the Island 1781; married (30th 11 mo. 1780) George Hussey son of Ebenezer and Miriam.
  iv Judith, born 25th 12 mo. 1760; married (29th 1 mo. 1784) Paul Hussey, son of William and Abigail.
   v Simeon, born 15th 5 mo. 1763.
  vi Albert, born 30th 9 mo. 1765.
 vii Lydia, born 16th 9 mo. 1768.
viii Eunice, born 6th 10 mo. 1775; married (2d 10 mo. 1794) David Mitchell, son of Richard and Hephzibah.

NATHANIEL [4] (Andrew [3] Nathaniel [2] Richard [1]) born March 3, 1724; married (7th, 9 mo. 1751) Anna Beard, daughter of John and Deborah; he died 5th, 11 mo. 1765. Their children were—

    i **Christopher**, born 22d 5 mo. 1754; died 7 mo. 1781.
   ii **William**, born 21st, 12 mo. 1756; probably married (August 22, 1779) Mehitable Mayo.
  iii **Rhoda**, born 22d, 5 mo. 1760.
  iv **Resolved**, born 14th, 7 mo. 1762; removed from the Island 27th, 9 mo. 1779.
   v **Charlotta**, born 22d, 6 mo. 1764; married (2d, 12 mo. 1790) George Newbegin, son of James and Phebe.

ABISHAI [5] (Robert [4] Benjamin [3] Richard [2] Richard [1]) son of Robert and Jedidah, born 25th, 5 mo. 1731; died 17th, 10 mo. 1770; married (27th, 12 mo. 1752) Lydia Macy, daughter of Robert and Abigail; she died 19th, 10 mo. 1765. Their children were—

   i **Phebe**, born 1752; married (8th, 12 mo. 1774) Francis Jenkins, son of Joseph and Ann; removed from the Island 1777.
  ii **Lydia**, born 1761.

HEZEKIAH [5] (David [4] Solomon [3] Richard [2] Richard [1] born 24th, 9 mo. 1737; died 3d, 1 mo. 1760; married (9th, 2 mo. 1758) Sarah Folger, daughter of Abishai and Dinah. They had but one child—

   i **Gideon**, born 30th, 5 mo. 1759; married (31st 5 mo. 1781) Hannah Barnard, daughter of Joseph and Mary.

GEORGE [2] (John [1]) son of Captain John, married Eunice Starbuck, daughter of Nathaniel and Mary; he died 17th, 2 mo. 1750; he was the only son of John to reside at Nantucket. Their children were—

i **Hephzibah,** born September 29, 1696; married first, Peleg Gardner, son of Nathaniel and Abigail; second (February 20, 1719) William Gardner, son of Richard and Mary.*

ii **Priscilla,** born January 30, 1698; married (December 8, 1720) Barnabas Pinkham, son of Richard and Mary.*

iii **Thomas,** born May 21, 1701; married (November 30, 1724) Hannah Swain, daughter of John and Catharine.*

iv **Grafton,** born April 27, 1707; married Abigail Coffin, daughter of Enoch and Beulah, of Edgartown.*

JEREMIAH [3] (John [2] John [1])

married Sarah Coffin, daughter of James and Love. Their children were—

i **George,** born at Newport, R. I., April 7, 1714.
ii **Daniel,** born at Nantucket December 8, 1715.
iii **John,** born March 26, 1718.
iv **Ruth,** born May 12, 1720.
v **Elisha,** born August 15, 1722.
vi **Sarah,** born October 26, 1724.
vii **Nathaniel,** born March 29, 1727.

THOMAS [3] (George [2] John [1])

born May 21, 1701; married (November 30, 1724) Hannah Swain, daughter of John and Catherine. Their children were—

i **Eunice,** born October 1, 1726.
ii **Anna,**† married (6th, 1 mo. 1763) Peter Fitch, son of Peter and Rachel.
iii **Elizabeth,** born July 23, 1732.
iv **Priscilla,*** married (10th, 10 mo. 1771) Nathaniel Coffin, son of Nathaniel and Mary.
v **Thomas,** born May 7 1736; married (7th, 2 mo. 1760) Anna Worth, daughter of John and Mary. He died in 1784, and by order of the Court his estate was divided among Thomas (eldest son) Alexander, Zephaniah, Abraham, Anna Fitch, Priscilla Coffin, and daughters of Eunice Pinkham (deceased).

---

*Thomas Gardner, Planter
†Friends' Records.

vi **Grindal,** born   ; married (June 9, 1732) Lois Ramsdell.
vii **Timothy,** born October 21, 1732.
viii **Mary,** born April 19, 1734.

GRAFTON [3] (George [2] John [1])
born April 27, 1707; married (probably in 1730) Abigail Coffin, daughter of Enoch and Beulah. Their children were—

i **George,** born June 10, 1731.
ii **Mary,** born July 6, 1733.
iii **Hephzibah,** born September 16, 1736
iv **Jemima,** born July 2, 1738.
v **Francis,** born April 18, 1741.
vi **Abigail,** born November 13, 1746.
vii **Eunice,** born July 20, 1750.
viii **Silas,** born September 5, 1753.

HUSSEY

The Husseys of Nantucket are descendants of Stephen Hussey, the son of Christopher. According to Mrs. Hinchman,* Christopher was the son of John Hussey and Mary Wood (or Moor), and was baptized in Dorking, Surrey, England, February 18, 1599. When a young man he spent some time in Holland where he met Theodate, the eldest daughter of Rev. Stephen Bachelor, who he desired to marry. Her father gave his consent contingent on their going to America with him. They arrived in Boston in 1632 on the ship William and Francis, settling first in Lynn, where Christopher's eldest son, Stephen, was the first child baptized by his grandfather in the church in Lynn.

Christopher early removed to Newbury, where he was one of the town's selectmen in 1636. In 1638, with his father-in-law, and others, he settled in Hampton, where he held several town offices. According to the best received opinion, he died in Hampton where, according to the record, he was buried March 8, 1636, leaving two sons and three daughters— **Stephen**, who married (October 8. 16-76) Martha Bunker, daughter of William; **John**, who married Rebecca Perkins; **Huldah**, who married John Smith; **Mary**; and **Theodata**.

Stephen was the only one to make his home in Nantucket. He was a sea-faring man, had lived at Barbadoes and had accumulated a little property. At the time of the organization of the Friends' Society, in 1708, he was one of the petitioners, a somewhat anomalous condition as he was a most persistent litigant. He several times held office and appeared to be quite a politician, and during the local turmoil following the temporary overturn of the New York government, he was severely denounced by Peter Folger for endeavoring to improperly affect the voting. He had his father's interest in the Island and acquired that of Robert Pike. Worth says,† that the Hussey and Pike lots "were on the west side of Trot's Swamp, but Stephen Hussey built three houses for himself and family, one on Federal Street near Chestnut, another at Monomoy and a third at Shimmoo." He died April 2, 1718, in the 88th year of his age. His wife died 21st, 9 mo. 1744. Their children were:

    i **Puella**, born October 10, 1677; married Shubael Gorham of Barnstable.

---

*Early Settlers of Nantucket, p. 50-1.
†Lands and Land Owners, p. 70. Patronymica Britannica says of the name—"According to Stapleton's Rotuli Scaccarii Normanniae Osbert de H. who was living in 1180 was so named from le Hozu, a fief in the parish of Grand Quevilly near Rouen. And one Henry de la Hosse, or Henze held inter alias, the sands of Hosse * * * In an old account of the Hussey family, the name is said to be Touasi de Hosa— from a boot of buskin" and the crest borne was a boot.

ii **Abigail,** born December 22, 1679; married Thomas Howes (April 5, 1700). He was drowned soon after.
iii **Sylvanus,** born May 13, 1682; married (8th 9 mo. 1723) Hepzibah Starbuck, daughter of Nathaniel and Dinah.*
iv **Bachelor,** born February 18, 1684-5; married (October 11, 1704) Abigail Halle.
v **Daniel,** born October 20, 1687; Daniels name is not mentioned in his father's will, executed in 1716 and he probably was not living
vi **Mary,** born March 24, 1689; married (16th, 4 mo. 1707) Jonathan Worth son of John Senior and, second, Ebenezer Barnard son of Nathaniel Senior, and Mary.
vii **George,** born June 21, 1694; married (12th 9 mo. 1717) Elizabeth Starbuck, daughter of Nathaniel Jr.
viii **Theodate,** born September 15, 1700; married (September 26 1726) James Johnson; died April 2, 1718, according to Savage.

SYLVANUS [2] (Stephen [1])

married twice—first Abial Brown, granddaughter of John Gardner Senior; second Hepzibah Starbuck daughter of Nathaniel and Dinah. He died 10th 2 mo. 1767; she died 31st 12 mo. 1764. Their children were:—

i **Seth,** born—married (9th 7 mo. 1742) Sarah Jenkins daughter of Matthew and Mary.
ii **Christopher,** born 3d 6 mo. 1724; married (August 11, 1743) Mary Coffin, daughter of Jonathan and Hepzabeth.†
iii **William,** born 10th 10 mo. 1725; married (January 27, 1746) Abigail Starbuck.
iv **Bachelor,** born 29th 11 mo 1728-9; married (29th 10 mo. 1748) Ann Coffin, daughter of Daniel and Mary.
v **Nathaniel,** born 2d, 11 mo. 1730-31; died 12th, 6 mo. 1769; married (6th, 10 mo. 1750) Judith Coffin, daughter of Francis and Theodate.
vi **Hephzibah,** born 14th 1 mo. 1732-3; married (28th 10 mo. 1749) Nathaniel Coleman son of Barnabas and Elizabeth.

---

*His first wife was Abial Brown, granddaughter of John Gardner Senior to whom he was married 7th, 12 mo. 1711-12.
†Christopher and Mary had a daughter Susanna who married (28th 1 mo. 1762) Thaddeus Gardner son of Reuben and Theodate.

HISTORY OF NANTUCKET 781

vii **Silvanus**, born 29th 11 mo. 1734-5; married (2d 12 mo 1756) Alice Gray, daughter of Jeremiah and Theodate.
viii **George**, born 12th 5 mo 1738; married (3d 2 mo 1757) Deborah Paddack, daughter of Daniel and Susanna.
ix **Joseph**, born 20th 5 1740; married (11th 12 mo. 1766) Mary Raymar, daughter of James and Sarah.*

BACHELOR [2] (Stephen [1])
born February 18, 1685; married (October 11. 1704) Abigail Halle. Under the terms of his father's will his (Stephen's) law books were to go to him for the use of his (Bachelor's) son Stephen, when he was 21. The children of Bachelor and Abigail were—

i **Mary**, born 9th 12 mo. 1706-7: died 2d. 2 mo 1758;† married (May 7, 1730) Peleg Swain son of Benjamin and Mary.
ii **Jedidah**, born 27th, 7 mo. 1708; died 6th, 8 mo. 1759; married (5th 2 mo. 1726) Benjamin Coffin son of Nathaniel and Damaris.
iii **John**, born 8th 8 mo. 1710; died 1749; married (4th 12 mo. 1733-4) Jedidah Coffin daughter of Joseph and Bethiah.
iv **Stephen**, born 14th, 8 mo. 1713; removed from the Island 6th mo 1737.
v **Huldah**, born 8th 12 mo. 1715-16; died 3d 4 mo. 1798; married (2d 11 mo. 1734-5) Simeon Bunker son of Jonathan and Elizabeth.
vi. **Ebenezer**, born 7th 12 mo. 1717-18.
vii **Paul**, born 12th 4 mo. 1720.
viii **Silvanus**, born 11th 3 mo. 1722.

DANIEL [2] (Stephen [1])
born October 20 1687; married (February 13, 1734-5) Sarah Gor-

---

*In his will, probated March 6, 1767, he also mentions sons x Obed and xi Jonathan (the latter of Dartmouth); grandsons Benjamin and Obed and Stephen and Daniel and Seth; granddaughters. Elizabeth Coffin, Rachel Mitchell, Eunice Worth and daughter in law. Sarah Hussey, daughters xii Rachel Coleman and xiii Hephzibah Coleman. The Friends Records show there was a daughter xiv **Rachel**, who married (8th 9 mo. 1733) Barnabas Coleman, son of John and Priscilla. Jonathan married (26th 12 mo 1738-9) Hephzibah Starbuck. daughter of Paul and Ann.
†The Town Records give as the first child **Christopher**, born 10th, 2 mo. 1706.

ham. He died in 1750; she died 18th 7 mo 1748. Their children were——

    i **Stephen**, born 2d, 4 mo. 1735; married (2d, 12 mo. 17-56) Rose Barnard, daughter of Matthew and Mary.
    ii **Elizabeth**, born 23d 2 mo. 1736-7; removed from the Island 1773; married (7th 2 mo 1754) Benjamin Coffin son of Benjamin and Jedidah.
    iii **Daniel**, born 10th 9 mo. 1739; died 30th 11 mo. 1768; married (4th 12 mo. 1760) Hephzibah Folger daughter of Abishai and Dinah.
    iv **Rachel**, born 13th 9 mo. 1741; married (6th 12 mo 1759) Jethro Mitchell, son of Richard and Mary.
    v **Eunice**, born 30th 9 mo. 1744;* removed from the Island 1771; married (9th 2 mo. 1764) Daniel Worth son of Joseph and Lydia.

According to the Friends Records that comprises all the children, but the Town Records also enumerate

    vi **David**, born 6th 9 mo. 1746.

GEORGE [2] (Stephen [1])

was born June 21, 1694 and married (12th 9 mo. 1717) Elizabeth Starbuck, daughter of Nathaniel Jr.; he died in (July) 1782: she died 9th 2 mo. 1770. Their children were—

    i **Christopher**, born 8th 4 mo. 1718;† died 7th 2 mo. 1721.
    ii **Rebecca**, born 20th 12 mo. 1719-20; died 8th 10 mo. 1721.
    iii **Deborah**, born 11th 8 mo. 1721; died 9th 2 mo. 1785; married (10th 2 mo. 1738) Peter Coffin, son of Paul and Mary.
    iv **Reuben**, born 17th, 5 mo. 1723; married (August 2, 1744) Elizabeth Woodbury.
    v **Lydia**, born 4th 5 mo. 1725; married (18th 9 mo. 1742) Clothier Peirce son of Clothier and Hannah.
    vi **Dinah**, born 8th 6 mo. 1727; died 20th 9 mo. 1763; married (22d 1 mo. 1743-4) Reuben Folger, son of Jonathan and Margaret.‡
    vii **Ruth**, born 21st 9 mo. 1728; married (5th 12 mo. 1746) Nathaniel Gardner, son of Nathaniel and Mary.

---

*By the Town Records this date is September 30, 1744.
†The Town Records give Christopher's birth as 18th, 6 mo. 1718.
‡His will probated August 2, 1782, mentions Dinah and her husband as removing to Nova Scotia in 1763.

HISTORY OF NANTUCKET 783

viii Elizabeth, born 10th, 7 mo. 1731; died 13th, 6 mo. 1805; married (6th 2 mo. 1749) Peleg Coffin son of Francis and Theodate.
ix Martha, born 19th 5 mo. 1733; married (5th 10 mo. 1751) David Swain, son of Richard and Elizabeth.
x George, born 11th 8 mo. 1736.
xi Jethro, born 18th 6 mo. 1738; married (October 16. 1766) Margaret Coffin, daughter of James and Priscilla.
xii Thomas, born 22d 12 mo. 1740; killed by a whale 1756.
xiii Paul, born 29th 5 mo. 1741; married (7th 2 mo. 1765) Margaret Barker daughter of Robert and Jedidah.

SETH [3] (Silvanus [2], Stephen [1])
married (9th, 7 mo. 1742) Sarah Jenkins, daughter of Matthew and Mary.* Their children were—

i Seth, born 5th, 7th mo. 1743; died 17th, 4 mo. 1745; married (31st 10 mo. 1765) Eunice Pinkham, daughter of James and Sarah.
ii Abigail, born 29th 8 mo. 1745; died 23d 7 mo. 1807; probably married (February 10,1763) Joseph Myrick.
iii Margaret, born 3d 12 mo. 1747; died 1749.
iv Sarah, born 5th 7 mo. 1750; removed from the Island 1st 1 mo. 1801; probably married (November 29. 1767) John Darling.
v Abial, born 5th 2 mo. 1752; died 29th 8 mo. 1773.
vi Mary, born 23d 10 mo. 1756; died 1759.

WILLIAM [3] (Silvanus [2], Stephen [1])
born 10th 10 mo. 1725; married January 27, 1746, Abigail Starbuck, daughter of Paul and Ann. Their children were—

i William, born 5th 3 mo. 1749; married (1st 2 mo. 1770) Sarah Burnell, daughter of Jonathan and Deborah.
ii Elizabeth, born 17th 8 mo. 1751; died 26th 7 mo. 1795; married (31st 12 mo. 1767) Silvanus Coffin, son of Richard and Ruth.

---

*Seth must have died prior to 1780 for his widow Sarah married (31st, 10 mo. 1782) Richard Mitchell, son of Richard and Elizabeth.

    iii **Catharine,** born 28th 7 mo. 1754; removed from the Island 31st 5 mo. 1779; married (7th 1 mo. 1773) Charles Coleman, son of Jethro and Lydia.
    iv **Laban,** born 29th 9 mo. 1756; died 14th 1 mo. 1779.
    v **Ruth,** born 17th 10 mo. 1758; married (7th 11 mo. 1776) Thaddeus Swain, son of David and Martha.
    vi **Paul,** born 18th 2 mo. 1761; married (29th 1 mo. 1784) Judith Gardner, daughter of Nathaniel and Ruth.
    vii **Anna,** born 23d 9 mo. 1763; married (9th 10 mo. 1805) Peter Barney, son of Benjamin and Jemima.
    viii **Seth,** born 13th 12 mo. 1765; married (1st 1 mo. 1795) Naomi Chase, daughter of Francis and Naomi.
    ix **Abigail,** born 9th 1 mo. 1769; died 2d 2 mo. 1792; married (3d 12 mo. 1789) David Greene, son of Joseph and Abigail.

    BACHELOR [3] (Silvanus [2], Stephen [1]) born 29th 11 mo. 1728-9; married (29th 10 mo. 1748) Ann (or Anna) Coffin, daughter of Daniel and Mary. Their children were—
    i **Hepsibah,** born 8th, 2 mo. 1751; died 18th 12 mo. 1760.
    ii **Tristram,** born 6th 2 mo. 1753; married (6th 11 mo. 1777) Sarah Folger, daughter of William and Ruth.
    iii **Mary,** born 2d 2 mo. 1755; died 27th 9 mo. 1780; married (30th 8 mo. 1774) Barzillai Swain, son of Francis and Mary.
    iv **Zaccheus,** born 18th 5 mo. 1760; married (July 23, 1780) Lydia Folger.
    v **Susannah,** born 25th 6 mo. 1762; married (July 28, 1786) Obed Barnard.
    vi **Lydia,** born 29th 7 mo. 1764; married (April 15, 1784) Alexander Coffin Jr.
    vii **Elizabeth,** born 20th 8 mo. 1766; married (October 25, 1781) Thomas Delano.
    viii **Moses,** born 19th, 11 mo. 1768; lost at sea 1785.
    ix **Peter,** born 26th 1 mo. 1775; married (July 5, 1794) Mary Moores.

    NATHANIEL [3] (Silvanus [2], Stephen [1]) born January 2, 1731; died July 6, 1769; married (6th 10 mo.

1750) Judith Coffin, daughter of Francis and Theodate. Their children were—

    i **Judith**, born 29th 8 mo. 1752; died 1752.
    ii **Francis**, born 31st, 3 mo. 1754; died 22d 7 mo. 1777.
    iii **Libbeus**, born 10th, 11 mo. 1755; died 1755.
    iv **David**, born 22d 2 mo. 1757; married (3d 2 mo. 1780) Lydia Swain, daughter of David and Martha.
    v **Phebe**, born 2d 9 mo. 1758; died 29th 8 mo. 1777; married (28th 11 mo. 1776) Edmund Gardner, son of Daniel and Provided.
    vi **Rachel**, born 28th 10 mo. 1760; married (30th 9 mo. 1779) Peregrine Folger, son of Jonathan and Lydia.
    vii **Peleg**, born 28th 12 mo. 1762; married (August 19, 1784) Temperance Swain.
    viii **Abraham**, born 28th 6 mo. 1765; died 7th 2 mo. 1788.
    ix **Nathaniel**, born 10th 1 mo. 1767; married, probably (July 17, 1790) Elizabeth Swain.
    x **Alexander**, born 15th 11 mo. 1769.

GEORGE [3] (Silvanus [2] Stephen [1])

born 12th 5 mo. 1738; married (3d 2 mo. 1757) Deborah Paddack, daughter of Daniel and Susanna. Their children were:—

    i **Rhoda**, born 16th 2 mo. 1758; married (4th 1 mo. 1776) Tristram Folger, son of Barzillai and Phebe.
    ii **Eunice**, born 26th 12 mo. 1759; married (2d 7 mo. 1778) Peleg Easton son of Peleg and Mary.
    iii **George Gorham**, born 17th 8 mo. 1762; married (29th 1 mo 1784) Lydia Chase, daughter of Francis and Naomi.
    iv **Uriel**, born 9th 10 mo. 1766; married (1st 10 mo. 1789) Phebe Folger, daughter of William and Ruth.
    v **Silvanus**, born 9th 4 mo. 1768; probably married December 25, 1794. Prudence Pease.
    vi **Susanna**, born 24th 4 mo 1771; married (30th 9 mo. 1790) Zenas Gardner, son of Paul and Rachel.
    vii **Deborah**, born 17th 9 mo. 1773; married (9th 9 mo. 1795) Robert Brayton, son of Israel and Elizabeth.
    viii **Alice** born 22d, 12 mo. 1777.
    ix **Rachel**, born 24th 3 mo. 1783; married (7th 12 mo. 1808) Joseph Austin, son of Jeremiah and Patience.

JOHN [3] (Bachelor [2] Stephen [1])

was born 8th 8 mo. 1710; died in 1749; married (4th 12 mo. 17-

33-4 Jedidah Coffin, daughter of Joseph and Bethiah. She died 11th 1 mo. 1799. Their children were:—

    i **Joseph,**——————
   ii **Robert,**   ; died 19th 7 mo. 1783; married (28th 2 mo. 1759) Lydia Swain, daughter of Richard and Elizabeth.*
  iii **Stephen,**   died 8th 2 mo. 1794; married (8th 11 mo. 1759) Elizabeth Swain, daughter of Richard and Elizabeth.†
  iv **Benjamin,**   ; married (1st 3 mo. 1763) Phebe Macy, daughter of Francis and Judith.
   v **Bethiah,**   ; died 9th 7 mo. 1791; probably married (June 1759) Bachelor Bunker.
  vi **Abigail,** probably married January 1763, Joseph Myrick.
 vii **Ruth,**
viii **Ebenezer,**

STEPHEN [3] (Daniel [2] Stephen [1]) born 2d 4 mo. 1735; married (2d 12 mo. 1756) Rose Barnard, daughter of Matthew and Mary. Their children were:—

   i **Sarah,** born 30th 1 mo. 1757.
  ii **Dinah,** born 12th 12 mo. 1764.
  iii **Abial,** born 25th 12 mo. 1767.
  iv **Aaron,** born 4th 6 mo 1770.
   v **Daniel,** born 2d 2 mo. 1774.
  vi **Eunice** born 15th 7 mo. 1780.

---

*Robert also married (6th, 1 mo. 1774) Elizabeth Wing, daughter of Joseph and Mary.
†Stephen and Elizabeth had a son John, who married (2d, 10 mo. 1783) Lydia Barnard, daughter of Christopher and Judith.

MACY

Thomas Macy, according to tradition, must have passed the earlier months of his sojourn on the Island with few if any English associates outside his own family. Tradition further says that early in the spring (Mr. Macy having removed in October or November) Edward Starbuck, returned to Salisbury or Dover and when he finally returned to Nantucket several neighbors came with him. It is difficult to see the basis for the story as it is told. Similarly tradition says that Mr. Macy returned to Salisbury and remained there awhile. There seems to be no evidence confirmatory of such a story.

Tradition has apparently aimed to establish a fact that Thomas Macy and his family and Edward Starbuck and Isaac Coleman settled in Nantucket in the fall of 1659, but there seems to be no available evidence to prove this assumption. Macy's letter, written in Salisbury to explain why he did not appear to answer the summons of the Court, was dated October 27, 1659. The decision of the Court in his case was not given until November 12. Some time would be required to perfect his plans after he learned the decision of the Court, (though it is doubtful if that seriously affected him) to move with his wife and four or more* children into a strange country inhabited only by Indians just at the opening of winter. Furthermore all meetings of the company prior to that of July 15, 1661, were held at Salisbury, the one of that date was held at Nantucket. At the meeting at Salisbury May 10, 1661 all apparently being present, it was decided that in the future the records of the Company should be kept at Salisbury by Robert Pike, and at Nantucket by Thomas Macy. It is more than probable that his permanent residence was not at Nantucket until 1661.

Mr. Macy's house lot was on the eastern side of Reed Pond, then a creek extending from the north shore south of the road.† Obed Macy says his house was moved to Wescot‡ and until very recently it stood in Macy's Lane. He seems to have been a man with good judgment and marked self control and his correspondence with Gov. Andros at the time of the "Insurrection," is in marked contrast to that of Gardner and Folger.

THOMAS MACY

married Sarah Hopcott, born in England in 1612, died in Nantucket April 19, 1682. Their children were—

    i Sarah, born at Salisbury, July 9, 1644; died 1645.
    ii Sarah, born at Salisbury, August 1, 1646, married (April 1, 1665) William Worth. Died 1701.

---

*Two sons, Francis and Thomas, died unmarried and probably formed part of his family.
†Land and Land Owners p 71.
‡Unpublished M. S.

  iii **Mary** born at Salisbury, December 4, 1648; died June 6, 1712; married (April 11, 1669) William Bunker, son of George and Jane.
  iv **Bethiah**, born at Salisbury 1650; died 1732; married (March 30, 1670) Joseph Gardner, son of Richard and Sarah.
  v **Thomas**, born at Salisbury, September 22, 1653; died, unmarried, December 3, 1675.
  vi **John**, born at Salisbury, July 14, 1655; died October 14, 1691; married   Deborah Gardner, daughter of Richard and Sarah.
  vii **Francis**, born in Salisbury, 1657; died 1658.

With the exception of the first Sarah and Francis, the children all died in Nantucket.

JOHN MACY [2] (Thomas [1])

born in Salisbury, July 14, 1635; died at Nantucket October 14, 1691; married   Deborah Gardner, daughter of Richard and Sarah. Their children were—

  i **John**, born   1675; died November 28, 1751; married (April 25, 1707) Judith Worth, daughter of John and Miriam.
  ii **Sarah**, born April 3, 1677; died March 18, 1748; married John Barnard, son of Nathaniel and Mary.
  iii **Deborah**, born March 3, 1679; died August 16, 1742; married   Daniel Russell.
  iv **Bethiah**, born April 8, 1683; died June 6, 1738; married first, (   ) Joseph Coffin, son of James and Mary—second, John Renuff.
  v **Jabez**, born   1683; died August 6, 1776; married (November 27, 1712) Sarah Starbuck, daughter of Jethro and Dorcas.
  vi **Mary**, born   1685; died June 27, 1717; married (1st, 9 mo. 1711) Solomon Coleman, son of John and Joanna.
  vii **Thomas**, born   1687; died March 16, 1759; married (June 18, 1708) Deborah Coffin, daughter of (Lieut.) John Coffin and Deborah.
  viii **Richard**, born September 22, 1689; died December 25, 1779; married, first, (November 8, 1711) Deborah Pinkham, daughter of Reuben and Mary; second, June 8, 1769) Alice Paddack, daughter of Joseph and Sarah.*

---

*Richard built the first wharf (1723) and the first windmill in Nantucket, Macy Genealogy, p. 81.

JOHN [3] (John [2] Thomas [1])

married (April 25, 1707) Judith Worth, daughter of John and Miriam. He died 28th, 11 mo. 1751; she died 8th, 11 mo. 1767. Their children were—

    i **Miriam**, born 16th, 2 mo. 1708; died August 2, 1736; married (10th, 9 mo. 1725) Zephaniah Coffin, son of Stephen and Experience.
   ii **Silvanus**, born 16th, 8 mo. 1709; died September 6. 1719; unmarried.
  iii **Seth**, born 22d, 8 mo. 1710; died July 6, 1790; unmarried.
  iv **Eliab**, born 20th, 12 mo. 1712; died April 1723; unmarried.
   v **David**, born 12th, 9 mo. 1714; married (6th, 1 mo. 1739-40) Dinah Gardner, daughter of Solomon and Anna.
  vi **Anna**, born 17th, 12 mo. 1717-8; died 13th, 12 mo. 1756; married (9th, 11 mo. 1734-5) Joseph Jenkins, son of Matthew and Mary.
 vii **Bethiah**, born 16th, 1 mo. 1719-20; died in infancy.
viii **John**, born 11th, 12 mo. 1721-22; married (13th, 8 mo. 1743) Eunice Coleman, daughter of Elihu and Jemima.
  ix **Judith**, born 20th, 3 mo. 1723; died 25th, 6 mo. 1795; married (1st, 3 mo. 1753) William Clasby, son of William and Abiel.
   x **Jonathan**, born 8th, 4 mo. 1725; died 17th, 6 mo. 1798; married (6th, 10 mo. 1744) Lois Gorham, daughter of Stephen and Elizabeth.
  xi **William**, born 23d, 1 mo. 1726-7; died 6th, 2 mo. 1753; married (13th, 9 mo. 1746) Mary Barney, daughter of Benjamin and Lydia.
 xii **Sarah**, born 25th, 6 mo. 1729; married (5th, 12 mo. 1746) Richard Gardner, son of Solomon and Anna.
xiii **Abigail**, born 26th, 5 mo. 1731; died 25th, 11 mo. 1763; unmarried.

David, John and Sarah removed to North Carolina in 1771.

JABEZ [3] (John [2] Thomas [1])

born in 1683; and married (November 7, 1712) Sarah Starbuck, daughter of Jethro and Dorcas. He died 6th, 8 mo. 1776; she died 28th, 10 mo. 1789. Their children were—

    i **George**, born 11th, 3 mo. 1720; died 9 mo. 1742; unmarried.

   ii **Eunice**, born 14th, 11 mo. 1721; married (4th 9 mo. 1742) Richard Beard, son of Richard and Dorothy who came from Devonshire Eng. They removed to New Garden, N. C., 21st, 5 mo. 1772.

  iii **Dorcas**, born 16th, 6 mo. 1724: died 29th, 2 mo. 1768; unmarried.

  iv **Jethro**, born 15th, 2 mo. 1728; married (11th, 8 mo. 1750) Hephzibah Worth, daughter of William and Mary; removed to North Carolina 17th, 10 mo. 1771.

   v **Daniel**, born 21st, 5 mo. 1731; died 28th, 3 mo. 1785: married (24th, 11 mo. 1755) Abigail Swain, daughter of Caleb and Margaret.

  vi **Matthew**, born 19th, 10 mo. 1732; married first, (27th, 2 mo. 1755) Abigail Coffin, daughter of Benjamin and Jedidah; second, (26th, 2 mo. 1761) Abigail Gardner, daughter of Barnabas and Mary; removed from the Island 23d, 9 mo. 1773.

 vii **Lydia**, born 18th, 9 mo. 1734; married (5th, 2 mo. 1756) Matthew Jenkins, son of Peter and Abigail.

viii **Sarah**, born 26th, 9 mo. 1737; died 17th, 11 mo. 1800; unmarried.

  ix **Jabez**, born 30th, 10 mo. 1739; died 9 mo. 1767; lost at sea; married (26th, 2 mo. 1767) Rachel Cartwright, daughter of Hezekiah and Abigail.*

THOMAS [3] (John [2] Thomas [1])

born in 1687, married Deborah Coffin, daughter of John and Deborah. He died 20th, 3 mo. 1759; she died 23d, 9 mo. 1760. Their children were—

   i **Joseph**, born 8th, 4 mo. 1709; died 28th, 2 mo. 1772; married (1728) Hannah Hobbs, daughter of Benjamin.

  ii **Robert**, born 20th, 11 mo. 1710; died 23d, 11 mo. 1771: married (January 3, 1731) Abigail Barnard, daughter of Benjamin and Judith.

  iii **Love**, born 9th, 2 mo. 1713; died 14th, 11 mo. 1767; married (21st, 12 mo. 1733-4) Joseph Rotch son of William and Hannah.

---

*The Friends Record states that Lydia, daughter of Jabez and Rachel, married (28th, 12 mo. 1786) Uriel Starbuck, son of Silvanus and Mary.

iv Francis, born 2d, 6 mo. 1715; died 21st, 5 mo. 1793; married (30th. 5 mo. 1738) Judith Coffin, daughter of Richard and Ruth.
v Nathaniel, born 20th, 8 mo. 1717; died 22d, 3 mo. 1783; married (16th, 2 mo. 1741) Abigail Pinkham, daughter of Shubael and Abigail.
vi Lydia, born 23d, 2 mo. 1720; removed from the Island 26th, 7 mo. 1779; married (31st. 1 mo. 1748) Jethro Coleman, son of John and Priscilla.
vii Elizabeth, born 9th, 6 mo. 1722; died 1st, 6 mo. 1765; married (14th, 11 mo. 1741) Francis Barnard, son of Benjamin and Judith.
viii Thomas, born 13th, 8 mo. 1724; died 1725.
ix Deborah, born 17th, 4 mo. 1726; died 22d, 11 mo. 1803; married, first—(29th, 4 mo. 1762) Benjamin Coffin, son of Nathaniel and Damaris; second, (31st. 1 mo. 1782) Edward Starbuck, son of Paul and Ann.
x Anna, born 7th, 4 mo. 1730; removed from the Island 27th, 12 mo. 1779; married (1st, 2 mo. 1753; Richard Worth, son of Richard and Sarah.
xi Hepzibah, born 22d, 10 mo. 1734; removed from the Island 23d, 9 mo. 1773; married (14th, 12 mo. 1752) Thomas Davis, son of John and Margaret.

RICHARD [3] (John [2] Thomas [1])
born 7 mo. 22. 1689; died 25th 12 mo. 1779; married first, (Nov. 8 1711) Deborah Pinkham, daughter of Reuben and Mary; second, (June 8, 1769) Alice Paddack, daughter of Joseph and Sarah. Deborah died 13th 12 mo 1767. Their children were:

i Lydia, born 10th, 6 mo. 1712; did not marry.
ii Zaccheus, born 7th 11 mo. 1713; died 27th 10 mo. 17-97; married (5th 10 mo. 1734) Hephzibah Gardner, daughter of Samuel and Patience.
iii Abraham, born 9th, 7 mo. 1715; died 4th, 7 mo. 1746; married (8th 4 mo. 1738) Anna Worth, daughter of Joseph and Lydia.*
iv Mary, born 26th 11 mo 1717; died 7th 6 mo. 1764; married (1st 4 mo. 1749) Benjamin Marshall, son of Joseph and Mercy.
v Caleb, born 28th 9 mo. 1719; died 18th 6 mo. 1798; married (8th 12 mo. 1749) Judith Gardner, widow of James, and daughter of Daniel and Abigail Folger.

*After the death of Abraham his widow married (16th, 10 mo. 1755) Tristram Swain, son of John and Mary.

vi **Judith,** born 14th 10 mo 1721; moved from the Island 29th, 6 mo. 1780; married (6th, 11 mo. 1742) Jonathan Bunker, son of Peleg and Susanna.
   vii **Ruth,** born 31st, 10 mo. 1723; died 8th, 9 mo. 1760; married (4th 8 mo. 1744) Joseph Starbuck, son of Paul and Ann.
  viii **Hannah,** born 21st 10 mo. 1725; died 18th 11 mo 1726.
    ix **Richard,** born 29th 6 mo. 1727; died 20th 4 mo. 1736.
     x **Priscilla,** born 28th, 10 mo. 1729; died 11th, 3 mo. 1746; unmarried.
    xi **Benjamin,** born 6th 7 mo. 1731; died 14th. 7 mo. 1780; married Abigail Brown, daughter of George and Abigail. They had no children.

DAVID [4] (John [3] John [2] Thomas [1])
born 12th 9 mo. 1714: married Dinah Gardner daughter of Solomon and Anna. They removed to North Carolina 1st 10 mo. 1771. Their children were—

   i **Stephen,** born 27th 3 mo. 1741; died 8th 2 mo. 1822. He married (4th 12 mo. 1760) Mercy Allen, daughter of Nathaniel and Mercy.*
  ii **Miriam,** born   ; died 6th 7 mo. 1780; married (28th 1 mo. 1762) Robert Gardner, son of Robert and Jedidah.
 iii **Anna,** born   ; married (29th 12 mo. 1763) Enoch Macy, son of Joseph and Hannah; removed from the Island 10th mo 1771.
  iv **Sarah,** born   ; married (1st 1 mo. 1767) Timothy Russell son of William and Mary; removed from the Island 23d 9 mo. 1773.
   v **Hepzibah,** born   ; unmarried.
  vi **Abigail,** born   ; married (1774) Benjamin Stanton, son of Henry and Lydia;† removed from the Island 1st 10 mo. 1771.
 vii **David** born   ; married Hannah White daughter of Isaac and Catherine.

---

*Stephen, apparently the oldest child of Stephen and Mercy, married (29th, 1 mo. 1784) Phebe Swain, daughter of David and Martha.
†Mrs. Hinchman states ("Early Settlers of Nantucket" p 279) that Abigail was grandmother of Edwin M. Stanton, U. S. Attorney General under James Buchanan, and Secetary of War under Abraham Lincoln from January 11, 1862, until after President Lincoln's Assassination. Authorities give Secretary Stanton's middle name as McMasters.

HISTORY OF NANTUCKET

JOHN, [4] (John, [3] John [2] Thomas [1])
born 11th 12 mo. 1720-21; married (13th 8 mo. 1743) Eunice Coleman, daughter of Elihu and Jemima. She died 28th 12 mo. 1768; he removed from the Island 18th 4 mo. 1771. Their children were:—

   i Bethiah, born 3d 8 mo. 1744; removed from the Island 22d 9 mo. 1773; married (31st 12 mo. 1761) Paul Macy, son of Joseph and Hannah. Removed from the Island 22d 9 mo. 1773.
   ii Judith, born 20th, 5 mo. 1746; married (31st, 12 mo. 1767) Reuben Bunker, son of Reuben and Mary; removed from the Island 27th 5 mo. 1771.
   iii Eliab, born 9th, 6 mo. 1748; did not marry; removed from the Island 18th 4 mo. 1771.
   iv Jemima, born 15th 5 mo. 1750; removed from the Island 27th 5 mo 1771; married Barzillai Gardner, son of Stephen and Jemima.
   v Eunice, born 12th 5 mo. 1752; died in infancy.
   vi John, born 9th 2 mo. 1754; married Rhoda Gardner, daughter of Stephen and Jemima.
   vii Elihu, born 20th, 11 mo. 1755; did not marry.
   viii Eunice, born 27th 12 mo. 1757; did not marry.
   ix Barachiah, born 24th. 2 mo. 1760; married (March 20, 1783) Lucinda Barnard, daughter of Benjamin and Eunice. (Eunice and Barachiah removed from the Island 18th 4 mo. 1771.)
   x Merab, born 30th 11 mo. 1761; married (January 8, 1783) Timothy Macy, son of Jethro and Hepzibah.
   xi Abigail, born 6th, 12 mo. 1763; did not marry.
   xii Micajah, born 25th 11 mo. 1764; did not marry.
   xiii Almy, born 5th, 11 mo. 1766; married Libni Barnard, son of Benjamin and Eunice.
   xiv Clement, born 24th, 12 mo. 1768.

JONATHAN [4] (John [3] John [2] Thomas [1])
born 8th 4 mo. 1725; married (6th 10 mo. 1744) Lois Gorham, daughter of Stephen and Elizabeth; he died 17th 6 mo. 1798; she died 10th 3 mo 1804. Their children were:—

   i Elizabeth, born 18th 8 mo. 1745; removed from the Island 26th 7 mo 1779; married (30th 12 mo. 1762) Elihu Coleman, son of Jethro and Lydia.
   ii Miriam, born 26th 6 mo. 1748; died 12 mo 1748.

    iii **Jonathan,** born 4th 11 mo. 1749; died 18th 6 mo 1816; married (3d 12 mo. 1778) Rose Pinkham, daughter of Reuben and Anne.
    iv **Barnabas,** born 16th. 4 mo. 1752; died 30th 4 mo. 1802; married (26th. 2 mo. 1784) Abiel Clasby, daughter of Joseph and Lydia.
    v **Solomon,** born 23d 6 mo. 1754; died 7 mo. 1755.
    vi **Susanna,** born 27th 5 mo. 1756; died 15th 8 mo. 1757.
    vii **Samuel,** born 3d 10 mo. 1758; died 16th 8 mo. 1761.
    viii **Peleg,** born 11th 11 mo. 1760; married (28th. 10 mo 1784) Sarah Starbuck, widow of Zaccheus and daughter of John and Sarah Wendell.
    ix **Judith,** born 18th 3 mo. 1763; died 10th 12 mo. 1799: did not marry.
    x **Samuel,** born 18th 2 mo. 1765; married (29th 6 mo. 17-86) first Lydia Folger, daughter of Walter and Elizabeth; second (7th 3 mo. 1833) Mary Clisby, daughter of William and Hepsabeth.
    xi **Seth,** born 9 mo. 1767; died 8 mo. 1768.

WILLIAM [4] (John [3] John [2] Thomas [1])
born 23d 1 mo. 1726-7; married (13th 9 mo. 1746) Mary Barney, daughter of Benjamin and Lydia; he died 6th 2 mo 1753; she died 11th, 7 mo. 1777. Their children were—

    i **Sarah,** born 10th, 9 mo. 1747; died 14th, 6 mo. 1749.
    ii **Lydia,** born 27th 7 mo. 1749; died 27th 3 mo. 1821; did not marry.
    iii **William,** born 29th 9 mo. 1751; died 17th 8 mo. 1814; married first (12th 12 mo. 1771) Anna Hussey daughter of Paul and Anna; second (9th 7 mo. 1807) Jedidah Barker daughter of Robert and Sarah.

JETHRO [4] (Jabez [3] John [2] Thomas [1])
born 15th 2 mo. 1728; married (11th 8 mo. 1750) Hephzibah Worth, daughter of William and Mary. The entire family removed to North Carolina 10th mo. 1771. Their children were—

    i **Hephzibah,** born 17th 10 mo. 1751; married Thomas Pierce.

ii **Mary,** born 13th 6 mo. 1754; married Samuel Coffin son of William and Priscilla.
iii **Jethro,** born 17th 10 mo. 1757; married (3d 4 mo. 1777) Susanna Wilcox, daughter of John and Hannah.
iv **Gayer,** born 11th 11 mo. 1757; married Anna Clasby, daughter of Charles and Anna.
v **Jedidah,** born 23d 11 mo. 1759; married Joseph Swain, son of Nathaniel and Bethiah.
vi **Timothy,** born 17th 7 mo. 1762; married (January 8, 1783) Merab Macy, daughter of John and Eunice.
vii **Elizabeth,** born 20th 5 mo. 1765; did not marry.
viii **Huldah,** born 1st, 5 mo. 1777; married (November 15, 1792) Asa Barnard, son of Tristram and Margaret.

DANIEL [4] (Jabez [3], John [2], Thomas [1])
born 21st 5 mo. 1731; married (24th 11 mo. 1755) Abigail Swain, daughter of Caleb and Margaret. He died 28th 3 mo. 1785; she died 2d 11 mo. 1788. Their children were—

i **Silvanus,** born 6th 12 mo. 1756; moved from the Island 2d 4 mo. 1801; married, first (30th 5 mo. 1782) Dinah Bunker, daughter of Paul and Hannah; second (3d 10 mo. 1798, Mary Foster, widow of John, daughter of Francis and Mary Swain.
ii **Lydia,** born 3d 3 mo. 1759; died 13th 7 mo. 1793; unmarried.
iii **Margaret,** born 20th 8 mo. 1761; removed from the Island 31st, 7 mo. 1800; married (2d, 8 mo. 1787) Obed Paddack, son of Jonathan and Kezia.
iv **Uriah,** born 7th 3 mo. 1764; married (27th 9 mo. 1787) Eunice Barney, daughter of Benjamin and Jemima.
v **Daniel,** born 26th, 3 mo. 1766; died 8th, 7 mo. 1768.
vi **Abigail, born 31st 5 mo.** 1770; died 16th 7 mo. 1799; married (28th 4 mo. 1791) Matthew Barney, son of Benjamin and Jemima.

MATTHEW [4] (Jabez [3], John [2], Thomas [1])
born 19th 10 mo. 1732; married (27th 2 mo. 1755) Abigail Coffin,

daughter of Benjamin and Jedidah. Abigail died 31st, 8 mo. 1758, and he married (26th 2 mo 1761) Abigail Gardner daughter of Barnabas and Mary. The entire family removed from the Island 23d 9 mo. 1773. Their children were—

By the first wife:

    i **Matthew**, born   1759; married Lydia Barnard, daughter of Benjamin and Eunice.

By his second wife:

    ii **George**, born   1762; married (1785) Matilda Folger, daughter of Reuben and Dinah.
    iii **Sarah**, born   ; married Stephen Springer.
    iv **Abigail**, born   ; married Joseph Coffin, son of Peter and Priscilla.
    v **Elizabeth**, born   ; married (   ) Libni Coffin, son of Libni and Hepzabeth.

JABEZ [4] (Jabez [3] John [2] Thomas [1])
born 30th 10 mo. 1739; married (26th 2 mo. 1767) Rachel Cartwright, daughter of Hezediah and Abigail. He was lost at sea in September 1767. They had one child:

    i **Lydia**, born 21st 12 mo. 1767; married (28th 12 mo. 1786) Uriah Starbuck, son of Silvanus and Mary; removed from the Island 3d 10 mo. 1799.

JOSEPH [4] (Thomas [3] John [2] Thomas [1])
born 8th 4 mo. 1709; died 28th 2 mo 1772; married (February 23, 1727-8) Hannah Hobbs daughter of Benjamin. Their children were:

    i **Mary**, born 15th, 7 mo. 1729; married (1st, 11 mo. 1753) Paul Way, son of John and Mary.
    ii **Thomas**, born 1st, 3 mo. 1731; married (24th, 2 mo. 1755) Mary Starbuck, daughter of Tristram and Deborah.
    iii **Bethiah**, born 3d, 4 mo. 1733; married (4th, 12 mo. 1755) Nathaniel Swain, son of Caleb and Margaret.
    iv **Joseph**, born 4th, 8 mo. 1735; married (8th, 12 mo. 1757) Mary Starbuck, daughter of William and Anna.

v Henry, born 22d, 8 mo. 1737; married (31st, 1 mo. 1760) Sarah Swain, daughter of Caleb and Margaret; second (March 24, 1791) Elizabeth Coffin, widow of Benjamin, daughter of Daniel and Sarah Hussey.

vi Paul, born 22d, 2 mo. 1740; married—first (31st, 12 mo. 1761) Bethiah Macy, daughter of John and Eunice; second, (26th, 1 mo. 1817) Deborah Coggeshall, daughter of Job and Deborah.

vii Enoch, born 11th, 2 mo. 1743; married (29th, 12 mo. 1763) Anna Macy, daughter of David and Dinah.

Joseph and his entire family removed to New Garden, N. C. about 1773.

ROBERT [4] (Thomas [3] John [2] Thomas [1])
born 20th, 11 mo. 1710; married (3d, 1 mo. 1731) Abigail Barnard, daughter of Benjamin and Judith. He died 23d, 11 mo. 1771; she removed from the Island 27th, 3 mo. 1775. Their children were—

i Lydia, born ———— 1733; died 19th, 10 mo. 1765; married (27th, 12 mo. 1752) Abishai Gardner, son of Robert and Jedidah.

ii Benjamin, born ———— 1735; lost at sea 1755; unmarried.

iii Judith, born 28th, 5 mo. 1737; removed from the Island 25th, 9 mo. 1775; married (16th, 11 mo. 1758) Benjamin Stretton, son of Caleb and Lois.

iv Nathaniel, born ————; removed from the Island 8th, 4 mo. 1773; married (5th, 2 mo. 1761) Hephzibah Macy, daughter of Zaccheus and Hephzibah.

v Elizabeth, born   ; removed from the Island 29th, 6 mo. 1772; married—first (1st, 3 mo. 1763) Alexander Movers, son of Thomas and Mary; second—(   ) William Coffin, son of Benjamin and Jedidah. Removed from the Island 29th, 6 mo. 1772.

vi Eunice, born   ; died in infancy.

vii Robert, born 16th, 1 mo. 1746; married—first (2d, 3 mo. 1772) Anna Jones, daughter of Silas and Anna; second (13th, 9 mo. 1798) Phebe Jenkins, daughter of Joseph and Ruth.

viii John, born 17th, 1 mo. 1748; removed from the Island 29th, 8 mo. 1774; married—first (3d 3 mo. 1768) Bethiah Cartwright, daughter of Hezadiah and Abigail; second (5th, 3 mo. 1794) Phebe Macy, daughter of Abraham and Priscilla.*

---

*John Macy, son of Robert Macy, of the fifth generation from Thomas Macy, signed his last will when he was eighty-eight years old and had nineteen children. Early Settlers of Nantucket, p. 283.

798   HISTORY OF NANTUCKET

 ix **Abigail,** born   ; removed from the Island 27th, 3 mo. 1775; married Thomas Butts.
 x **Deborah,** born   ; died 30th, 4 mo. 1771; married (28th, 12 mo. 1769) Jonathan Cartwright, son of Hezediah and Abigail.
 xi **Mary,** born   ; removed from the Island 27th, 3 mo. 1775; unmarried.
 xii **Eunice,** born 19th, 1 mo. 1757; removed from the Island 29th, 8 mo. 1774; married Francis Bunker, son of Shubael and Lydia.
 xiii **Benjamin,** born 19th, 1 mo. 1757; unmarried.

FRANCIS [4] (Thomas [3] John [2] Thomas [1])
born 2d, 6 mo. 1715; died 21st, 5 mo. 1793; married (30th, 5 mo. 1738) Judith Coffin, daughter of Richard and Ruth; she died 15th, 5 mo. 1799. Their children were—

 i **Love,** born 7th, 6 mo. 1740; died 7th, 1 mo. 1808; married (8th, 2 mo. 1759) James Cartwright, son of Hezediah and Abigail.
 ii **Reuben,** born 8th, 7 mo. 1742; married—first (28th, 5 mo. 1767) Anna Barnard, daughter of Robert and Hepzabeth; second, Judith Myrick, widow of Jethro, daughter of Thomas and Judith Jenkins.
 iii **Phebe,** born 11th, 7 mo. 1744; removed from the Island 23d, 6 mo. 1787; married (1st, 3 mo. 1763) Benjamin Hussey. son of John and Jedidah.
 iv **Seth,** born 21st, 10 mo. 1747; lost at sea 1768; unmarried.
 v **Francis,** born 23d, 11 mo. 1750; married—first (in London) Hannah Mackrell, of Pool England; second (June 1798) Elizabeth Brown, daughter of Joseph and Mary.*
 vi **Judith,** born 19th, 10 mo. 1751; married (4th, 2 mo. 1773) Benjamin Coffin, son of Benjamin and Rebecca.
 vii **Anna,** born 11th, 1 mo. 1754; married (29th, 11 mo. 1774) Tristram Jenkins, son of Peter and Abigail.
 viii **Ruth,** born 16th, 6 mo. 1760; married Obadiah Folger, son of Barzillai and Phebe.
 ix **Deborah,** born 6th, 2 mo. 1762; died 26th, 8 mo. 1790; unmarried.
 x **Lydia,** born 12th, 7 mo. 1764; removed from the Island 26th, 9 mo. 1791; married (2d, 9 mo. 1784) Edward Starbuck, son of Edward and Damaris.

---

*Early Settlers of Nantucket, p. 283.

NATHANIEL [4] (Thomas [3] John [2] Thomas]1[ )
born 20th, 8 mo. 1717; died 22d, 3 mo. 1783; married (16th, 2 mo 1741) Abigail Pinkham, daughter of Shubael and Abigail; she died 1st, 9 mo. 1810. Their children were—

    i Shubael, born 27th, 2 mo. 1743; married (4th, 2 mo. 1762) Eunice Gardner, daughter of Robert and Jedidah.
    ii Tristram, born 26th, 2 mo. 1745; died 1781; married (31st, 10 mo. 1765) Miriam Barnard, daughter of William and Mary.
    iii George, born 6th, 7 mo. 1747; died 25th, 10 mo. 1773; married (28th, 12 mo. 1769) Margaret Paddack, daughter of Paul and Anna.
    iv Deborah, born 11th, 3 mo. 1750; died 30th, 8 mo. 1752.
    v Nathaniel, born 15th, 1 mo. 1753; married—first Elizabeth Broch, daughter of William and Elizabeth; second Mercy Dunham, daughter of Jethro and Mercy.*
    vi Eunice, born 19th, 2 mo. 1755; died 17th, 1 mo. 1784; married (   ) Solomon Coffin, son of Zephaniah and Abigail.
    vii Peter, born 3d, 2 mo. 1757; married (28th, 11 mo. 1780) Sarah Folger, daughter of Timothy and Abial.
    viii Phebe, born 31st, 1 mo. 1759; died 5th, 12 mo. 1803; married—first (9th, 7 mo. 1778) Paul Barnard, son of William and Mary; second (9th, 9 mo. 1790) Paul Worth, son of John and Mary.
    ix Elizabeth, born 16th, 7 mo. 1763; married (1st, 3 mo. 1787) Barzillai Macy, son of Caleb and Judith.
    x Thomas.
    xi Abishai, born 23d, 10 mo. 1770; married (July 19, 1794) Phebe Worth, daughter of Andrew and Judith.

ZACCHEUS [4] (Richard [3] John [2] Thomas]1[ )
born 7th, 12 mo. 1713; died 27th, 10 mo. 1797; married (5th, 10 mo. 1734) Hephzibah Gardner, daughter of Samuel and Patience. She died 27th, 6 mo. 1795. Their children were—

    i Mary, born 14th, 9 mo. 1735; died 8th, 5 mo. 1784; married (1st, 3 mo. 1753) John Ray, son of Samuel and Mary.
    ii Hannah, born 30th, 10 mo. 1737; married (30th, 8 mo. 1756)Reuben Swain, son of Stephen and Eleanor.

---

*Early Settlers of Nantucket, p. 284.

  iii **Phebe**, born 16th, 1 mo. 1740; removed from the Island 27th, 4 mo. 1772; married (1st, 1 mo. 1756) William Stanton, son of Samuel and Sarah.
  iv **Richard**, born 22d, 4 mo. 1742; married (4th, 10 mo. 1759) Miriam Coffin, daughter of Hephaniah and Abigail.
  v **Hepsibah**, born 26th, 6 mo. 1744; removed from the Island 28th, 4 mo. 1772; married (5th, 2 mo. 1761) Nathaniel Macy, son of Robert and Abigail.
  vi **Priscilla**, born 25th, 9 mo. 1746; died 26th, 6 mo. 1818; married—first Enoch Ray, son of Samuel and Mary; second (8th, 12 mo. 1808) Micajah Coffin, son of Benjamin and Jedidah.
  vii **Ruth**, born 12th, 4 mo. 1751; married (1st. 12 mo. 1768) Thomas Barnard, son of Thomas and Sarah.
  viii **Deborah**, born 18th, 1 mo. 1755; married Daniel Ray, son of Samuel and Elizabeth.
  ix **Latham**, born 7th, 2 mo. 1759; married (2d, 10 mo. 1777) Lydia Russell, daughter of John and Ruth.

  The above list of the names of the children of Zaccheus and Hepsibah Macy is taken from the Friends Records. Mrs. Hinchman has in addition*—x **David**, xi **Abishai**, xii **Lydia**, xiii **Jemima**, and xiv **Samuel**, neither of whom married.

  ABRAHAM [4] (Richard [3] John [2] Thomas [1]) born 9th, 7 mo. 1715; died 4th, 7 mo. 1746; married (8th, 4 mo. 1738) Anna Worth, daughter of Joseph and Lydia. Their children were—

  i **Abraham**, born 7th, 8 mo. 1739; he removed from the Island 25th, 4 mo. 1774; married (3d, 12 mo. 1761) Priscilla Bunker, daughter of Samuel and Priscilla.
  ii **Simeon**, born 30th, 11 mo. 1742-3; died 1764; unmarried.
  iii **Anna**, born 24th, 10 mo. 1744; married (10th, 12 mo. 1761) Edward Allen, son of Ebenezer and Christian.
  iv **Reuben**, born 14th, 1 mo. 1747; removed from the Island 7th, 5 mo. 1772; married—first (31st. 12 mo. 1767) Elizabeth Bunker, daughter of Samuel and Priscilla; second (September 21, 1774) Ruth Howard, daughter of Edward and Phebe.

---

*Early Settlers of Nantucket, p. 285.

CALEB [4] (Richard [3] John [2] Thomas [1])
born 28th, 9 mo. 1719; died 18th, 6 mo. 1798; married (8th, 12 mo. 1749) Judith Gardner, widow of James, and daughter of Daniel and Abigail Folger. She removed from the Island 29th, 4 mo. 1819. Their children were—

i Kezia, born 22d, 5 mo. 1751; died 30th, 6 mo. 1752.
ii Elisha, born 17th, 5 mo. 1753; died 2d, 4 mo. 1806: married (8th, 9 mo. 1774) Phebe Gardner, daughter of Jonathan and Miriam.
iii Silvanus,* born 15th, 12 mo. 1756; married (July 3. 1779) Anna Pinkham, daughter of Daniel and Eunice.
iv Barzillai, born 6th, 9 mo. 1759; died 1st 8 mo. 1789: married (1st, 3 mo. 1787) Elizabeth Macy, daughter of Nathaniel.
v Obed, born 15th, 1 mo. 1762; married (2d, 2 mo. 1786) Abigail Pinkham, daughter of Daniel and Eunice.
vi Caleb, born 20th, 3 mo. 1764; died 18th, 8 mo. 1834: did not marry.
vii Judith, born 16th, 9 mo. 1766; died 14th, 3 mo. 1789: unmarried.
viii Kezia, born 22d, 9 mo. 1768; died 7th, 4 mo. 1770.
ix Ruth, born 31st, 8 mo. 1771; married (9th, 11 mo. 1796) Job Chase, son of Benjamin and Martha.

---

*An unnamed child born 2d, 9 mo. 1755, lived but a day.

STARBUCK

EDWARD STARBUCK

Nathaniel Barney says of Edward Starbuck "He was a man of great firmness and his influence among the Indians was so great that if at any time suspicion or alarm arose among the early settlers he was always in requisition to explain the apparent causes thereof and suggest a palliation for their rude and inexplicable action, which served to allay the fears of the more timid. His wife's name was Katharine Reynolds. He died 4th 12 mo. 1690, aged 86."*

There seems to be no record regarding his wife, but as the early records of births, marriages and deaths kept by William Worth seem to be quite complete and her name does not appear in them the presumption is that she died before the family removed to Nantucket.† That he was well esteemed among the Indians as mentioned by Mr. Barney is evidenced by the deeding of Coatue to him by Wannackmamack and Nicanoos "of our free and voluntary willes." Tradition says that Edward Starbuck was a man of commanding presence.

It is stated that the spring following his coming to Nantucket with Thomas Macy, he returned to Dover and vicinity and persuaded several to accompany him back to Nantucket.

Various incidents in his life have already been related. When he came to the Island he occupied a house which he built at Maddeket. His house lot as laid out was about 1000 feet square, extending northward from the head of Hummock Pond to Maxcy's Pond.‡

Children of EDWARD STARBUCK and KATHERINE REYNOLDS

    i **Nathaniel,** born in 1635; died 6th 6 mo. 1719; married 1662 Mary Coffin, daughter of Tristram.
    ii **Dorcas,** born   : married William Gayer.
    iii **Sarah,** born   ; married—first William Story; second, Joseph Austin; third, Humphrey Varney as his second wife.
    iv **Abigail,** born   ; married Peter Coffin, son of Tristram and Dionis.
    v **Esther,** born   ; was Humphrey Varney's first wife.
    vi **Jethro,** one son, was killed May 27, 1663, at the age of twelve years by the overturning of a cart.

Edward Starbuck died 4th 12 mo. 1690 aged 86 years.

---

*Unpublished M S.
†The probabilities are that she died in Dover.
‡Nantucket Lands and Land Owners p. 75. There is a tradition that on one occasion the Indians were in an ugly mood and threatened trouble. He was sent for and unhesitatingly went among them. So much regard they had for him that he soon quieted them.
    William Gayer who married Dorcas Starbuck is stated to be direct in descent from Edward I of England.

NATHANIEL [2] (Edward [1])

son of Edward and Katherine born 1635; married (1662) Mary Coffin, daughter of Tristram and Dionis;* died 6th 6 mo. 1719. She died 13th 9 mo. 1717. Their children were—

   i **Mary**, born 30th 3 mo. 1663;† married James Gardner son of Richard and Sarah.

   ii **Elizabeth**, born 9th 9 mo. 1665; married—first (August 15, 1682) Peter Coffin, son of Peter and Abigail; second, Nathaniel Barnard, son of Nathaniel and Mary.

   iii **Nathaniel**, born 8th 9 mo. 1668; married (November 20, 1690) Dinah Coffin, daughter of James and Mary; died January 29, 1753.

   iv **Jethro**, born December 14, 1671; married (December 6, 1694) Dorcas Gayer, daughter of William and Dorcas; died August 12, 1770.

   v **Barnabas**, born 1673; died 21st 9 mo. 1732; unmarried.

   vi **Eunice**, born April 10, 1674; married ( ) George Gardner, son of John and Priscilla; died 12th 7 mo. 1766.

   vii **Priscilla**, born 1676; married ( ) John Coleman, son of John; died March 14, 1762.

   viii **Hephzibah**, born April 2, 1680; married ( ) Thomas Hathaway of Dartmouth; died 7th 2 mo. 1740.

   ix **Ann**, born ; unmarried.

   x **Paul**, born ; unmarried.

NATHANIEL [3] (Nathaniel [2]. Edward [1])

born August 9, 1668, married (November 20, 1690) Dinah Coffin, daughter of James and Mary. He died 9th 2 mo. 1753; she died 1st 8 mo. 1750.‡ Their children were—

   i **Mary**, born 31st 10 mo. 1692; died 22d 7 mo. 1763; married (1st 12 mo. 1710-11) Jethro Folger, son of John.

---

*At the time of his death Nathaniel Starbuck was doubtless one of the wealthiest, if not individually the wealthiest men on the Island. He owned three full shares of land, having purchased a share of Stephen Greenleaf. His wife was one of the ablest women who ever lived on Nantucket and her advice and influence were noteworthy factors in the conduct of affairs. She was the leading spirit in the organization of the Society of Friends.

†Mary Starbuck was the first English child born on Nantucket.

‡Nathaniel was for several years Town Clerk and was also Clerk of the Friends' Meeting.

804   HISTORY OF NANTUCKET

    ii **Paul,** born 29th 8 mo. 1694; died 20th 5 mo. 1759; married (26th, 9 mo. 1718) Ann Tebbets. His second wife (29th, 10 mo. 1737) was Kezia Folger, widow of Jethro Gardner, daughter of Peter Folger, and his third, Elizabeth Coffin, (28th, 8 mo. 1750) daughter of William and Susanna Stretton, widow of Daniel Coffin.

    iii **Priscilla,** born 25th 8 mo. 1696; died 1 mo. 1728; married (6th 10 mo. 1717) Shubael Coffin, son of Stephen Jr. and Experience.

    iv **Elizabeth,** born 27th 9 mo. 1698; died 9th 2 mo. 1770; married (12th 9 mo. 1717) George Hussey, son of Stephen and Martha.

    v **Hephzibah,** born 8th 9 mo. 1700; died 31st 12 mo. 1764; married (8th 9 mo. 1723) Silvanus Hussey son of Stephen and Martha.

    vi **Abigail,** born 28th, 6 mo. 1704; died 31st, 12 mo. 1777; married—first (18th 9 mo. 1723) Thomas Howes, son of Thomas and Abigail; second (7th, 7 mo. 1741) John Way.

    vii **Benjamin,** born 16th 7 mo. 1707; died 3 mo 1731, lost at sea; married (31st 10 mo. 1730) Dinah Coffin daughter of Experience (widow). He died 16th 2 mo. 1731.

    viii **Tristram,** born 18th 6 mo. 1709; died 29th 11 mo. 1789; married (10th 12 mo. 1729) Deborah Coffin, daughter of Samuel and Miriam.

    ix **Ruth,** born 24th 12 mo. 1714-15; died 5th 10 mo. 1772; married (3d 12 mo. 1731-2) John Russell, son of Daniel and Deborah.

    x **Anna,** born 12th 9 mo. 1716; died 18th 12 mo. 1785; married (10th 11 mo. 1733-4) Peter Barnard, son of Nathaniel and Judith.

    JETHRO [3] (Nathaniel [2], Edward [1])
born December 14, 1671; died August 12, 1770; is said to have attained the greatest age of anyone who ever lived on Nantucket;* married (December 6, 1694) Dorcas Gayer, daughter of William. She died 11th, 10 mo. 1747. Their children were—

    i **Sarah,** born 20th, 10 mo. 1697; died 27th, 10 mo. 1789; married (27th 9 mo. 1712) Jabez Macy, son of John and Deborah.

---

*He was for many years (30) a member of the Board of Selectmen.

ii **William,** born 22d 5 mo. 1699; died 17th 10 mo. 1760; married first (9th 10 mo. 1720) Anna Folger, daughter of Peter and Judith; second (28th 8 mo. 1751) Lydia Coleman, daughter of Jeremiah and Sarah.
iii **Eunice,** born 4th 12 mo. 1701-2; died 9th 10 mo. 1745; married (2d 2 mo. 1724) Daniel Pinkham, son of Richard.
iv **Lydia,** born 15th 7 mo. 1704; died 2d 4 mo. 1751; married (31st 1 mo. 1722) Benjamin Barney of Rhode Island.
v **Thomas,** born 12th, 10 mo. 1706; died 5th, 7 mo. 1777; married (2d, 10 mo. 1726) Rachel Allen, daughter of Edward and Ann.
vi **Dorcas,** born 13th, 2 mo. 1710; died 10 mo. 1710.
vii **Jemima,** born 2d 5 mo. 1712; removed from the Island 27th 4 mo. 1761; married (31st 8 mo. 1728) Silvanus Allen, son of Edward and Ann.
viii **Mary,** born 8th 7 mo. 1715; died 24th 10 mo. 1780; married (26th, 12 mo. 1731) Richard Mitchell, son of Richard and Elizabeth.

PAUL [4] (Nathaniel [3] Nathaniel [2] Edward [1]) born 29th 8 mo. 1694; died 20th 5 mo. 1759; married Ann Tebbets; she died 29th 7 mo. 1736. Their children were—

i **Edward,** born 28th 11 mo. 1719; died 11th 12 mo. 1798; married (7th 11 mo. 1742) Damaris Worth, daughter of William and Mary. He married again (31st 1 mo. 1782) Deborah Macy, daughter of Thomas and Deborah.
ii **Hephzibah,** born 22d 7 mo. 1721; removed from the Island 25th 5 mo. 1743; married (26th 12 mo. 1738-39) Jonathan Hussey, son of Silvanus and Abiel.
iii **Joseph,** born 26th 6 mo.* 1723; died 24th 10 mo. 1760; married (4th 8 mo. 1744) Ruth Macy, daughter of Richard and Deborah.
iv **John,** born 16th 2 mo. 1725; lost at sea 1755; married Abigail Calef, widow of Peter and daughter of Nathaniel Woodbury.
v **Samuel,** born 15th 1 mo. 1727; removed from Island 19th 3 mo. 1795; married (1st 12 mo. 1749) Abigail Barney, daughter of Benjamin and Lydia.

*There are occasionally slight discrepancies between the Records of the Friends' Society and those of the Town Clerk. The Town Records give Joseph's birth-place as 26th, 6 mo. 1723 and the Friends Records give the 5 mo.

  vi **Abigail,** born 10th 12 mo. 1728; married William Hussey, son of Silvanus and Abiel.
  vii **Elizabeth,** born 26th 12 mo. 1730-31; married (29th 9 mo. 1750) Tristram Coffin, son of Tristram and Mary.
  viii **Mary,** born 2d 8 mo. 1734; removed from the Island 27th 2 mo. 1800; married (8th 11 mo. 1753) Richard Coffin, son of Richard and Ruth.* She died in 1807.
  ix **Anna,** born 22d 7 mo. 1736; removed from the Island 29th, 10 mo. 1770; married first, Reuben Pinkham son of Theophilus; second Thomas Smith.

Paul Starbuck was married three times; the above named children are all by the first wife; there were no children by the second wife; by the third wife, Elizabeth who died 6th, 1 mo. 1780, he had—

  x **Dinah,** born 24th, 8 mo. 1752; died 29th, 11 mo. 1788; married (11th, 7 mo. 1776) William Jenkins, son of Peter and Abigail.

BENJAMIN [4] (Nathaniel [3] Nathaniel [2] Edward [1]) born 16th, 7 mo. 1707; was lost at sea 3 mo. 1731; married (31st, 10 mo. 1730) Dinah Coffin, who removed from the Island 30th, 5 mo. 1785. They had but one child—

  i **Benjamin,** born 5th, 10 mo. 1731; he removed from the Island 27th, 2 mo. 1775. Married Hepsabeth Bunker, daughter of Stephen; second Sarah Gardner, widow of Samuel and daughter of Thomas Jenkins.
  ii **Thaddeus,** married Mary Brock, daughter of William and Elizabeth.

TRISTRAM [4] (Nathaniel [3] Nathaniel [2] Edward [1]) born 18th, 6 mo. 1709; died 29th, 11 mo. 1789; married (10th, 12 mo. 1729) Deborah Coffin, daughter of Samuel and Miriam, who died 9th, 6 mo. 1789. Their children were—

  i **Christopher,** born 21st, 1 mo. 1731; died 29th, 9 mo. 1815; married (12th 10 mo. 1751) Mary Barnard, daughter of Benjamin and Judith.

---

*The record states that she also married Isaac Kelley.

ii Zaccheus, born 1st, 2 mo. 1733; died 9th, 1 mo. 1766; did not marry.
iii Mary, born 30th, 4 mo. 1735; removed from the Island 3 mo. 1781; married first, (24th, 2 mo. 1755) Thomas Macy, son of Joseph and Hannah; second, (26th, 2 mo. 1767) Abishai Gardner, son of Robert and Jedidah.*
iv Lydia, born 30th, 4 mo. 1735; died 30th, 1 mo. 1809, married—first, Joseph Clasby, son of William and Abiel; second, Eliphalet Gardner, son of James and Susanna.
v Deborah, born 19th, 1 mo. 1739; died 13th, 10 mo. 1781; married (10th, 11 mo. 1757) Job Coggeshall, son of Caleb and Mercy.†

WILLIAM [4] (Jethro [3] Nathaniel [2] Edward [1]) born 22d, 5 mo. 1699; died 17th, 10 mo. 1760; married—first (9th, 10 mo. 1720) Anna Folger, daughter of Peter and Judith; who died 6th, 9 mo. 1748; second, (28th, 8 mo. 1751) Lydia Coleman, daughter of Jeremiah and Sarah. Their children were—

By Anna—

i Nathaniel, born 16th, 8 mo. 1722: lost at sea 1755.
ii Eunice, born 7th, 6 mo. 1728; died 26th, 4 mo. 1750; married (3d, 11 mo. 1744) Stephen Barnard, son of Ebenezer and Mary.
iii Jethro, born 29th, 1 mo. 1732; died 13th, 5 mo. 1806; married—first (27th, 2 mo. 1755) Anna Upham, daughter of Jonathan and Ruth. He married, second, (7th, 6 mo. 1770) Ann Coffin, daughter of Jonathan and Hephzibah Hussey.
iv Judith, born 10th, 8 mo. 1734; removed from the Island 29th, 9 mo. 1774; married (6th, 12 mo. 1753) Joseph Worth, son of Joseph and Lydia.
v Mary, born 15th, 7 mo. 1738; removed from the Island 29th, 9 mo. 1774; married (8th, 12 mo. 1757) Joseph Macy, son of Joseph and Hannah.

By his second wife—

vi Anna, born probably in 1752.

---

*Mary was married again (1st, 3 mo. 1781) to James Mitchell, son of Richard and Elizabeth.
†There was also another daughter who died at the age of 8 years.

THOMAS [4] (Jethro [3] Nathaniel [2] Edward [1])
born 12th, 10 mo. 1706; died 5th, 2 mo. 1777; married (2d, 10
mo. 1726) Rachel Allen, daughter of Edward and Ann; she died
31st, 5 mo. 1789. Their children were—

    i **Silvanus**, born 16th, 6 mo. 1727; died 9th, 5 mo. 1813; married (16th, 11 mo. 1745) Macy Howes, daughter of Thomas and Abigail.

    ii **William**, born 27th, 2 mo. 1732; died 3d, 6 mo. 1812; married (10th, 5 mo. 1753) Mary Folger, daughter of Daniel and Abigail.

    iii **Rachel**, born 20th, 4 mo. 1735; died 29th, 8 mo. 1775; married (7th, 2 mo. 1754) Paul Gardner, son of Solomon and Anna.

    iv **Elizabeth**, born 13th, 4 mo. 1738; died 24th, 9 mo. 1821; married (13th, 1 mo. 1757) Walter Folger, son of Barzillai and Phebe.

    v **Thomas**, born 22d, 8 mo. 1742: died 13th, 12 mo. 1830; married (10th, 12 mo. 1761) Dinah Trot, daughter of Benjamin and Priscilla.

    vi **Gayer**, born 9th, 9 mo. 1744; removed from the Island 28th, 3 mo. 1774; married Rachel Folger, daughter of Peter and Christian.

    vii **Hezekiah**, born 10th, 2 mo. 1749; removed from the Island 29th, 8 mo. 1785. He married—first, Mary Thurston of Rhode Island; second, Judith Macy. He had no children.

EDWARD [5] (Paul [4] Nathaniel [3] Nathaniel [2] Edward [1])
born 28th, 11 mo. 1719; died 11th, 12 mo. 1798; married (7th, 11
mo. 1742) Damaris Worth, daughter of William and Mary; she
died 1st, 10 mo. 1780. Their children were—

    i **Paul**, born ————; married (4th, 2 mo. 1768) Mary Coffin, daughter of Jonathan and Eunice; removed from the Island 23d, 9 mo. 1773.

    ii **William**, born 29th, 12 mo. 1748; removed from the Island 26th, 10 mo. 1772; married in North Carolina.

    iii **Matthew**, born 1 mo. 1750;* removed from the Island 27th, 4 mo. 1795; married—first, (10th, 12 mo. 1772; Rose Barnard, daughter of Shubael and Susanna; second, (28th, 11 mo. 1776; Lydia Barney. daughter of Benjamin and Jemima; third, (9th, 10 mo. 1806) Anna Swain, daughter of Richard and

---

*Matthew was one of Paul Jones's men on the Bon Homme Richard.

Anna; fourth, Anna Macy, daughter of Enoch and Anna. Matthew's family formed a part of the large emigration from Nantucket to North Carolina from 1770 to 1790, which eventually extended through East Tennessee to the middle West.

iv Mary, born 18th, 8 mo. 1756; married (November 16, 1776) John Cartwright, son of Hezekiah and Abigail.

v Edward, born 2d, 11 mo. 1759; married (2d, 9 mo. 1784) Lydia Macy, daughter of Francis and Judith.

JOSEPH [5] (Paul [4] Nathaniel [3] Nathaniel [2] Edward [1]) born 26th, 5 mo. 1723; died 24th, 10 mo. 1760; married (4th 8 mo. 1744) Ruth Macy, daughter of Richard and Deborah, who died 8th, 9 mo. 1760. Their children were—

i Nathaniel, born 20th, 6 mo. 1745; married (31st, 10 mo. 1765) Eunice Barnard, daughter of Peter and Anna.*

ii Hephzibah, born 6th, 7 mo. 1749; removed from the Island 25th, 4 mo. 1771; married (29th, 1 mo. 1767) Libni Coffin, son of William and Priscilla.

iii Phebe, born 18th, 4 mo. 1752; removed from the Island 7th, 5 mo. 1772; married (1st, 12 mo. 1768) Elihu Bunker, son of Samuel and Priscilla.

iv Joseph, born ———— 1755; died ———— 1756.

SAMUEL [5] (Paul [4] Nathaniel [3] Nathaniel [2] Edward [1]) born 15th, 1 mo. 1727; married (1st, 12 mo. 1749) Abigail Barney, daughter of Benjamin and Lydia. He removed with his family to Milford Haven, Wales, in 1795. Their children were—

i Daniel, born 20th, 8 mo. 1751; married (7th, 9 mo. 1773) Alice Vaughan of Rhode Island.

ii Samuel, born 29th, 9 mo. 1762; married (27th, 11 mo. 1783) Lucretia Folger, daughter of Timothy and Abiel.†

---

*Nathaniel also married, second Sally Fullington; third Patience Miller, widow of Elihu and daughter of Robert Coffin.

†Samuel Jr. removed to Milford Haven (Wales) after the Revolutionary War and there established a whale fishery which was for a while very successful.

CHRISTOPHER [5] (Tristram [4] Nathaniel]3] Nathaniel [2] Edward [1[) born 21st, 1 mo. 1731; died 29th, 9 mo. 1815; married (12th, 10 mo. 1751) Mary Barnard, daughter of Benjamin and Judith, who was born 18th, 8 mo. 1729 and died 6th, 4 mo. 1817. Their children were—

    i Miriam, born 19th, 11 mo. 1752; died 7th, 11 mo. 1817; did not marry.
   ii Benjamin, born 16th, 2 mo. 1755; died 27th, 7 mo. 1772.
  iii Zaccheus, born 29th, 6 mo. 1757; married (October 7, 1780) Sarah Wendell, daughter of John and Sarah.*
  iv Christopher, born 25th, 1 mo. 1760; died 15th, 5 mo. 1762.
   v John, born 25th, 10 mo. 1761; died 7 mo. 1781.†
  vi Mary, born 3d, 2 mo. 1764; died 6th, 11 mo. 1765.
 vii Tristram, born 13th, 5 mo. 1767; married (2d, 12 mo. 1790) Miriam Joy, daughter of David and Phebe.
viii Judith, born 15th, 10 mo. 1769; married (25th, 2 mo. 1790) Zaccheus Macy, son of Richard and Miriam.
  ix Nathaniel, born 6th, 3 mo. 1772; did not marry; died 26th, 11 mo. 1854.

JETHRO [5] (William [4] Jethro [3] Nathaniel [2] Edward [1]) born 29th, 1 mo. 1732; died 13th, 5 mo. 1806; married—first (27th, 2 mo. 1755) Anna Upham, daughter of Jonathan and Ruth, who died 28th, 3 mo. 1769; second, (7th, 6 mo. 1770) Ann Coffin, daughter of Jonathan and Hephzibah Hussey, who died 28th, 5 mo. 1814. Their children were—

    i Nathaniel, died in infancy.
   ii Jethro, born 25th, 9 mo. 1757; married (28th, 12 mo. 1780) Elizabeth Starbuck, daughter of William and Mary.
  iii William, died in infancy.
  iv Anna, born 15th, 3 mo. 1764; died 11th, 9 mo. 1764.
   v Obed, born 23d, 7 mo. 1766; died 13th, 4 mo. 1773.
  vi William, born 20th, 3 mo. 1769; died 18th, 9 mo. 1769.

By Ann, his second wife—

 vii Anna, born 21st, 1 mo. 1773; married (May 2, 1793) Daniel Hussey, son of William and Sarah.

---

*Zaccheus and Sarah had no children.
†Was taken prisoner of war by the British while on his way to Turk's Island during the Revolution for a cargo of salt, carried to Portsmouth, England, where he died of small pox in Fortune jail. Zaccheus, Barnabas Starbuck and John Yeomans were also taken prisoners of war in another vessel and all three died in Halifax jail.

HISTORY OF NANTUCKET 811

viii **Paul,** born 19th, 11 mo. 1776; married, in England, Ann Patten.
ix **Jonathan,** born 11th, 1 mo. 1781; died 6 mo. 1783.
x **Phebe,** born 8th, 2 mo. 1783; married (May 8, 1806) Isaac Gardner, son of Francis and Anna.

SILVANUS [5] (Thomas [4] Jethro [3] Nathaniel [2] Edward [1])
born 16th, 6 mo. 1727; died 9th, 5 mo. 1813; married (16th, 11 mo. 1745) Mary Howes, daughter of Thomas and Abigail, who died 19th, 9 mo. 1826. He was prominent on the Board of Selectmen during the period of the Revolution and for many years was clerk of the Proprietors of Common and Undivided Lands. Their children were—

i **Howes,** born 1st, 7 mo. 1746; died 25th, 8 mo. 1848.
ii **Barnabas,** born 14th 5 mo. 1748; died 11th, 12 mo. 1781.
iii **William,** born 6th, 9 mo. 1750; died 24th, 12 mo. 1752.
iv **Abigail,** born 5th, 3 mo. 1753; died 15th, 4 mo. 1787: married (November 1, 1771) **David Barnard,** son of Peter and Anna.
v **Lydia,** born 7th, 12 mo. 1755; married (October 7, 1775) Elisha Barnard, son of Peter and Anna.
vi **Hephzibah,** born 3d, 7 mo. 1758; removed from the Island 2d, 11 mo. 1809; married (July 11, 1789) David Barnard.
vii **David,** born 10th, 10 mo. 1760; married (28th, 9 mo. 1786) Phebe Cartwright, daughter of James and Love. He is said to have been the first whaleman to bring a cargo of sperm oil from the Pacific Ocean.* He was then sailing from Dunkirk, France.
viii **Uriah,** born 18th, 1 mo. 1765; removed from the Island 3d, 10 mo. 1799; married (28th, 12 mo. 1786) Lydia Macy, daughter of Jabez and Rachel.
ix **Mary,** born 26th, 11 mo. 1767; removed from the Island 31st, 5 mo. 1832.
x **Moses** born 19th, 2 mo. 1770.
xi **Matilda,** born 16th, 10 mo. 1772; died in Ohio 2d, 9 mo. 1829.

WILLIAM [5] (Thomas [4] Jethro [3] Nathaniel [2] Edward [1])
born 27th, 2 mo. 1732; died 3d, 6 mo. 1812; married (10th, 5 mo.

---
*F. C. Sanford's M. S.

1753) Mary Folger, daughter of Daniel and Abigail. Their children were—

    i Kezia, born 1st, 4 mo. 1754; removed from the Island 23d, 6 mo. 1787; married (29th, 9 mo. 1785) Ebenezer Jenkins, son of Peter and Abigail.
    ii William, born 24th, 6 mo. 1756; died 1 mo. 1779.
    iii Phebe, born 16th, 6 mo. 1758; died 22d, 9 mo. 1759.
    iv Elizabeth, born 7th, 8 mo. 1760; died 28th, 2 mo. 1787; married (28th, 12 mo. 1780) Jethro Starbuck, son of Jethro and Anna.
    v Judith, born 10th, 9 mo. 1762; married (29th, 11 mo. 1781) Eliakim Coffin, son of Benjamin and Rebecca.
    vi Obed, born 3d, 11 mo. 1764; died 18th, 5 mo. 1786.
    vii Laban,* born 25th, 11 mo. 1766; died 1st, 2 mo. 1787.
    viii Kimbal, born 22d, 1 mo. 1771; married (7th, 1 mo. 1796) Mary, widow of   and daughter of Seth and Susanna Coffin.
    ix Clarinda, born 3d, 10 mo. 1773; removed from the Island 28th, 9 mo. 1797.
    x Lydia, born 28th, 10 mo. 1777.
    xi Elisha, born 3d, 2 mo. 1780; married (1801) Betsey Coffin.

---

*A child was born 14th, 7 mo. 1769 who lived less than a day.

SWAIN

According to Savage, Richard Swain came to America in the Truelove in 1635, being then about thirty-four years old, and settled in Rowley. He had in April "perhaps his wife Elizabeth in the Planter, his sons William and Francis in the Rebecca, and his daughter Elizabeth in the Susan and Ellen, under care of various friends." He was one of the original proprietors of the Island.

Mr. Worth says of him* "He was not an educated man and his signatures are by mark. His house lot was on both sides of the cove formed by the north westerly extension of Hummock Pond. He never held any Town office, but performed labor for the Town in relation to sheep and cattle. He was married before coming to America and had four children by that marriage. The wife, Jane, had two children, John and Richard. The latter is said to have moved to New Jersey but he was administrator of his father's estate."

Richard Senior died April 14, 1682. His wife, Jean, died October 31, 1662, the first death on record in Nantucket.

JOHN [2] (Richard [1])

was the only son of Richard who removed to Nantucket, and from him all Nantucket Swains are descended. Before coming to the Island he had married Mary Wyer, daughter of Nathaniel and Sarah. Their children were—

    i Mary, born —— probably before the family removed to Nantucket; married Joseph Nason.
    ii John, born September 1, 1664; married Experience Folger, daughter of Peter.
    iii Stephen, born November 21, 1666.
    iv Sarah, born July 13, 1670; married Joseph Norton.
    v Joseph, born July 17, 1673; married Marah Sibley of Salem.
    vi Elizabeth, born May 17, 1676; married Joshua Sevolle.
    vii Benjamin, born July 5, 1679; married (10th, 5 mo. 1705) Mary Taylor.
    viii Hannah, married Joseph Tallman.
    ix Patience, married Samuel Gardner, son of James (27th. 10 mo. 1713-14).

*Of the name Patronymica Britannica says "It is a Scandinavian personal name of great antiquity, introduced here under the Danish rule. Domesday shows us several persons (tenants in chief and otherwise) called Svain, Suain, Suanus, Suuen, Swen or Sueno, some of whom are specifically stated to have held lands under Edward the Confessor Suain of Essex, supposed by Morant to have been of Danish origin, was ancestor of the famous Henry de Essex, temp Henry II."

JOHN [3] (John [2] Richard [1])

born September 1, 1664; married Experience Folger, daughter of Peter. In his will, which was drawn June 22, 1738, and probated March 2, 1739, he names his wife, his daughters, (i) **Ruth Upham**, wife of Jonathan, (ii) **Katherine Wyer**, and (iii) **Hannah Gardner**, children of deceased daughter (iv) **Priscilla Bunker**, wife of Daniel, (married November 14, 1717) and sons (v) **William**, (vi) **John**, (vii) **Eliakim**, (viii) **Stephen** and (ix) **George**.

Katherine and Robert Wyer were married July 5, 1720.
Hannah and Thomas Gardner were married November 30, 1724.
Stephen probably married (November 24, 1723) Eleanor Ellis.
John married (6th, 1 mo. 1711-12) Mary Swett.

JOSEPH [3] (John [2] Richard [1])

born July 17, 1673: married Marah Sibley, of Salem. Their children were——

    i **Peter**, born June 22, 1697; married (January 10, 1719) Elizabeth Ellis.
    ii **Richard**, born August 16, 1698; married (October 12, 1722) Elizabeth Gardner.
    iii **Caleb**, born probably about 1700; married (7th 12 mo. 1726-7) Margaret Paddack, daughter of Joseph and Sarah.

BENJAMIN [3] (John [2] Richard [1])

born July 5, 1679; married (10th, 5 mo. 1705) Mary Taylor. His will was probated September 2, 1757. Their children were—

    i **Jethro**, married (July 24, 1734) Dorcas Rider.
    ii **Peleg**, married (May 7, 1730) Mary Hussey.
    iii **Patience**, married (September 10, 1738) Jonathan Russell.
    iv **Christopher**.
    v **Nathaniel** had died prior to 1757 leaving Lydia (16) and Abigail (18); married (February 27, 1738-39) Jane Smith.

WILLIAM [4] (John [3] John]2[Richard [1])

born October 2, 1688; married (29th, 1 mo. 1727) Jemima Coffin, daughter of Peter and Elizabeth. He died 1st, 3 mo. 1770; she died 6th, 4 mo. 1766. Their children were—

HISTORY OF NANTUCKET

i **Hephzibah**, born 18th, 10 mo. 1727; died 27th 5 mo. 1785; married (3d, 11 mo. 1744) Benjamin Pinkham, son of Shubael and Abigail.

ii **William**, born 21st, 1 mo. 1729-30; married (29th, 10 mo. 1767) (widow) Mary Gardner, daughter of Philip and Mehitable Pollard.

iii **John**, probably born in 1731; married, probably, (January 19, 1750) Lydia Bunker.

JOHN [4] (John [3] John [2] Richard [1])

By his will, which was drawn 4th. 7 mo. 1736, and probated July 2, 1744 he left a wife Mary (Swett daughter of Moses) four sons and six daughters:

i **Elijah**, who married (July 23, 1735) Susanna Cathcart.

ii **Seth**, married (8th 9 mo. 1750) Abigail Coffin, daughter of Richard and Ruth.

iii **Francis**, married (31st, 11 mo. 1736-7) Mary Paddock, daughter of Nathaniel and Ann.

iv **Tristram**, married—first (6th 8 mo. 1743) Phebe Coffin, daughter of Richard and Ruth; second (16th 10 mo. 1755) Anna (Macy) Worth daughter of Joseph and Lydia Worth.

v **Christian**, married first (April 23 1731) Peter Folger son of Nathan and Sarah; second, (28th 2 mo. 1770) Peter Jenkins son of Matthew and Mary.

vi **Ruth**, probably married (March 9, 1737-8) William Russell.

vii **Priscilla**, married (12th 11 mo. 1743) Hezekiah Gardner son of Jethro and Kezia.

viii **Anna**, married (1st 12 mo. 1768) Jethro Folger, son of Jethro and Mary.

ix **Eunice**, married (26th 2 mo. 1756) William Coleman, son of Elihu and Jemima.

x **Jemima**, married (February 6, 1752) James Coffin, son of Jonathan and Hepzabeth.

At the time of the death of the father the five last named daughters were minors. The widow subsequently married (31st 8 mo. 1748) Samuel Gardner, son of James and Mary.

ELIAKIM [4] (John [3] John [2] Richard [1])

married first (April 18, 1717) Elizabeth Arthur, daughter of John;

second (October 27, 1742) Abigail Woodbury. Their children were—

    i **Charles**, born April 2, 1719; married (November 6, 1740) Elizabeth Coffin, daughter of Nathan and Lydia.
    ii **Zaccheus**, born March 18, 1721.
    iii **Priscilla**, born November 9, 1723; married (February 22, 1749) Barnabas Long.
    iv **Hannah**, born June 10, 1726.*
    v **Rachel**, born May 12, 1729; married (January 3, 1750) John Ramsdell.
    vi **Lydia**, born February 9, 1731-2; probably married (December 13, 1750) Reuben Coleman.
    vii **Timothy**, born October 16, 1734; probably married (October 27, 1774) Dinah Gardner.

By Abigail, his second wife—

    viii **Hannah**, born June 6, 1743.

STEPHEN [4] (John [3] John [2] Richard [1]) married (November 24, 1723) Eleanor Ellis. The record shows but one child—

    i **Reuben**, who married (30th 8 mo. 1756) Hannah Macy, daughter of Zaccheus and Hephzibah.

GEORGE [4] (John [3] John [2] Richard [1]) married (5th 12 mo. 1729) Love Paddock, daughter of Nathaniel and Ann. He died 8th 12 mo. 1797; she died 28th 7 mo. 1792. Their children were—

    i **Daniel**, born 1st 9 mo. 1731;†
    ii **Phebe**, born 12th, 1 mo. 1734; died 8th, 1 mo. 1794; married (25th 2 mo. 1754) Stephen Barnard, son of Ebenezer and Mary.

---

*Hannah doubtless died young.
†There seems to be some discrepancy between the Friends Records from which the accompanying births are copied and the Town Records. The latter give the following birthdates; Daniel 1st, 7 mo. 1731; Phebe 12th 8 mo. 1733; Love 16th 8 mo. 1739; George 23d 7 mo. 1744.

HISTORY OF NANTUCKET 817

iii **Anna,*** born 16th 10 mo. 1739; died 1st 3 mo. 1741.
iv **Love,*** born 16th 10 mo. 1739; married (8th 2 mo. 1759) Timothy Barnard, son of Timothy and Mary; removed from the Island 23d. 9 mo. 1773.
v **George,** born 25th 9 mo. 1744; died 9 mo. 1766.

RICHARD [4] (Joseph [3], John [2], Richard [1])
born August 16, 1698; married (October 12, '1722) Elizabeth Gardner. Their children were—

i **Anna,** married (23d, 12 mo. 1741) Thomas Bunker, son of Benjamin and Deborah.
ii **Joseph,** married (2d. 11 mo. 1745) Elizabeth Paddock, daughter of Daniel and Susanna.
iii **Jonathan,** married—first (3d 1 mo. 1747) Hephzibah Folger, daughter of Jethro and Mary; second (4th, 10 mo. 1753) Margaret Folger, daughter of Eleazer and Mary.
iv **David,** married (5th 10 mo. 1751) Martha Hussey, daughter of George and Elizabeth.
v **Richard,** married (8th 3 mo. 1753) Anna Gardner, daughter of Robert and Jedidah.
vi **Lydia,** married (28th 2 mo. 1758) Robert Hussey, son of John and Jedidah.
vii **Elizabeth,** married (8th 11 mo. 1759) Stephen Hussey, son of John and Jedidah.
viii **Mary,** married (3d, 2 mo. 1763) Joseph Mitchell, son of Richard and Mary.
ix **Hephzibah,** married (7th 1 mo. 1762) Silas Paddack, son of Eliphalet and Naomi.

CALEB, [4] (Joseph [3] John [2] Richard [1])
born ————; married (7th 12 mo. 1726-7) Margaret Paddock, daughter of Joseph and Sarah; he died 25th 7 mo. 1785; she died 26th 5 mo. 1789. Their children were:—

i **Susanna,** born 16th, 1 mo. 1728; died 7th, 1 mo. 1800; probably did not marry.
ii **Nathaniel,** born 1729 or 1730; removed from the Island 23d 9 mo. 1773; married (4th. 12 mo. 1755) Bethiah Macy, daughter of Joseph and Hannah.

*Twins.

iii Silvanus, born 2d 4 mo. 1731; died 7th 6 mo. 1763; married (6th. 12 mo. 1753) Hannah Worth, daughter of William and Mary.
iv Abigail, born 24th 3 mo. 1734; died 2d 11 mo. 1788; married (24th. 11 mo. 1755) Daniel Macy son of Jabez and Sarah.
v Mary, born 1735; removed from the Island 31st 5 mo. 1779;married (8th 11 mo. 1764) Shubael Coffin, son of Zephaniah and Miriam.
vi Sarah, born 1738; removed from the Island 29th 8 mo. 1785; married (31st 1 mo. 1760) Henry Macy, son of Joseph and Hannah.
vii Judith, born 1741; removed from the Island 30th. 10 mo. 1775; married first (28th 1 mo. 1762) Christopher Barnard, son of Peter and Anna; second (9th 7 mo. 1772) Thomas Worth, son of Joseph and Lydia.
viii Margaret, born 25th 8 mo. 1743; married (6th 12 mo. 1764) Nathaniel Barnard, son of Peter and Anna.
ix Anna, born 19th 4 mo. 1746; died 20th 7 mo. 1802; married (28th. 6 mo. 1792) Prince Gardner, son of Robert and Jedidah.
x Deborah, born probably 1748 or 1749; married Elisha Folger, son of Richard and Sarah.

PELEG [4] (Benjamin [3], John [2], Richard [1]) born   ; married (May 7, 1730) Mary Hussey, daughter of Bachelor and Abigail. Their children were—

i Martha, born September 20, 1730; married, probably, (September 26, 1751) John Baker.
ii Benjamin, born December 5, 1733; probably married (October 6, 1757) Elizabeth Johnson.
iii Peleg, born October 28, 1735; married (January 7, 1759) Rachel Chadwick.
iv Batchelor, born October 2, 1738.
v Micajah, born October 12, 1743; married (April 2. 1769) Eunice Bunker.
vi Paul, born August 17, 1742.

REUBEN, [5] (Stephen [4] John [3] John [2] Richard [1]) born   ; married, first (probably 1744) Elizabeth

; second (30th 8 mo. 1756) Hannah Macy, daughter of Zaccheus and Rephzibah. He removed with Hannah from the Island 5th 5 mo. 1796; Elizabeth died 11th 3 mo. 1755. Their children were:—

By Elizabeth—

    i John, born 3d 5 mo. 1745; married (2d 1 mo. 1766) Mary Gardner, daughter of Nathaniel and Ruth.
    ii Howland, born 16th 9 mo. 1747; died 12th 1 mo. 1772; married (7th 1 mo. 1768) Jemima Gardner, daughter of Stephen and Jemima.
    iii Deborah, born 21st 1 mo. 1749; married (29th 12 mo. 1768) Seth Coleman, son of Barnabas and Rachel.
    iv Rebecca, born 5th 5 mo. 1752; died 19th 12 mo. 1809;
    v Elizabeth, born 28th 1 mo. 1755; died 17th 6 mo. 1778; married (30th 8 mo. 1774) Matthew Barnard, son of Matthew and Mary.

By Hannah—

    vi Hephzibah, born 29th 5 mo. 1757;
    vii Shubael, born 27th 4 mo. 1764.
    viii Margaret, born 8th 7 mo. 1766.
    ix Jemima, born 2d 2 mo. 1766.
    x Samuel, born 26th 5 mo. 1771.
    xi Franklin, born 7th 3 mo. 1774.
    xii Hannah, born 27th 3 mo. 1778.
    xiii Ruth, born 28th 10 mo. 1781.

DANIEL [5] (George [4], John [3], John [2], Richard [1]) born 1st, 9 mo. 1729; married (January 31, 1745) Elizabeth Wyer. Their children were—

    i Simeon, born September 17, 1745.
    ii William, born February 14, 1747; married (December 30, 1773) Eunice Barnard.
    iii Jedidah, born December 11, 1749.
    iv Henry, born October 15, 1750.

SETH [5] (John [4] John [3] John [2] Richard [1]) was born ; died 6 mo. 1757; married (8th. 9 mo.

1750) Abigail Coffin, daughter of Richard and Ruth. Their children were—

    i **Andrew**, born 1st 2 mo. 1754.
    ii **Matthew** born 24th 3 mo. 1756.

FRANCIS [5] (John [4] John [3] John [2] Richard [1]) was born ; married (31st 11 mo. 1736-7) Mary Paddock, daughter of Nathaniel and Ann. He died probably in December 1783, and his will was probated January 2. 1784. The will was drawn up August 13. 1783 and is noteworthy as reading the "Seventh Year of American Independence." His wife died 26th 4 mo. 1775. Their children were—

    i **Deborah**, born 30th. 3 mo. 1739;* died 16th 7 mo 1771; married (3d 3 mo. 1757) Thomas Worth, son of Joseph and Lydia.
    ii **Ruth**, born 22d 8 mo. 1741; married (6th. 12 mo. 1759) Reuben Russell, son of John and Ruth.
    iii **Francis**, born 10th 11 mo. 1745; married (29th 1 mo. 1767) Lydia Barker, daughter of Robert and Jedidah.
    iv **Barnabas**, born 1st 6 mo. 1749;
    v **Barzillai**, born 19th 3 mo. 1752; died 25th 12 mo. 1777; married (30th 8 mo. 1774) Mary Hussey daughter of Batchelor and Anna.
    vi **Shubael**, born 26th 6 mo. 1775; died in 1781 abroad.
    vii **Mary**, born 25th 11 mo. 1757:
    viii **Seth**, born 6th 11 mo. 1759; died 18th. 10 mo. 1760.

TRISTRAM [5] (John [4] John [3] John [2] Richard [1]) born ; married first (6th 8 mo. 1743) Phebe Coffin, daughter of Richard and Ruth, who died 9th 4 mo 1754; second (16th. 10 mo. 1755) Anna Macy widow of Abraham and daughter of Joseph Worth and Lydia. The children were:

By Phebe

    i **Margaret**, born 5th 6 mo. 1745; died 1780; married (1st 1 mo. 1767) Charles Jenkins, son of Thomas and Judith.

*Here is also a slight discrepancy from the Town Records which give the date of Deborah's birth as 30th 1 mo. 1739; that of Ruth as 22d, 6 mo. 1741; and that of Francis as 10th, 9 mo. 1745.

ii **Tristram**, born 13th 12 mo. 1747; married (28th 12 mo. 1769) Rachel Bunker daughter of Samuel and Priscilla.
iii **Abishai**, born 5th 2 mo. 1750; died 7 mo. 1780; married first (1st. 3 mo. 1770) Lydia Barnard, daughter of Shubael and Susanna, second (4th 8 mo. 1774) Susanna Coffin, daughter of Joseph and Eunice.
iv **Lydia**, born 13th 6 mo. 1752; married (7th 2 mo. 1771 Benjamin Barnard, son of Benjamin and Judith.

By Anna

v **Phebe** born 31st 7 mo. 1760; married (5th 9 mo. 1776) Abishai Barnard, son of Abishai and Hannah.
vi **Seth**, born 3d 12 mo. 1761; died 10 mo. 1780.

NATHANIEL [5] (Caleb [4] Joseph [3] John [2] Richard [1]) born in 1729 or 1730; married (24th, 11 mo. 1755) Bethiah Macy, daughter of Joseph and Hannah. Their children were [i] **Joseph**, [ii] **Elihu**, [iii] **Silvanus**, [iv] **Caleb**, [v] **Thomas**, [vi] **Lydia**. The entire family removed from the Island 23 d 9 mo. 1773.

SILVANUS [5] (Caleb [4], Joseph [3], John [2], Richard [1]) born 2d 4 mo. 1731; married (6th 12 mo. 1753) Hannah Worth, daughter of William and Mary. He died 7th 6 mo. 1763; she died 30th 7 mo. 1820. Their children were—

i **Silvanus**, born 3d 9 mo. 1754; died 10th 10 mo. 1754.
ii **Abial**, born 29th 9 mo. 1755; died 11th 1 mo. 1828.
iii **Miriam**, born 8th 5 mo. 1757: married (27th 2 mo. 1777) Abishai Paddack, son of Jonathan and Kejiah.
iv **Hannah**, born 22d 5 mo. 1759; removed from the Island 21st 5 mo. 1772.
v **Judith**, born 23d 1 mo. 1762; died 6th 4 mo. 1841.

JOSEPH [5] (Richard [4], Joseph [3], John [2], Richard [1]) married (2d 11 mo. 1745) Elizabeth Paddock, daughter of Daniel and Susanna. He died 8 mo. 1767. Their children were—

  i **Anna**, born 12 9 mo. 1746; died 14th 6 mo. 1747.
  ii **Joseph**, born 27th 6 mo. 1752; died 15th 12 mo. 1821; married (6th 1 mo. 1774) Phebe Barney, daughter of Benjamin and Huldah.
  iii **Elizabeth**, born 27th 1 mo. 1758; died 16th 7 mo. 1759.
  iv **Elizabeth**, born 8th 12 mo. 1761; married (30th 11 mo. 1780) Obed Coleman, son of Barnabas and Rachel.
  v **Eunice**, born 6th 4 mo. 1765.

JONATHAN [5], (Richard [4], Joseph [3], John [2], Richard [1]) born ——————; died 23d 8 mo. 1803; married first (3d 1 mo. 1747) Hephzibah Folger, daughter of Jethro and Mary; second (4th 10 mo. 1753) Margaret Folger, daughter of Eleazer and Mary. Hephzibah died 18th 2 mo. 1750; Margaret died 2d 2 mo. 1822. Their children were—

By Hephzibah—

  i **Paul** born 17th 10 mo. 1748; probably married (March 28, 1771) Susanna Chase.

By Margaret—

  ii **Richard**, born 26th 7 mo. 1754; died 30th 10 mo. 1766.
  iii **Albertus**, born 3d 1 mo. 1756; removed from the Island 27th 6 mo. 1785; married (March 15, 1776) Lydia Barnard.
  iv **Hephzibah**, born 6th 9 mo. 1757; died 8th 11 mo. 1759.*
  v **Jonathan**, born 22d 5 mo. 1759; died 8th 10 mo. 1760.*
  vi **Ruel**, born 9th 3 mo. 1761; died 20th 12 mo. 1762.
  vii **Mary**, born 20th 3 mo. 1763; died 24th 6 mo. 1784.
  viii **Gideon**, born 14th 3 mo. 1765; died 27th 10 mo., 1782, lost at sea.
  ix **Jonathan**, born 25th 4 mo. 1769; married (31st 3 mo. 1791) Rachel Fish, daughter of Stephen and Ruth.
  x **Richard**, born 1st 12 mo. 1771; died 7th 6 mo. 1802.
  xi **Hezekiah**, born 28th 2 mo. 1774; removed from the Island 1st 5 mo. 1800.
  xii **Frederick**, born 26th 7 mo. 1778; removed from the Island 2d 5 mo. 1805; married (9th 4 mo. 1801) Ann Coffin, daughter of Jonathan and Abigail.

DAVID [5] (Richard [4], Joseph [3], John [2], Richard [1]) was born ——————; he married (5th 10 mo. 1751) Martha

*The Town Records give the date of Hephzibah's death as March 11 and Jonathan's as November 8.

Hussey, daughter of George and Elizabeth. He died 14th 2 mo. 1782; she removed from the Island 3d 12 mo. 1795. Their children were—

    i Thaddeus, born 25th 10 mo. 1752; married (7th 11 mo. 1776) Ruth Hussey, daughter of William and Abigail.
    ii Merab, born 7th 10 mo. 1755; died 3d 2 mo. 1842; married (5th 1 mo. 1775) Abishai Bunker, son of Abishai and Dinah.
    iii Thomas, born 7th 11 mo. 1757; died 9 mo. 1759.
    iv Lydia, born 6th 2 mo. 1760; married (3d 2 mo. 1780) David Hussey, son of Nathaniel and Judith.
    v Valentine, born 17 9 mo. 1762; married (28th 9 mo. 1786) Mary Barnard, daughter of Shubael and Ruth.
    vi Phebe, born 22d 8 mo. 1765; married (29th 1 mo. 1784) Stephen Macy, son of Stephen and Mercy.
    vii Elizabeth, born 10th, 10 mo. 1767.
    viii Gilbert, born 20th 5 mo. 1770.
    ix David, born 28th 7 mo. 1772; died 11 mo. 1775 (?).
    x Josiah, born 7th 10 mo. 1774; died 4 mo. 1775.
    xi David, born 24th 6 mo. 1776; died 25th 4 mo. 1795; married (8th 1 mo. 1795) Margaret Barnard, daughter of Nathaniel and Margaret.

RICHARD [5] (Richard, [4] Joseph, [3] John, [2] Richard [1]) born   ; married (8th 3 mo. 1753) Anna Gardner, daughter of Robert and Jedidah. Their children were—

    i Hephzibah, born 3d 7 mo. 1754; married (6th 3 mo. 1799) Edward Freeman, son of Edward and Hannah.
    ii Elizabeth, born 9th 9 mo. 1756.
    iii Gilbert, born 9th 4 mo. 1759; died 27th 4 mo. 1762.
    iv Anna, born 25th 6 mo. 1762; married (9th 10 mo. 1806) Matthew Starbuck, son of Edward and Damaris.
    v Matilda, born 25th 1 mo. 1765; died 27th 10 mo. 1786.
    vi Richard Gardner, born 5th 8 mo. 1774; married (4th 4 mo. 1799) Judith Chase, daughter of Francis and Naomi.

JOHN* (England)

was born   ; married Patience Skiffe, daughter of Nathan and Sarah probably in 1705. Their children were—

---

*This John was born in England and is known in the Records as "John Swain, England." The exceeding duplication in given names seems quite as puzzling in contemporary times as in later years as there are several instances of a special name to indicate some particular John or Thomas or William in the Town Records.

i **Dinah**, born September 5, 1706; married (August 12, 1730) Hugh Cathcart.
　　ii **Chapman**, born July 13, 1708; married (July 19, 1739) Sarah Meader.
　　iii **Deborah**, born September 15, 1710; married Richard Chadwick.
　　iv **Hannah**, born September 4, 1713; married (　　　　).
　　v **Anne**, born June 29, 1716; married (November 9, 1742 Samuel Cartwright.
　　vi **Oliver**, born June 9, 1720.

　　In his will John Swain "England," calls himself a weaver. He devises certain property to the "eldest son in succession in each branch forever."

CHAPMAN (John-England)

born July 13, 1708; married (July 19, 1739) Sarah Meader. Their children were—

　　i **Patience**, born September 23, 1742.
　　ii **Joseph**, born August 19, 1744.
　　iii **John**, born February 2, 1747.
　　iv **Zephaniah**, born February 2, 1750.
　　v **Judith**, born April 14, 1753.
　　vi **Ephraim**, born June 26, 1755.

WORTH

WILLIAM WORTH

was born in England about 1640. He came to Nantucket as a "Half Share" man in 1662 to pursue the occupation of a Sailor. He married (April 1, 1665) Sarah, the daughter of Thomas and Sarah Macy. They had but one child—a son, John. His wife died ──────────── 1701, and he married twice subsequently but had no other children. He died ──────────── 1724. He was quite active in Nantucket affairs having been five times chosen a Selectman, three times an Assistant Magistrate, four times Assessor, and for many years Clerk of the Court. The earliest Vital Records are in his hand writing and a large number of marriages were solemnized by him, the marriage service for many years being a civil and not a religious contract. The Worth homestead was in the No-Bottom Pond section.*

Patronymica Britannica says of the name that it is " a very usual termination for family names as Longworth, Ainsworth, Whitworth, Hepworth. It is possibly identical with the South German Worth. North German wuurt a plot of ground surrounded with water but elevated above it or secured with dykes or piles * * * The old expression in those days What is he worth? meant Has he land? If he had secured a Worth to himself he was called a worthy person."

JOHN [2] (William [1])

born May 19, 1666; married (September 22, 1684) Miriam daughter of Richard Gardner. His wife died about 1700, after which he removed to Marthas Vineyard. There he was twice married. By his first marriage he had one son and two daughters. The children by his first wife, with the exception of Nathaniel, all settled in Nantucket. They were—

    i **Jonathan**, born October 31, 1685; married (16th, 4 mo. 1707) Mary Hussey, daughter of Stephen.

    ii **Nathaniel**, born September 8, 1687; married at the Vineyard.

    iii **Judith**, born December 22, 1689; married John Macy, son of John.

    iv **Richard**, born May 27, 1692; married (2d, 5 mo. 1729) Sarah Hoag, daughter of Joseph and Sarah.

    v **William**, born November 27, 1694; married Mary Butler, daughter of Thomas.

---

*H. B. Worth, Nantucket Lands and Land Owners.

  vi **Joseph,** born probably 1696; married (September 8, 1720) Lydia Gorham, daughter of Shubael.
 vii **Mary.** born probably in 1696; married (24th, 3 mo. 1722) Ebenezer Barnard.

JONATHAN [3] (John [2] William [1])

born October 31, 1685; married (16th 4 mo. 1707) Mary Hussey, daughter of Stephen. He died 26th 7 mo. 1719. Their children were

  i **Miriam,** born 2d 1 mo. 1710; married (5th 10 mo. 1728) Jonathan Clark.
  ii **John,** born 15th 2 mo. 1713; married (6th 12 mo. 1734-5) Mary Gardner, daughter Solomon and Anna.
 iii **Christopher,** born 24th 9 mo. 1717; married (25th 10 mo. 1738) Dinah Paddock, daughter of Nathaniel and Ann.
 iv **Ezekiel,*** born—3 mo. 1719;

RICHARD [3], (John [2] William [1])

born May 27, 1692; married (2d 5 mo. 1729) Sarah Hoag daughter of Joseph and Sarah.
 Their children were—

  i **Richard,** born 11th 2 mo. 1730; married (1st 2 mo. 1753) Anna Macy, daughter of Thomas and Deborah.
  ii **Joseph,** born 30th 5 mo. 1731; died 2d 7 mo. 1732.
 iii **Sarah,** born 23d 9 mo. 1732; removed from the Island.
 iv **Francis,** born 21st 1 mo. 1735; married (5th 2 mo 1756) Mary Gardner, daughter of Barnabas and Mary; removed from the Island 28th, 11 mo. 1771.†
  v **Lyonel,** born 8th 2 mo. 1737; removed from the Island 26th 3 mo. 1759, returned, and again removed 30th 4 mo. 1801.
 vi **Walter,** born 18th 10 mo. 1738; died 9th 7 mo 1739.
 vii **Anna,** born 26th 6 mo. 1740; removed east.
 viii **William,** born 5th 6 mo. 1742; removed east.

---

  *The entry in the Town Records is "Ezekiel alias Jonathan."
  †Their children were (i) Francis, born 9th 12 mo 1756 and (ii) Phebe, born 26th 1 mo. 1780. The family removed from the Island 28th 11 mo. 1771.

WILLIAM [3] (John [2] William [1])
born November 27. 1694; married (probably in 1717) Mary Butler, daughter of Thomas. He died 16th 10 mo. 1780; she died 8 mo. 1756. Their children were:—

    i Judith, born 28th 6 mo. 1718; died 1 mo. 1739.
   ii Jemima, born 5th 1 mo. 1719-20 removed from the Island 28th, 9 mo. 1772; married (7th 8 mo. 1742) Stephen Gardner son of Solomon and Anna.
  iii Sarah, born 23d 3 mo. 1721; died 27th 4 mo. 1797.
  iv Damaris, born 2d 8 mo. 1722; died 1st 10 mo. 1780; married (7th 11 mo. 1742) Edward Starbuck, son of Paul and Ann.
   v Jonah, born 4th 10 mo. 1723;
  vi Miriam, born 19th 8 mo. 1725; died 7th 9 mo. 1816;
 vii Hephzibah, born 9th 9mo. 1726; removed from the Island 17th 10 mo. 1771; married (11th 8 mo. 1750) Jethro Macy, son of Jabez and Sarah.
viii Hannah, born 15th 10 mo. 1728; died 30th 1 mo. 1820; married (6th 12 mo. 1753) Silvanus Swain, son of Caleb and Margaret.
  ix Matthew, born 26th 2 mo. 1730; married (4th 4 mo. 1765) Sophia Folger, daughter of Eleazer and Mary.
   x Jedidah, born 1731; died 1731.
  xi Edmund, born 1733; died 1733.

JOSEPH [3] (John [2] William [1])
born probably in 1696; married (September 8, 1720) Lydia Gorham. He died 14th 7 mo. 1790; she died 1st 3 mo. 1763. Their children were:—

   i Anna,* born 23d 5 mo. 1721; married first (8th 4 mo. 1738) Abraham Macy, son of Richard and Deborah. Second (16th 10 mo. 1755) Tristram Swain, son of John and Mary.
  ii Abigail,* born 23d 5 mo. 1721; died 24th 4 mo. 1788; married first (1st 4 mo. 1738) George Bunker, son of Jonathan and Elizabeth; second (9th, 12 mo. 1743-4) Benjamin Bunker, son of Jabez and Hannah.
  iii Nathaniel, born 4th 7 mo. 1723; died 20th 6 mo. 1806; married (20th 9 mo. 1759) Abigail Swain, widow of Seth Swain daughter of Richard and Ruth Coffin.
  iv Reuben, born 13th 7 mo. 1725; removed from the Island 3d 12 mo. 1795; married (30th 9 mo. 1749) Mary Allen, daughter of Silvanus and Jemima.

*Twins.

828   HISTORY OF NANTUCKET

    v **Silvanus,** born 27th 6 mo. 1727; married (16th 9 mo. 1749) Rachel Allen daughter of Silvanus and Jemima.
   vi **Joseph,** born 29th 9 mo. 1729; removed from the Island 29th 9 mo. 1774; married (6th 12 mo. 1753) Judith Starbuck, daughter of William and Anna.
  vii **Lydia,** born 12th, 12 mo. 1731; died 17th, 7 mo. 1776; married (8th, 12 mo. 1749) Peleg Bunker, son of Jabez and Hannah.
 viii **Miriam,** born 22d 4 mo. 1734; died 15th, 11 mo. 1763; married (5th 10 mo. 1751) Jonathan Gardner, son of Barnabas and Mary.
  ix **Thomas,** born 1st 11 mo. 1736; removed from the Island 30th 10 mo. 1775; married first (3d 3 mo. 17-57) Deborah Swain, daughter of Francis and Mary; second (9th 7 mo. 1772) Judith Barnard, widow of daughter of Caleb Swain and Margaret.
   x **Daniel,** born 10th 12 mo. 1739; removed from the Island 25th 4 mo. 1771; married (9th 2 mo. 1764) Eunice Hussey, daughter of Daniel and Sarah.*
  xi **William,** born 4th 1 mo. 1741; married (1763) intention published to Ruth Folger.
 xii **Shubael,** born 6th 5 mo. 1745; marriage intention with Bethiah Jenkins published January 14, 1769.

    JOHN [4] (Jonathan [3] John [2] William [1])
born 15th 2 mo. 1713; married (6th 12 mo. 1734-5) Mary Gardner. Their children were:—

    i **Stephen,** born 8th 8 mo. 1735; died in infancy.
   ii **Seth,** born 9th 8 mo. 1738; probably married (December 1763) Huldah Coleman.
  iii **Anna,** 5th 6 mo. 1741; married (7th 2 mo. 1760) Thomas Gardner, son of Thomas and Hannah.
  iv **Abigail,** born 13th 8 mo. 1743; married (3d 1 mo. 17-65) Christopher Bunker, son of John and Mary.
   v **Jonathan,** born 25th 7 mo. 1745.
  vi **Mary,** born 4th 10 mo. 1747; removed from the Island 1780; married (28th 10 mo. 1768) Reuben Morton.
  vii **John,** born 6th 4 mo. 1750; married (probably) (September 5, 1773) Jemima Swain.
 viii **Eunice,** born 9th 7 mo. 1752.
  ix **Paul,** born 24th 11 mo. 1754; married (9th 9 mo. 1790) Phebe Barnard, daughter of Nathaniel and Abigail Macy.

---

*Chief Executive Officer Worth Bagley of the U. S. Torpedo Boat Winslow, who was the first U. S. naval officer to be killed in the Spanish War, was a descendant of Daniel Worth and Eunice Hussey, daughter of Daniel and Sarah (Gorham) Hussey, the family removing to North Carolina about the time of the Revolution.

x **Miriam**, born 19th, 3 mo. 1757.
xi **Asenath**, born 19th 5 mo. 1760; married (November 2 1784) Owen Coleman.

CHRISTOPHER [4] (Jonathan [3] John [2] William [1])
born 24th. 9 mo. 1717; married (25th 10 mo. 1738) Dinah Paddock, daughter of Nathaniel and Anna. Their children were—

    i **Judith**, born 25th 7 mo. 1739; removed from the Island 27th 2 mo. 1775; married (2d 2 mo. 1758) Daniel Folger, son of Daniel and Abigail.
   ii **Andrew**, born 29th 6 mo. 1741; married (9th 2 mo. 1763) Judith Coleman, daughter of Barnabas and Rachel.
  iii **Phebe**, born 18th 10 mo. 1743; removed from the Island 31st 5 mo. 1785; married (3d 12 mo. 1761) Benjamin Folger, son of Timothy and Anna.
  iv **Elizabeth**, born 1st 2 mo. 1746; removed from the Island 29th 11 mo. 1779; married (10th 2 mo. 1763) Nathan Folger, son of Barzillai and Phebe.
   v **Dinah**, born 17th 5 mo. 1748; died 7th 6 mo. 1775.
  vi **Christopher**, born 30th 6 mo. 1750.
 vii **Uriah**, born 5th 4 mo. 1755;

RICHARD [4] (Richard [3] John [2] William [1])
born 11th 2 mo. 1730; married (1st 2 mo. 1753) Anna Macy, daughter of Thomas and Deborah. The Friends Records state that the family went "into the country" in 1799 where the father died. The widow returned to Nantucket. The children were—

  i **Richard**, born 17th 6 mo. 1755; married (3d 4 mo. 1777) Elizabeth Folger, daughter of Walter and Elizabeth.
 ii **Elizabeth**, born 3d. 11 mo. 1765.

FRANCIS [4] (Richard [3] John [2] William [1])
born 21st 1 mo. 1735; married (5th 2 mo. 1756) Mary Gardner daughter of Barnabas and Mary. Their children were:—

 i **Francis**, born 9th 12 mo. 1756.
 ii **Phebe**, born 26th 1 mo. 1760.
The entire family removed from the Island in 1771.

 REUBEN [4] (**Joseph [3] John [2] William [1]**)
born 13th 7 mo. 1725; married (30th 9 mo. 1749) Mary Allen, daughter of Silvanus and Jemima. His wife died 4th 6 mo. 1785 and he removed from the Island in 1795. Their children were:—

 i **Reuben**, born 3d 7 mo. 1750; died 3d 6 mo. 1784; married (7th 12 mo 1772) Lydia Gardner daughter of Simeon and Sarah.
 ii **Charles**, born 29th 12 mo. 1752; died 29th 12 mo. 1753.
 iii **George**, born 12th 3 mo. 1755; died 27th 9 mo. 1756.
 iv **Mary**, born 19th, 8 mo. 1757; died 30th 8 mo. 1759.
 v **Job**, born 10th 9 mo. 1759; died 13th 11 mo. 1760.
 vi **Elizabeth**, born 29th 12 mo. 1761; married (1st 4 mo. 1784) Libni Gardner, son of Paul and Rachel.
 vii **Mary**, born 31st 5 mo. 1764; died 14th 6 mo. 1785.
 viii **Lydia**, born 13th 9 mo. 1766; removed from the Island in 1795.
 ix **Adino**, born 11th 9 mo. 1768; died 5th 8 mo. 1772.

 SILVANUS [4] (**Joseph [3] John [2] William [1]**)
born 27th 6 mo. 1727; married (16th 9 mo. 1749) Rachel Allen daughter of Silvanus and Jemima. Their children were:—

 i **Miriam**, born 19th 4 mo. 1752; died 8 mo. 1769.
 ii **Puella**, born 5th 12 mo. 1754.
 iii **Gideon**, born 9th 1 mo. 1757.
 iv **Solon**, born 25th 2 mo. 1760.
 v **Drusilla**, born 4th 12 mo. 1761.
 vi **Rachel**, born 29th 10 mo. 1764.
 vii **Christina or Christian**, born 19th 10 mo. 1766; married Samuel Stubbs 1785.

 JOSEPH [4] (**Joseph [3] John [2] William [1]**)
born 29th 9 mo. 1729; married (6th 12 mo. 1753) Judith Star-

buck, daughter of William and Anna; the entire family removed from the Island in 1774. Their children were:—

    i **Jethro**, born 3d 9 mo. 1754.
    ii **Eunice**, born 30th 8 mo. 1756.
    iii **Matilda**, born 14th 10 mo. 1758.
    iv **Charles**, born 17th 6 mo. 1761.

THOMAS [4] (Joseph [3] John [2] William [1]) born 1st 11 mo. 1736; married (3d 3 mo. 1757) Deborah Swain, daughter of Francis and Mary. All the family excepting the wife, who died 16th 7 mo. 1771, and eldest son removed from the Island in 1775. Thomas married a second time (9th 7 mo. 1772) his second wife being Judith Barnard, widow of Christopher and daughter of Caleb and Margaret Swain. The children were:—

By Deborah

    i **David**, who removed from the Island in 1777.
    ii **Lydia**
    iii **Barzillai**

By Judith

    iv **Deborah**, born 26th 4 mo. 1773.
    v **Sylvia**, born 12th 7 mo. 1776.

DANIEL [4] (Joseph [3] John [2] William [1]) born 10th 12 mo. 1739; married Eunice Hussey. Their children were [i] **Job**, [ii] **Stephen**, [iii] **Elihu** [iv] **Zenas**. The family removed from the Island in 1771.

RICHARD who came from New Jersey*
born   ; married (October 18, 1722) Lydia Swain. Their children were:—

    i **Benjamin**, born August 28, 1723; married (7th 9 mo. 1745) Mary Folger, daughter of Shubael and Jerusha.

---

*Doubtless grandson of the original New Jersey Worth.

ii Priscilla, born February 23, 1726; married (November 20, 1746) David Upham.
iii Eunice, born February 22, 1729; married first (16th 9 mo. 1749) Joseph Gardner son of Ebenezer and Judith; second (28th 7 mo. 1767) Benjamin Taber son of Benjamin and Susanna.
iv Mary, born July 9, 1731;

BENJAMIN [4] (Richard [3] John [2] William [1]) born August 28, 1723; married (7th 9 mo. 1745) Mary Folger. Their children were:*

i Francis, born 18th 12 mo. 1746.
ii Benjamin, born 11th 10 mo. 1748; married (30th 11 mo 1769) Phebe Coffin, daughter of John and Anna.

---

*Benjamin probably died prior to 1750 for his widow married (12th, 10 mo. 1751) Peleg Coleman, son of Solomon and Deliverance.

Note:
The subject index, whaling index, and addendum (original pages 833–843, 845–852 and 873–874) were deleted from this reprinted edition.

GENEALOGICAL INDEX

A plus sign, +, following the page number signifies that the name occurs more than once on the page.

BARNARD

Abigail .. 661, 671, 672, 674, 675, 677, 679, 681
Abishai ...... 673, 674, 677+, 682
Alice 681
Andrew 406, 679
Anna ...... 672, 674+, 675, 676, 677, 679, 680, 682
Ann 674
Avis 675

Benjamin ...... 188, 190, 194, 323, 539, 661, 672, 674, 676+, 680+, 682
Barzillai 683
Benjamin Jr. 259
Bethiah 670

Charles 678
Christopher .... 675, 681+, 682
Charles D. 344
Charles F. 344
Charles H. 294
Cromwell .... 323, 539+, 541, 542, 543, 679

David 403, 675, 679
Deborah 674, 677, 679, 683
Dorcas .... 671+, 672

Ebenezer 671, 673, 678
Edwin 446, 447, 448, 451, 465,
Eleanor 661, 671
Elisha 675
Elizabeth .... 672, 673, 674, 675+, 676, 677+, 679, 680, 681, 683
Enoch 681
Eunice .... 672, 673, 674, 675, 676, 678+, 679, 680, 681, 682+

Francis .... 109+, 673, 676, 677
Franklin S. 347
Frederick 393, 429, 434, 440
Frederick W. 344

George 678
Gilbert 683

Hannah 661, 670, 671, 673, 677, 681
Henry 678, 679

Hepzibah .... 671, 673, 674, 675, 676+, 679, 680, 682+
Hezekiah 320, 383, 408, 411, 541, 542, 603, 605, 637, 640, 675, 682
Hopcot 676

Isaiah 677

Joanna .... 662, 670+
James 295, 560, 580
Job 683
John .. 25, 97, 99+, 112+, 182, 197, 315, 389, 661, 670+, 671, 673, 675, 681
Jemima 671, 673, 677
Jethro 678
Jonas 190
Jonathan .. 182, 197, 674, 677, 679+
Jonathan E. 294
Joseph .... 113, 117, 185, 259, 674, 681+
Judith .... 661, 671+, 672, 674, 675+, 676+, 677, 680+, 681
Jonathan Jr. 394
John F. 344

Katharine 677

Libni 679
Love 676, 683
Lucretia 682, 683
Lydia .... 673, 675+, 677, 678, 680+, 682+

Margaret .... 553, 675, 678, 682+
Martha 673
Mary ...... 542, 575, 661+, 670+, 671+, 672, 673+, 674+, 675+, 676+, 678+, 679+, 679, 680+, 681, 682, 683
Matthew .. 108+, 671, 674+, 675, 681
Miriam 678
Moses J. 679

Nathaniel 53, 62, 75, 126, 395, 670+,
Nathaniel Jr. .. 99+, 671+, 672+, 673, 674, 675, 677+, 682

Obed 241, 403, 404, 405, 678, 680

HISTORY OF NANTUCKET

Paul 259, 678
Peter 328, 672, 675
Phebe ...... 673, 677+, 678+, 680, 683+

Rebecca 677
Reuben 203, 258, 295, 677, 680, 683
Rhoda 677
Robert ...... 19, 21, 23+, 25, 553, 661, 665, 670+, 671, 673, 674
Rose 675, 680
Ruth 673, 674, 676, 680, 682

Samuel 671, 682
Sarah 537, 661, 671, 672, 674, 675, 677, 680
Seth 678
Shubael .... 115, 117, 185, 190, 191, 204, 222, 225, 232, 238, 257, 266, 295, 386, 536, 674+, 680+, 681
Shubael Jr. 294
Stephen .... 661, 671, 672, 673, 676, 678+, 682
Susan 542
Susanna ...... 674+, 676, 679, 680+

Thaddeus 188
Thomas .... 18+, 19, 20, 21, 132, 330, 410, 660, 661, 667+, 670+, 672, 675, 676+, 679, 681
Thomas H., ... 347
Timothy ...... 672, 676+, 679, 682, 683
T. G. 330
Tristram .... 287, 393, 413, 677, 678, 679 ....

Uriah 683

Valentine 676

William .. 238,. 403, 673, 676, 678, 679
William F. 344

Zaccheus (?) 421

BUNKER

Abial 693, 695
Abigail .... 660, 685, 686+, 687, 689, 690, 692, 694+, 695.
Abishai .... 691, 695+
Abner 687
Abraham 696
Alexander 462, 467, 694

Alexander D. 428, 435, 441, 445, 448, 456
Alfred 344
Andrew 689
Ann .... 684+
Anna .... 688+, 690, 692, 693, 694
Asa G 617
Axel D. 294

Bachelor .... 689, 694+
Barnabas 691, 696
Barzillai 692
Batchelor 259
Benjamin .... 100, 117, 685+, 687+ 692
Bethiah ...... 686, 689+, 690, 694+
Bethuel 696

Caleb .... 114, 685, 688+
Caleb Jr. 111
Calvin 323, 421, 428, 429, 432, 434, 539
Charles .... 386, 601, 614, 630, 691, 696+
Charles C. 347
Christopher 265, 315, 393, 685
Cromwell .... 461.
Christian 660

Daniel 439, 539, 659, 685, 688, 695
David .... 315, 487, 687, 694+
David 2d 471, 476
Deborah .... 659, 684, 685+, 687, 688, 690, 691+, 694, 696
Desire 686, 688, 689
Dinah 686, 691, 692, 695. 696

Ebenezer 695
Eber 393
Eliab 694
Elihu 691, 696
Elijah 692
Elisha 394, 553, 685, 690
Elizabeth ...... 500, 618, 658, 684+, 686, 687, 689, 691, 693, 694+, 696
Edward M. 618
Esquire 122
Eunice .... 688+, 691, 693, 694

Francis 395, 689, 695

George .... 97, 99, 100+, 101, 103, 105, 259, 404, 635, 658, 659+, 684+, 685+, 685+, 686, 689
George 2d .... 436+
George Marshall .... 637+, 638
George Jr. 287
Gilbert 695

Hannah .... 659, 685, 687+, 691

Henry 265, 439, 442, 539
Henry C. .... 471+
Hepzibah ...... 688, 690, 691, 692, 693+, 695, 696+
Hezekiah 691
Huldah 686, 689, 694
Isaiah 394, 694
Jabez .... 105, 533, 618, 659, 685+, 687
James .. 295, 417, 425, 435, 686, 689+
James H. 483
Jane 656, 658, 659, 660, 684
Jesse 415
Job 188, 190, 693
John .. 152+, 295, 356, 431, 635, 684, 685+
Jonathan ...... 664, 684, 685, 686+, 689, 690+
Joshua 239, 259, 685
Joseph 109, 688, 694
J—— 316
Judith .. 686+, 687+, 689, 690+, 692

Kezia 690, 692

Latham 294, 692
(Lawson) 694
Lawton
Lois 693
Lydia ...... 543, 618, 686, 687, 689+, 690, 691, 692+, 693, 695

Martha .... 684+
Margaret .... 685+, 690
Mary .... 259, 658, 660, 684+, 685+, 686, 687, 688, 689, 691+, 695, 696+.
Merab 695, 696
Matthew 690
Miriam 690, 692, 694, 695

Nathan 695
Nathaniel 315, 687, 690
Naomi 687, 695

Obed .... 182, 197, 209, 372, 389, 395, 476, 687, 693 ..
Obed R. 463, 480
Owen 393, 573

Patience 686
Paul 107, 109, 110, 442, 687, 691, 693
Peggy 553
Peleg 109, 117, 265, 389, 394, 659, 684, 685, 686, 687, 690, 692
Peter ...... 265, 376, 377, 687, 692+
Phebe .... 573, 576, 685, 688, 690, 691+, 694, 696+

Prince 693
Priscilla ...... 647, 685+, 686, 687, 688+, 690, 691, 694, 696
Puella 695

Rachel 691, 696
Reuben 687
Reuben R. 272, 287, 395
Richard 688, 694
Rufus 693
Ruth 686, 688, 690, 695
R. R. 330
R. S. (Capt.) 326

Samuel .. 441, 444, 647, 687, 690
Sarah 618
Seth 691
Shubael 365, 689, 695
Silvanus 259, 688
Silas 687, 691, 696
Simeon .... 686+, 689, 689+
Solomon 197, 694
Sophia 618
Susanna 659, 684, 686, 692, 693
Susannah 690

Thaddeus .... 696+
Thomas ... 111, 115, 116, 117, 316, 659, 685+, 688+, 694+
Timothy 692
Tristram 393, 688

Uriah 182, 197, 375, 408, 409, 411, 413, 415, 693
Uriel 389

Way 693
William ... 26+, 27+, 28, 32, 50, 172, 274, 658, 659+, 663, 684+, 688+, 690+
William Cushman 638
William R 394
Watts
Zacchariah 686, 688, 689
Zacchary 389
Zephaniah 696
Z 550

COFFIN

Aaron 453
Abel 715
Abial 726, 727
Abigail ...... 73, 533, 618, 655, 662, 664, 698, 699+, 701, 703+, 705, 706, 708, 709, 710, 711, 712, 713, 716+, 717+, 718, 719+, 724, 725+, 726, 727+, 728, 730
Abihu 719

Abijah 723
Abishai 721
Abner 708, 716, 721
Abraham 716
Absalom 418, 421, 426, 432
Albert 726
Albert C. 345
Alexander ... 200+, 444, 461, 636+, 706+
Alexander G. 542
Alexander H. 342
Alexander Jr. 263
Alfred M. 481
Allen 579, 654, 698
Alpheus 395, 405, 409, 413, 647, 729
Alvin C. 348
Ammiel 730
Andrew 315, 712, 719
Ann 550, 712, 722
Anna .. 571, 618, 625, 626, 700, 702, 707, 710, 716, 718, 719, 724, 725
Anne 705
Ariel 294, 425, 429, 433
Arnold 726

Barna 295
Barnabas .. 202, 277, 703, 717, 723+, 727
Bartlett 274, 356, 394, 404, 708, 720, 721, 729
Barzillai 269, 418, 420, 426, 431, 446, 449, 727
Barzillai S. 345
Benjamin .... 259, 290, 292, 294, 302, 311, 533, 617, 664, 701, 702, 704, 705, 706, 713+, 716+, 727
Benjamin A. 347
Beujamin F. .... 439, 444, 448+
Benjamin J. 345
Benjamin Jr. 110
Benjamin 2d 116, 272
Benjamin S. 345
Benoni 704
Bethiah 664, 700, 706, 719
Bethuel 723
Betsy 553
Beulah 701, 707, 705
Brown 295, 389
Brown Jr. 294

Caleb 553, 730
Catharine 705, 712
Charles 647, 705, 714, 728
Charles F. 456
Charles G. 337, 341, 580
Charles 3d 277
Charles W. 453, 457, 463, 464
Christian .. 701, 704, 707, 709, 720

Christopher 377, 717, 722, 727
Clement 274, 726
Cromwell 295, 553, 706

Damaris 700, 704
Daniel .... 208+, 209+, 256, 286, 290, 297, 323, 393, 539, 617, 702, 707, 710+, 717, 720+, 727
David .... 709+, 722+
David G. 345
David Jr. 258
David U. 460
David W. 449, 455
Deborah .... 543, 655, 656, 659, 664, 699+, 700+, 701, 705, 708, 709+, 711+, 714, 715, 716+, 723+, 726, 729
Dinah 664, 666, 700, 704, 711, 714, 718, 725, 730
Dionis .... 655+, 698, 702
Dorcas 704, 706

Eben 148, 246
Ebenezer .. 99+, 188, 190, 203, 222, 256, 295, 332, 355, 664, 700, 705, 708
Eber 389, 729
Edward 323, 395, 409, 700, 703, 712
Edwin 446, 451
Edy 442, 446
Eleanor 664, 700
Eliab 730
Elias 202, 203, 533, 705, 717, 718
Eliel 719
Elihu 188, 258, 432, 438, 449, 456, 463, 713, 716, 717, 722, 723
Elijah 258, 403, 719
Eliphalet 700
Elisha .... 109+, 356, 376, 434, 704, 714+, 715, 726+
Elizabeth ...... 542, 553, 574, 606, 618, 655, 661, 662, 664, 666, 667, 698, 700, 701, 702+, 703, 704,, 709+, 710+, 712+, 713, 716+, 717, 718, 719+, 720+, 721, 722+, 723, 724, 726, 729+
Elizabeth R. 608
Enoch 99, 720
Enoch (Martha's Vineyard)
      .... 701, 708
Ephriam 707, 713
Eunice .... 532, 574, 618, 703, 706, 710, 713, 714, 718, 719, 724+, 727, 728+, 729, 729.
Experience 664, 701, 702, 710

Francis .... 705, 717, 718+, 728, 729

HISTORY OF NANTUCKET 857

Francis C. 467
Francis Jr. 274
Francis 2d 433, 466
Frederick 389, 724
Fred S. 461
Fred W. 467

Gardner 288, 581
Gayer 705
George 355, 356, 625, 704, 713, 714
George A. .... 469+
George C. 348
George D. 466, 467
George G. 295
George H. 345
George H. 2d 345
George W. 343
Gideon 722
Gilbert .... 266, 271, 320, 330, 539, 604, 605+, 636, 726, 727
Gorham 271, 295

Hannah 618, 701, 703, 704, 706, 708, 711, 715
Henry .... 256, 377, 550, 633, 707, 720+
Henry F. 347
Henry S. 592
Hepsah 618
Hephzibah ...... 550, 701, 702, 709, 715, 720, 724+, 725
Hepsibah 729
Hepza 574
Hepzabeth .... 707+, 710, 713
Hepzibah 721, 723, 724, 725, 730
Hezekiah .... 107, 708, 719+
Hope 700, 701, 705, 707
Huldah 721, 727

Isaac .... 265, 274, 281, 282, 286+, 290+, 295, 296, 297, 300, 301, 302, 576, 606, 617, 640, 700, 705, 716
Isaiah 711, 716, 727

James ..19, 21, 29, 32, 53, 64, 69, 73+, 74+, 75, 78, 80, 82, 87, 88, 89, 90, 93, 97, 98+, 111, 114, 140+, 142, 148, 274, 282, 295, 310, 323, 355, 553, 666, 635, 655, 659, 663, 664, 667, 699, 700+, 703, 704, 707, 714, 715, 717
James C. 450
James G. 451
James J. 294
James Jr. 96
Jane 706, 713

Jared .... 637+, 728
Jedidah 705, 707, 715, 716, 718, 727, 728
Jemima .... 703, 707, 708+, 713, 719, 721+, 722
Jennett 553, 712, 715
Jesse 389, 427, 433
Jerusha 708, 721
Jethro 111, 281, 421, 428, 616, 699, 703, 711, 713
Joan 655
Joanna 700, 712
Job 258, 281, 418, 420, 435, 411, 729
John .... 21, 29, 53, 64, 103, 108, 111, 130, 133, 148, 172, 253, 550, 655, 664, 699+, 700+, 701, 703, 705+, 709, 710+, 711+, 722, 724, 725
John B. 345
John F. 539
John G. .... 444, 446+, 542
John L. 542
John Jr. 701
John 2d 110
Jonathan .. 108, 155, 157, 356, 377, 389, 550, 553, 664, 701, 707+, 710+, 713, 714, 720, 724+, 727
Jonathan 377, 389
Joseph .... 97+, 98+, 115, 117, 550, 573, 635, 664, 700, 706+, 708, 716, 719, 721, 722, 729
Joshua .... 272, 393, 436, 442, 446, 459, 704, 707, 714+, 720,, 726
Joshua 2d 450
Josiah 105, 151, 165, 181, 182, 187, 197, 259, 553, 635, 703, 711, 712
Judith .... 647, 700, 702, 705, 706+, 708, 711, 712, 714, 715, 717, 718, 720+, 726, 730

Katharine 618, 716
Kezia .... 181, 182, 192, 205+, 220, 221, 224, 227, 538, 709, 711, 722+,
Kimball 706

Laban 394, 719, 728
Lettice 717
Levi 717
Libbeus 719
Libni 709, 723
Linzee 487
Love 664, 700, 703, 706, 717, 718, 720
Lovey 729
Lurana 715
Lydia ...... 543, 701, 705, 708, 711+, 713, 714, 716, 717, 719+, 720, 721, 723, 728+

Margaret 703, 708, 712, 713, 714, 715, 717, 727
Mark 618, 647
Martha W. 607
Mary ...... 73, 550, 553, 578, 616, 655, 656, 658, 667, 699+, 700+, 701+, 702, 703, 704, 705, 705, 706+, 707+, 709+, 710+, 711+, 712+, 713, 714, 715, 716, 717, 718+, 719+, 720, 723, 724, 724, 725+, 726+, 727, 729+, 730
Matilda 728
Matthew 710, 717, 723
Mehitable 702
Merab 718
Mercy 706, 718
Micah 109, 156, 706
Micajah .... 211, 215, 216, 259, 271+, 272, 287, 636+, 716, 727
Miriam .... 701, 707, 708, 709, 710, 721, 722, 723, 725+, 728, 729
Moses 274, 726

Nabby 618
Nathan 106, 113, 115, 152, 182, 197, 202, 203, 204, 230, 256, 259, 356, 365, 704, 713, 714
Nathaniel .... 95, 190, 211, 251, 393, 606+, 664, 700, 703, 704, 705+, 715, 716+, 726+
Nathaniel 2d 115, 117, 211
Noah 729

Obed 723
Obediah .... 258, 323, 428, 434, 539, 717, 722.
Oliver C. 342
Oliver 706
Owen .... 496+

Farnal 711
Parnel .... 709+
Parnell .... 700, 712+
Patience 721
Paul .. 393, 395, 702, 711, 716, 725
Peleg 248, 386, 705, 718, 720, 728
Peleg Jr. .... 259, 636+, 640+
Peleg 2d 238, 239, 377
Pernal 724
Peter .... 18, 19, 20, 21, 23, 32, 52+, 53 (57 Mr) 61, 62, 73, (99 Lt) 99, 132, 355, 430, 432, 437, 441, 442, 444, 448, 449, 455, 655, 661, 667, 667, 698, 699+, 701, 702+, 703, 707, 708, 710, 711+, 721, 722, 726
Peter F. 298, 299, 301, 302, 347
Peter Jr. 666, 699

Phebe .... 542, 618, 708, 716, 717 721+, 722, 723+, 725, 726, 727 728, 729
Philip C. 347
Polly 573
Prince 2d 448, 706, 718, 728
Priscilla ...... 553+, 703, 704, 707 708, 709+, 710, 712, 713, 714+ 716, 720, 721, 723+

Rachel .... 713, 714, 726+
Ralph 726
Rebecca .... 542+, 704, 705, 715, 720, 723, 727
Rebekah .... 715+, 726
Reuben 441, 625, 715, 724
Richard ...... 106+, 108, 109, 112, 113+, 115, 152, 155, 157, 163, 202, 356, 394, 698, 705, 710, 711, 717+, 723
Robert III 543, 550, 700, 703, 708, 712, 713, 721
Robert Jr. 258
Rufus 347
Ro(w)land 345, 504
Roland W. 347
Ruth .... 73, 259, 553, 664, 700, 701, 704+, 705, 706, 709, 712, 713, 716, 717, 717+, 722+

Sally 553
Samuel .... 100, 174, 175, 701, 703, 708, 709, 723+
Sarah 704, 709, 712, 722, 727, 728
Seth 266, 271, 287, 405, 715, 716, 722
Seth Jr. 434, 440
Sheffield 716
Shubael .. 123, 259, 266, 271+, 272, 287, 356, 386, 393, 395, 536, 636, 710, 719, 725, 730+
Silvanus 188, 190, 192, 201, 243
Simeon 188, 190, 714, 723
Simeon Jr 272
Solomon 389, 726, 730
Solomon Jr. 315
Stephen ...... 29, 34, 99, 128, 656, 658, 659, 702+, 725, 729+
Stephen Jr. .. 96, 99, 100, 532, 666, 667, 702, 710
Susan 542, 618
Susanna .... 659, 702, 703, 707, 711, 712+, 714, 715+, 722, 725, 729
Sylvanus 431, 717

Thaddeus .. 266, 284, 393, 394, 442, 447, 456, 559, 560, 636, 637, 640
Thaddeus Jr. 294
Theodate 705, 718
Thomas 330, 706, 716, 723, 728

HISTORY OF NANTUCKET 859

Thankful 719
Thomas E. 345
Thomas R. 345
Thomas 2d ... 455, 459, 466, 472, 478
Timothy .. 117, 203, 204, 256, 572+, 710, 721
Timothy G. 286
Timothy R. 455, 511
Tristram .. 17, 18+, 19+, 20+, 21+, 22+, 23, 27+, 28+, 29+, 32, 33+, 43+, 44, 46, 64, 67+, 68, 69, 70, 71, 72, 73, 78+, 119, 123, 126+, 132, 133, 134, 137, 140, 172, 236+, 353, 547, 606, 608, 654, 656, 667+, 697+, 698+, 699, 700, 701, 703, 708, 709+, 723, 734+
Tristram.. Jr. ... 19, 21, 23, 32, 53, 536, 663

Uriah 719, 721

Valentine 203, 256, 258, 706

Walter 717
William .... 107, 112, 114, 182, 264, 275, 284, 286+, 287+, 288+, 289+, 290, 292, 293, 295, 560, 602, 604, 605, 606, 607, 608+, 628, 637, 655, 705+, 709, 715, 718, 723+, 724, 728+
William B........... 419, 426, 539
William H. 429, 431, 436
William Jr. 334
William J. 617, 629
William 2d 294, 393
William T. 315

Zaccheus 708, 718, 719
Zebbedee 229
Zebdiel 393
Zebulon 184
Zenas 266, 299, 304, 305, 307, 603, 727
Zephaniah ...... 103, 167, 710, 725+
Zimri 434, 496

COLEMAN

Aaron 739
Abial 737
Abiel 736, 737
Abigail .... 732, 734+, 735, 737+, 738, 739
Abishai 635, 739
Alexander 323
Alfred 347
Andrew 241, 389, 737
Ann 658, 665, 731, 732

Anna 734, 735, 736, 738
Asa 457

Barnabas ...... 733+, 735, 736, 737
Barzillai 403
Benjamin .. 328, 395, 731, 732, 734
Benjamin A. 442, 446, 451, 457, 471
Bethuel 738

C ————— 194, 197, 256
Charles .... 197+, 294, 423, 736
Charles E. 628
Christopher 734, 736, 737, 738

Daniel 734, 739
David 294, 389, 738
David B. 345
Deborah .... 732, 736+, 739
Deliverance 732, 734

Eben 451
Elihu .... 620, 621+, 627, 647, 534, 670, 733, 735, 735+
Elizabeth .... 733, 734+, 735, 736+, 737+, 738, 739+
Eliza 542
Ellenwood Bunker 639
Enoch 733, 737
Eunice ... 553, 734, 735+, 736+, 737, 738+

Francis 734, 738

Gardner 739
George .... 241, 258, 734, 738+

Henry 466
Hephzibah 736
Hepzibah 734, 737, 738
Hepzibeth 739

Isaac .... 17, 19, 126, 660, 661, 665, 670, 731+, 732

James 456, 458, 464, 469, 474
James B. 542
Janet 739
Jean 99
Jeremiah .... 732, 733+
Jemima 733, 735
Jethro 733, 733, 733, 736
Joanna 665, 731, 732
Johanna 733
Job 341, 342, 737
John ... 23+, 69, 107, 112, 117, 132, 140, 647, 665+, 731+, 732+, 733, 734, 737
John Jr. 107, 531, 666
John B. 451, 455, 460, 542
John Franklin 542
John 2d 116
Jonathan 111

HISTORY OF NANTUCKET

Joseph ...... 24, 99, 130, 553, 665, 731, 732+
Joseph G. 542
Judith 736, 738
Katharine 736
Libni 738
Lydia .... 542, 733+, 734, 735+, 736, 737+, 738, 739

Margery 665, 731
Mary .... 665, 731+, 732+, 733, 734+, 735, 736, 737, 738
Mehitable 734, 739
Miriam 738, 739
Moses 739

Nathan 122
Nathaniel .. 188, 647, 733, 734, 738+

Obediah 738
Obed 737

Paul 735, 738
Peleg 734, 738
Persis 733
Peter 733
Phebe 732, 733, 735, 738, 739
Prince 389, 394, 421
Priscilla ...... 531, 647, 732+, 733, 734, 735+, 737, 739

Rachel .... 733, 736+
Rebecca .... 736+
Rebekah 736
Richard L. 618
Robert G. 498
Rowland 277
Ruth 733, 735, 737

Sarah 628, 732, 733, 736
Seth 736
Silas 739
Silvanus 272, 733, 736, 737
Simeon 271, 272, 389, 636, 736
Solomon ...... 258, 732, 734+, 739+
Solomon Jr. 389
Stephen 393, 738
Susanna .. 543, 570, 665, 731+, 733, 739
Sylvia 739

Thaddeus .... 738+
Thomas .. 21, 23+, 34, 55, 664, 665+, 667, 731+, 732
Thomas Jr. 345
Timothy 635
Tobias 665, 731, 732

William 110, 190, 295, 464, 617, 735, 737

William Jr. 295
William M. 345

Zenas 581
Zenas M. ...... 472, 477, 480, 482+, 483

FOLGER

Aaron .... 754+
Abiah 740, 741
Abial 749
Abiel .... 749+
Abigail .. 742+, 743, 744, 746, 748+, 752, 754
Abishai ... 106, 108, 117, 148, 153, 157, 163, 168, 148, 153, 155, 157, 163, 356, 361, 749+
Abraham 751
Alfred 341
Alexander 755
Amy 751
Anna .... 743, 744+, 746, 748, 750+, 751+, 755
Arnold 755
Andrew 748
Asa 256, 258, 752

Barnabas *................... 755
Barnard 752
Barzillai .. 197, 257, 259, 403+, 447, 744, 750+
Barzillai T. 342, 455, 460, 466
Benjamin .... 190, 211, 222, 224, 225, 248, 258, 259, 323, 429, 431, 433, 539, 567, 574, 744, 747, 753+
Benjamin Franklin 616, 750
Benjamin H. 347
Bethiah .... 670, 740, 741, 742+, 743
Bethsheba 741
Betsey 568, 569, 570
Brown 393

Capt. * 198
Catharine 616, 745
Charles 286, 487, 742, 750
Charles C. 348
Charles F. .... 345+
Charles G. 345
Charles James 754
Christian .... 744+
Christopher 393, 750
Clarinda 754
Clement 295, 755
Cleona 754

Daniel .... 215, 434, 441, 621, 741, 743+, 748, 749, 754

*Probably Capt. Timothy Folger

David 277, 395, 405, 414, 746
David G. 349
Deborah .... 742+, 746, 747
Dinah .... 746+, 749+, 751, 752, 755
Dorcas 740
Edward
Edward R. 348
Eleazer .. 22, 27, 100+, 103, 115, 127, 131, 172, 174, 526, 605, 606, 616+, 617, 661+, 670, 741+, 742
Ebenezer 752
Eleazer Jr. 97, 99
Elihu 751
Elijah 751
Eliphaz 742, 748
Elisha .. 190+, 277, 394, 424, 430, 622, 741, 747, 748+, 754
Elisha Jr. .. 294, 323, 419, 436, 539
Ellery C. .... 345+
Esther 744
Elizabeth .... 745+, 750+, 752, 754+ 755
Eunice 744, 745, 748, 753, 755
Experience 660, 741
Ezekiel 754

Francis 755
Francis E. 345
Franklin 752
Frederick 109, 113, 114, 115, 117, 118, 211, 215, 216, 254, 386, 617, 743

George .... 200, 232, 259, 749, 755+
George B. 466, 471
George F. 345
George Gill .... 638+
George Howland 638
Gideon 286, 297, 637, 742, 755
Gilbert 403, 405, 406, 750
Giles 316
Gorham 748

Hannah 742
Henry 197, 345, 365
Henry B. 467
Hepsabeth 567
Hephzibah .. 744, 746, 749, 751, 753, 754, 755
Hepzibah 753
Hezekiah 752
Hiram 472, 477

Isaac .... 328, 637+
Isaac H. 345, 631
Isaac Hussey 639
Isaiah 753

James 347, 348, 747

Jane 743
Jared 751
Jedidah .... 742, 744+, 751
Jerusha 742, 747
Joanna 740, 747
Jemima .... 747, 753+
Jethro 114, 533, 742, 744, 745, 751
Job 258, 753
John ...... 97, 258, 670, 542, 661, 741+, 744, 747, 749
John M. 468, 473
Jonathan .... 259, 742, 743, 745+, 746+, 752+
Jonathan Jr. 117
Joseph 295, 751
Joseph W. 469
Judith ... 661, 741, 743+, 744, 745, 747, 748+, 749, 750, 753, 754+, 755

Keziah .... 743, 748+

Latham 752
Leah 744
Lebbeus 751
Love 575, 747
Lucretia 750
Lydia .. 542, 744, 745, 746+, 747+, 751, 752+, 753+, 754, 755+

Margaret 742, 743, 745, 750, 751
Martha 746
Matilda 752
Mayhew .... 755+
Merab 752
Mary .... 661, 670, 740+, 741+, 742, 743+, 744+, 745+, 747+, 478, 749, 750+, 751+, 752+, 753
Mary Ann 618
Meribah 740
Miriam 750
Moses 754

Nathan .... 102+, 103, 356, 741, 743, 750
Nathaniel 393, 742, 744, 748
Nancy F. 628

Obadiah .. 241, 256, 271+, 272, 320 752
Obadiah 3d 258
Obed ...... 258, 265, 393, 539, 636+, 752
Obed 2d 323, 539
Owen 259, 294, 744

Patience 741
Paul 745, 748
Peleg 617, 743
Peregrine 259, 752

Peter..17, 20, 21+, 22+, 24, 25, 29, 33, 51+, 52, 53+, 55, 56+, 57+, 58, 59, 63+, 64+, 67, 128, 133+, 134, 135, 136, 137, 214, 225, 236, 351, 670+, 740+, 741, 743, 744+, 748
Philip H. 330, 511
Phebe .... 744, 747+, 750+, 752, 753+, 754+, 755
Priscilla .... 742+, 745

Rachel 744, 746, 748
Rebecca 744, 745, 752, 754, 755
Reuben .... 114, 117+, 258, 744, 749
Reuben 746, 748, 751
Reuben C. 345
Reuben Pinkham .... 639+
Reuben S. 345
Rhoda 750
Richard 277, 415, 418, 742, 755
Robert 209, 258, 294, 749
Ruth .... 743, 744, 746+, 749, 752, 755

Sally 753
Sarah .... 618, 741+, 742, 743, 749+, 750, 751, 755+
Samuel B. 628
Seth ...... 257, 280, 295, 365, 395, 403, 404+, 406, 423, 747+, 752+
Shubael .. 110+, 356, 742, 747+, 753+
Silvanus 749
Simeon 258, 753
Sophia 743
Stephen 257, 258, 743, 748
Solomon 269, 422, 575, 746
Solomon Jr. 411, 415
Susanna .... 746+, 750, 753
Susan 755
Susannah 755
Sylvanus 259, 277, 746

Thaddeus 294, 409
Thomas 393, 752
Timothy ...... 113, 114, 117, 118, 181, 206+, 210, 211+, 212+, 215, 219+, 220, 221+, 222, 224+, 225+, 227, 228+, 232+, 233+, 234, 235, 236, 237, 238, 246, 247+, 249+, 250, 251, 253, 259, 277, 374, 384, 386+, 394, 414, 636, 744, 745, 749+, 750, 753+
Timothy Jr. 560
Tristram .... 259, 405, 406, 410, 414, 420, 435, 750, 751+

Uriah 345
Urian 742

Walter .... 117, 222, 224, 225, 232, 233, 238, 266, 294, 331, 536, 624, 647, 750, 754+,
Walter Jr. .. 267, 287, 288, 330, 636, 640, 652, 754+
William .... 232, 259, 328, 393, 749, 755+
William C. 618
William C. 2d 474
William T. .... 345+
Zaccheus 742, 747, 748

GARDNER

Errors in the previous edition on pages 759 and 764 of the Gardner genealogy have been corrected in the present edition. James Gardner, Junior, had only one wife (Susannah Gardner, daughter of Nathaniel and Abigail) and not four, as the earlier edition stated.

Aaron 393, 773
Abel .. 108, 167, 202, 760, 766, 767
Abial 774
Abiel 758
Abigail .... 553, 759, 763+, 764 765, 766+, 767+, 770, 775, 778+
Abishai 316, 761, 768, 776
Abraham 773
Ab'm 295
Albert 286, 295, 320, 560, 775
Albert C. .... 456+
Alexander .... 214, 236, 258, 386, 636+, 773+, 777
Alex'r 236, 414
Alexander E. 330
Alexander F. 347
Alfred H. 345
Amaziah .. 264, 395, 408, 410, 411, 412, 413, 430, 433
Amy .... 553+
Andrew .... 356, 760, 766+
Anna .. 624, 758, 760, 763, 764, 766, 767+, 768, 769, 770, 772+, 773+, 774+, 776, 777+
Annie 765
Archelus 773
Arthur H. 627, 632
Arthur Hinton .... 639+
Barnabas .. 108, 202, 759, 763, 764, 772
Barney 393
Barzillai 770, 773
Benjamin .. 356, 443, 542, 618, 637+, 638+, 757+, 758, 761+, 764, 775

HISTORY OF NANTUCKET

Benjamin C. 468
Bethiah 757, 758
Bethuel 760, 767
Beulah 761

Caleb 393, 760
Calvin 393
Capt. 198
Charles .... 295, 316, 393, 619, 760, 767+
Charles F. 330
C. F. 330
Charles P. 347
Charles W. 345
Charlotta 776
Christopher 766, 769, 776

Damaris 756, 757
Daniel 294, 762, 774, 777
David 108, 114, 761, 769, 770
Deborah .... 756, 758, 761, 764+, 768
Dinah .... 761, 764, 770+
Dorcas 771

Eben 151
Ebenezer .... 102+, 174, 356, 532, 760, 765+
Edmund 295, 416, 440, 485, 487, 774
Edward C. 345, 586
Edward J. 294
Edward M. 618, 630
Eliab 771
Elihu 110, 764
Elijah 770
Eliphalet .... 764, 774+
Elisha 777
Elisha P. F. 345
Elizabeth ...... 233, 259, 553, 574, 618, 758, 759, 761+, 764, 766+, 767+, 769, 771, 771, 772, 773+, 774, 775, 777
Enoch 328, 761
Ephraim 766, 767
Eunice .. 757, 760, 763, 764, 765+, 766, 767, 768, 769, 772, 773, 775+, 775, 776, 777, 778,

Francis 393, 569, 570, 775, 778
Francis C. 347
Francis M. 480
Franklin 393
Frederick 618
Freeman 287, 772, 774

Gayer 767
George .... 96, 97, 99, 272, 393, 549, 550, 619, 666, 757+, 771, 776, 777, 778
George 2d 286, 297, 636, 757
George W. .... 418, 421, 423, 430, 434, 439, 442, 462, 478 ....

George Washington .... 637+
Gideon .... 246, 259, 265, 281, 282, 287+, 320, 640, 775, 776
Grafton 103, 106, 108, 114, 152, 181, 152, 181, 283, 330, 345, 406, 407, 411, 421, 426, 553, 777, 778
Grindall 553, 568, 778

Hannah ...... 543, 618, 659, 661, 758, 760, 761, 762, 763, 770, 773+, 776, 777+
Hannah Maria 542
H. B. 294
Henry 3d 581
Hephzibah 767, 768, 770, 777, 778
Hepsabeth 567
Hepzabeth 760
Hepzibah .... 553, 762+, 763
Hezekiah B. 560, 758, 759, 762, 770, 771, 773, 776
Hiram 347
Hope 664, 757
Hope Macy 758
Howard 345
Huldah 772

Isaac .. 292, 418, 452, 455, 459, 487+, 770
Isaiah 768

James .... 115+, 395, 664, 756, 757, 759+, 762, 764, 765+, 766, 767, 775
James 2d 117
Jared 272
Jedidah ...... 761+, 763, 768, 769+
Jemima .... 761, 762, 763, 766, 768, 770+, 772, 778
Jeremiah .. 103, 165, 635, 757, 777
Jerry 573
Jesse 330
Jethro .... 393, 395, 759, 762, 763+, 768, 772
Job 393
John .. 75, 78, 80, 87, 89, 91, 96, 108, 136+, 137+, 138, 139, 140, 148, 171, 172+, 487, 516, 527, 549, 552+, 659, 592, 593, 597, 662, 664+, 756+, 757+, 777
John Jackson 639
John Jr. 109
John C. 345
John 2d .... 113, 116+, 511
John J. .... 442, 445, 447, 451, 458, 471 ..
Jonathan ...... 759, 763+ 771, 772
Joseph .... 198, 259, 351, 356, 756, 757+, 758, 760, 765, 767, 775
Joseph P. .... 345+
Josiah 258, 551, 552, 766

Joshua 182, 553, 766, 767
Judith, ... 553, 661, 760+, 762+, 765+, 770, 771, 774, 775

Kate 573
Katharine .... 767+
Kezia 759, 762, 764, 773

Latham 257, 406
Leah 758
Levi .... 203+, 256
Libni 771
Lois 778
Love 757, 761, 767, 768
Lucy 574
Lydia .. 576, 618, 758+, 761, 764, 765, 768+, 769, 771, 772, 774, 755+, 776

Mary .. 525, 526+, 542, 553, 618, 757, 758+, 759+, 760+, 761+, 762, 763+, 764+, 766+, 768, 769, 770+, 771, 774, 775, 778+
Margaret .... 760+, 765, 775
Matthew 762, 773
Mehitable 757, 759, 765, 776
Merab 771
Micajah .. 271+, 272, 284+, 285+, 286, 287, 288, 289, 290, 389, 394, 399, 433, 636
Miriam .... 757, 758, 763, 764, 768, 769, 770, 772+, 772, 773+
Moses .... 773+

Naomi .... 769+, 773
Nathan 766, 767, 772
Nathaniel .. 215, 258, 532, 659, 661, 757+, 759, 760, 766+, 775+, 776, 777
Noah 773

Obediah 761
Obed 760
Oliver C..................... 625
Owen 774

Parnel 774
Patience .. 758, 759+, 760, 762, 763, 764
Paul ...... 109, 214, 225, 232, 236, 300, 576, 761, 770, 771+
Paul Jr. 536
Peleg 553, 760, 762, 765, 773
Pernal 771
Peter 356, 570, 758, 761, 762
Phebe .... 766, 767, 772, 773, 774+, 776
Prince 182, 197, 539, 542, 768
Priscilla .. 553, 664, 756, 757+, 763, 766, 767, 773, 777+
Provided 762, 774

Rachel .. 542, 757, 759+, 761, 764+, 771+, 773, 774+, 775
Rebecca .... 572+, 768+
Rebekah 761
Resolved 776
Reuben .... 189, 190, 233, 258, 259, 761, 769+, 775
Rhoda 770, 776
Richard .. 97+, 98, 99, 100, 171, 172, 277, 331, 342, 351, 355+, 525, 605, 635, 664+, 756+, 758+, 761, 770, 771
Robert .... 761, 768+
Robert B. 345
Robert Jr. 269, 418, 420
Roland C. 347
Rosanna 773
Ruth .... 757, 758, 760+, 764, 765, 766, 767, 770, 773, 775, 777

Sally 574
Samuel 316, 660, 759, 762, 765, 769
Sarah .... 215, 525, 526, 664+, 756+, 757+, 761+, 764+, 765, 766, 767, 770+, 771, 772, 773, 776, 777
Seth 110, 764, 772
Shubael .... 233, 258, 395, 553, 760+, 766, 767, 768, 769, 775
Shubael 2d 395
Silas 774, 778
Silvanus 761, 771
Simeon 109, 764, 775
Solomon .... 99, 109, 110, 111,, 758, 760, 761, 766, 771+, 182, 190, 197, 218, 389, 394, 766, 770+
Stephen 18. 761
Susanna .... 549, 759, 763, 765+, 769, 771, 774+
Susannah 760, 763, 764, 768, 772, 775

Thaddeus .... 258, 769+, 772
Theodate .... 761, 769+
Thomas .. 526, 618, 766, 777+, 777+
Thomas M. 343, 347, 459
Timothy 760, 778
Tristram 395, 765, 775

Uriah .. 109, 203, 239, 256, 294, 765

Walter 258, 768, 774
William .. 570+, 572, 758, 762+, 770, 775, 776
William B. 459
William H. 331, 334, 460

Zaccheus .... 763, 772+
Zacchary 766
Zecchariah 259
Zenas 539, 771

Zimri	274
Zephaniah	777

HUSSEY

Aaron	786
Abial	780, 783, 786
Abigail	780+, 781, 783+, 784, 786
Abraham	785
Albert	294
Albert M.	346
Alexander	785
Alice	781, 785
Ammiel	389
Anna	784+
Ann	780, 784
Augustus	349
Bachelder	100, 780
Bachelor	780, 781, 784
Batchelder	190, 191, 232
Batchelor	185, 190, 191, 232, 248, 259, 533
Barzillai	395, 413
Benjamin	211, 214, 215, 219, 222, 225+, 233, 236, 239, 241, 393, 395, 542, 781, 786
Benjamin F.	443, 447
Benjamin R.	445+, 450, 456
Bethiah	786
Catharine	784
Charles 2d	295
Charles W.	479, 480+, 481+
Christopher	20, 53, 109+, 110, 115, 118, 132, 259+, 354, 658, 661, 667, 779+, 780, 781, 782
Christopher Jr.	230
Christopher B.	290, 293
Christopher C.	543, 614
Cyrus	543, 647
Cyrus M.	501, 502, 503+, 504
Daniel	621, 780, 781+, 782, 786
David	782+, 785
David J.	542
Deborah	781, 782, 785+
Dinah	782, 786
Ebenezer	395, 781, 786
Edward B.	316, 348
Edward B., Jr.	475, 481
Elizabeth	542, 780, 781, 782+, 783+, 784, 785, 786+
Eunice	781, 782, 783, 785, 786
Francis	202, 295, 785
Francis F.	329
George	103, 106, 111, 193, 356, 386, 636, 780, 781, 782, 783, 785
George C.	346
George Jr.	187
George 2d	117+, 222, 225
George Gorham	640, 785
George G.	265
Gorham	395, 542
Hannah	543
Hepsibah	784
Hepsibeth	542, 546
Hephzibah	780+, 782
Huldah	779, 781
Isaac B.	454, 457, 463, 470
Isaiah	395
Jedidah	781+, 786
Jethro	783
John	448, 779+, 781, 785
John Jr.	451, 457, 462
Jonathan	781+
Joseph	192, 259, 786
Joseph S.	348, 781
Josiah	286, 290, 294, 504, 601, 602
Judith	543, 780, 784, 785+
Laban	784
Libbeus	785
Lydia	543, 576, 647, 782, 784+, 785+, 786
Lydia Barnard	581
Lydia G.	542
Lydia M.	542
Margaret	783+
Maria	618
Martha	658, 779, 783
Mary	553, 618, 779, 780+, 781+, 783, 784+
Moses	784
Nancy	542
Naomi	576, 784
Nathaniel	780, 784, 785
Obed	105, 109, 111, 112+, 233, 274, 323, 553, 781+
Obed B.	323, 539
Obed (Capt)	109
Oliver F.	346
Paul	197, 203+, 204, 256, 258, 295, 487, 781, 783, 784
Peleg	389, 395, 785
Peter	275, 286, 288, 294, 560, 784
Phebe	618, 785+, 786
Prudence	785
Puella	779
Rachel	542, 781+, 782, 785+
Rebecca	779, 782
Reuben	782

HISTORY OF NANTUCKET

Rhoda 785
Robert 182, 197, 288, 786
Robert B. 348, 543, 631
Roland 487, 539, 637
Roland B. 631
Rose 782, 786
Ruth 782, 784, 786

Sally 576
Samuel B. 631
Sarah .... 780, 781+, 783+, 784, 786
Seth .... 780, 781, 783+, 784
Shubael 426, 429, 435, 439
Silvanus .. 102, 106, 182, 198, 332, 355, 356, 533+, 781+, 785
Stephen .... 46, 52+, 56, 57+, 64, 67, 75+, 95, 97, 114, 116, 117+, 118+, 130, 141+, 171+, 173+, 177, 181+, 185, 187, 190, 191, 193, 195, 201, 211+, 214, 217, 222, 238+, 239, 251, 253, 254, 256, 518, 528, 531, 615, 635, 636, 658, 661, 779+, 781+, 782, 786+
Susanna 780, 785
Susannah 784
Sylvanus .... 780+
Sylvanus Jr. 601

Temperance 785
Thaddeus 295
Theodate .... 662, 779+, 780
Thomas 316, 346, 783
Thomas W. 451
Tristram 266, 784

Uriel 785

Valentine 330, 581

William .. 230, 232, 294, 780, 783+

Zaccheus 560, 784

MACY

Abiel 794
Abigail .. 789, 790+, 791, 792+, 793, 795+, 796+, 797, 798, 799, 801,
Abishai 799, 800
Abraham .... 618, 791+, 800+
Alexander 295, 442, 446, 451
Alice 788, 791
Almy 793
Anna .... 789, 791+, 792, 794, 797, 797, 798+, 800+, 801
Andrew M. 617, 630
Arthur 349

Barachiah 793
Barnabas 794
Barzillai 801

Benjamin 792, 797, 798
Bethiah .... 654, 788+, 789, 793, 796, 797+

Caleb .... 259, 791, 801+
Catharine 576
Charles 294, 295, 438
Charles C. 346
Charlotte 618
Clement 793

Daniel .... 790+, 795+
Daniel P. 618
David .... 110, 789+, 792+ 800
David R. 316
Deborah..788+, 790, 791+, 797, 798+, 799, 800
Dinah 789, 792, 795
Dorcas 790

Edmund 389
Edward B. 346
Eliab 789, 793
Elihu 793
Elisha 618, 801
Elizabeth .. 791, 793, 795, 796, 797+, 798, 799+, 800, 801
Enoch 797
Eunice .... 323, 539, 789, 790, 793+, 795, 797, 798, 799+
Eunice Coffin 618

Francis .... 111, 113, 115, 117, 229, 265, 267, 286, 297, 323, 393, 395, 539, 654, 788, 791, 798+
Francis G. 624
Francis Gardner .... 637+

Gayer 795, 796
George 790, 796, 790
George Nelson 343, 346
Gorham 295, 316, 323

Hannah .... 618, 790, 792+, 796, 798, 799
Henry 797
Henry G. 349
Hepsibah 800
Hephzibah .... 790, 791, 794+, 797, 799
Hepzibah 791, 792
Huldah 795

Jabez 788, 789, 790, 796
James 592
James H. 346
Jemima 793, 800
Jedidah 794, 795
Jethro .. 75+, 97, 102, 103, 147, 172, 269, 421, 425, 533, 654, 788+, 789+, 793, 793, 790, 794, 795
John 797

HISTORY OF NANTUCKET 867

John B. 323
John P. 539
John R. 328, 581
John W. 328, 346
Joseph .... 294, 790, 796+
Josiah 323, 539
Jonathan 239, 789, 794
Judith .... 618, 788, 789+, 791+, 792, 793, 794, 797, 798+, 801+

Kezia .... 801+
Latham 800
Lois 789
Love 790, 798
Lucinda 793
Lucretia 618
Lydia .. 790, 791+, 794+, 795, 796+, 797, 798, 800+

Margaret 795, 799
Mary .... 542, 647, 654, 658+, 788+, 789, 791, 794+, 795+, 796+, 798, 799
Mary Ann 618
Matilda 796
Matthew ....+....... 790, 795, 796
Merab 793, 795
Mercy 792, 799
Micajah 793
Miriam 789, 792, 793, 799, 800

Nathaniel .. 109, 110+, 189, 791, 797, 799+

Obed .. 536, 539, 610, 618, 642, 801

Paul .... 603, 605+, 618, 797
Peleg 272, 794
Peleg Jr. 272
Peter ... 222, 248, 295, 539, 618, 799
Peter Jr. 295
Phebe .... 797+, 798, 799+, 800, 801
Priscilla .... 792, 800+

Rachel 618, 790 796
Reuben 229, 242, 393, 395, 618, 798, 800
Rhoda 793
Richards .. 439, 442, 533, 535, 788, 791, 792, 800
Robert .... 790, 797+
Rose 794
Ruth .... 792, 798, 800+, 801

Samuel .... 539, 794+, 800
Samuel H. 539
Samuel M. 300, 323
Sarah .... 134, 654+, 661, 787+, 788, 789+, 790, 792, 794+, 796, 797, 799
Seth 259, 789, 794, 798
Shubael 799

Silvanus.. 266, 271, 295, 297+, 300+, 301, 302, 539, 624, 653, 789, 795, 801
Simeon 295, 800
Solomon 794
Stephen .... 792+
Stephen Jr. 393
Susanna 794

Thomas (60 Mr) (61 Mr) .... 21+, 22+, 23+, 24, 27, 28, 29+, 33, 39+, 50+, 51, 52, 53+, (54 Mr), (55 Mr) (56 Mr), 58, 59, (60 Mr) (61 Mr), 62, 63, 97, 100, 101, 103+, 109, 132+, 133, 134+, 140, 152, 172+ 174 516, 517, 539, 546+, 547, 605, 618, 653, 654+, 658, 686, 667+, 787+, 788+, 790, 791, 796, 799
Thomas M. 618
Timothy 795
Tristram 256, 799

Uriah 539, 795

William .... 266, 536, 789, 794+
William C. 339
William H. 346
William Henry 346
William W. 323, 539

Zaccheus .. 107, 109, 112, 117+, 119, 259, 352+, 598+, 642, 791, 799

STARBUCK

Abigail 658, 662, 667, 802, 804, 805, 806, 809, 811
Albert W. 347
Alice 809
Alexander 514
Ann 803, 804, 805, 807, 810, 811
Anna ..666, 804, 805, 806, 807+, 808+, 810+
Barnabas .. 204, 531, 532, 666, 803, 810, 811
Benjamin .... 804, 806+, 810

Charles 294
Charles E. 474, 479
Charles Henry 588
Christopher ...... 111, 115, 116, 118 211, 215, 216, 219, 239, 251, 386, 806, 810+
Clorinda 812

Damaris 805, 808
Daniel 230, 809

David .... 295, 296+, 297, 300, 301, 395, 399, 652, 811
David Joy 349
Deborah 804, 805, 806, 807
Dinah .... 666, 803+, 804, 806+, 808
Dorcas .. 22, 531, 658, 666, 802, 803, 804, 805

Edward .. 21+, 22+, 27+, 29, 32, 33, 34, 43, 50, 52, 55, 65, 114+, 117, 126, 129, 133+, 134, 171, 172, 340, 351, 393, 395, 516, 517, 546, 547, 653, 655, 656+ 657+, 658, 667+, 802+, 805, 808, 809
Elisha .. 295, 320, 329, 500, 581, 812
Elizabeth .... 666, 803, 804+, 806+ 808, 810, 812
Esther 802
Eunice .... 803, 805+, 807, 809

Frederick C. 580

Gayer 808
George B. 347

Henry 462, 467, 475
Hephzibah .. 803, 804, 805, 809, 811
Hepsabeth 506
Hepzibeth 666
Hezekiah .... 623+, 808
Howes 811

Jemima 805
Jethro .... 100, 103, 144, 531, 532, 533+, 658, 666, 802, 803, 804, 807, 810+
Jethro Jr. 536, 810
John 277, 377, 805, 810
Jonathan 811
Joseph .... 294, 576, 805, 809+
Judith 807, 808, 810, 812

Katharine .... 655, 656, 802+
Kezia 804, 812
Kimball 295, 539, 542, 543, 812

Laban 812
Levi 294, 409
Lucretia 809
Lucy 618
Lydia .. 572, 805+, 807+, 808, 809, 811+, 812

Mandana A. 580
Matilda 811
Matthew 257, 395, 406, 808
Mary .. 21, 50, 133, 517, 518, 520, 522, 523, 524, 526, 528, 530, 531, 623+, 647, 665+, 802, 803+, 805, 806+, 807+, 808+, 809, 810, 811+, 812+
Miriam .... 543, 810+

Moses 811
Nathaniel .. 23, 27, 29, 53, 64, 98, 127, 128, 355, 520, 523, 525, 526+, 528, 529+, 531, 533, 534, 547, 655, 658, 661, 662, 665, 667, 802, 803+, 807, 809+, 810+
Nathaniel Jr. .... 97, 98, 526, 528, 529, 531, 532+, 621, 664, 666, 803+

Obed 433, 438, 441, 444, 447, 449, 465, 812
Owen 257

Paul .. 152, 357, 533, 666, 803, 804, 805, 806, 808, 811
Phebe .... 809, 811+, 812
Priscilla 666, 803, 804

Rachel .... 805, 808+
Reuben 258, 294, 413, 458
Reuben F. 463, 472
Rose 808
Ruth 804, 805, 809

Sally 576
Samuel .. 115, 117+, 188, 190+, 192, 198, 211+, 212, 214, 215, 216, 218, 220, 221, 224, 226, 227, 239, 241, 253, 254+, 255, 300, 389+, 805, 809+
Sarah .... 658, 802, 804, 810+
Simeon 409, 414
Silvanus .. 214, 219, 225, 236, 808, 811

Thaddeus 806
Thomas .... 623, 805, 808+
Tristram .. 147, 295, 804, 806, 810
T. & H. 328

Uriah 811

William .. 214, 225, 236, 805, 807. 808+, 810+, 811+, 812
William C. 340
William Coffin 638, 640
William Hadwen 564

Zaccheus .... 807, 810+

SWAIN

Abial 821
Abigail 814, 815, 818, 820
Abishai 218, 821
Abner 295
Abraham 429, 434, 441, 446, 475
Abertus 822
Alexander 460

HISTORY OF NANTUCKET 869

Alfred 639
Alice 618
Andrew 393, 820
Ann 658, 822
Anna .... 596, 618, 815+, 817+, 818, 820, 822, 823+
Anne 824

Barnabas 188, 320, 389, 820
Barney 192, 197
Barzillai .. 182, 197, 202, 204, 442, 446, 505+, 820
Batchelor 818
Benjamin .. 97, 434, 660, 813, 814, 818
Bethiah 817, 821

Caleb 814, 817, 821
Calvin 480
Chapman .... 110, 175, 824+
Charles 316, 816
Charles Bunker 639
Charles B. 2d .... 347, 467, 472+
Charles B. 3d 348
Charles F. 347
Christian 815
Christopher 814
Clinton 347

Daniel .... 316, 816+
Daniel 2d 260
David .. 395, 413, 422, 424, 817, 822, 823+
David 2d .. 419, 431, 436, 442, 448
Deborah 818, 819, 820, 824
Dinah 816, 824
Dorcas 814

Edmond 617
Edward 295
Edward M. 348
Edw. 474
Eliakim 814, 815
Eleanor 814, 816
Elihu 821
Elijah 815
Elizabeth .... 658, 660, 813+, 814+, 815, 817+, 818+, 819+, 821, 822+, 823+
Emeline 618
Ephraim 824
Eunice 543, 571, 618, 815, 818, 819, 822
Experience 660, 813, 814

Francis .... 182, 658, 813, 815, 820+,
Franklin 819
Frederick .. 441, 444, 448, 453, 822

George .... 618, 814, 816+, 817
George 2d .. 418, 420, 423, 428, 437
George H. 480

Gideon 539, 822
Gilbert .... 823+
Hannah .. 660, 813, 814, 816+, 816+, 818, 819+, 821+, 824
Henry 819
Hepza 569
Hephzibah .... 815, 817+, 819, 822+, 823
Hezekiah 539, 542, 822
Howland 819
Howse 393

James 258, 316
Jane 133, 134, 658, 659, 814
Jacob C. 347
Jean 813
Jedidah 819
Jemima .... 814, 815, 819+
Jethro 814
John .. 21, 23, 26, 27, 33, 43, 53, 64, 65, 67, 96, 127, 128, 132, 162+, 172+, 174, 182, 275, 295, 348, 356, 528, 531, 579, 615, 658, 660+, 667, 813+, 814+, 815+, 819
Jonathan .. 111, 280, 418, 421, 817, 822+
Jonathan 2d .. 424, 429, 435, 444, 449, 536
John (England) .... 102, 823+, 824
Joseph .. 111, 316, 813, 814, 817, 821+, 822, 824
Joseph B. 542
Josiah .... 638+, 823
Judith 818, 821, 823, 824

Katharine 814

Louisa A. 652
Love .... 618, 816+, 817
Lydia .. 542, 618, 814, 815, 816, 817, 820, 821+, 822, 823

Marah 813, 814
Margaret .... 542, 814, 817+, 818, 819, 820, 822, 823
Martha 618, 658, 817, 818, 822
Mary .. 571, 618, 658+, 660+, 813+, 814+, 815+, 817, 818+, 819, 820+, 822
Matilda 823
Matthew 393, 820
Merab 823
Micajah 295, 443, 542, 818
Miriam 821

Nathaniel 814, 817, 821

Obed .. 316, 344, 440, 443, 456, 638
Obed B. 542
Obed 2d 470, 475
Oliver 824

Oliver C. 468, 473
Owen 295, 417, 419, 592, 593

Parnell 572
Patience 660, 813, 814, 823, 824
Paul 818, 822
Peleg .... 484, 613, 814, 818+
Peter 814
Peter F. 462
Phebe .. 815, 816+, 820, 821, 822, 823
Priscilla 814, 815, 816

Rachel 543, 816, 818, 821
Rebecca 819
Reuben 323, 428, 663, 816, 818
Reuben 2d 295, 433, 439, 442
Richard .. 21, 22, 53, 127, 129+, 132,
 133, 134, 658, 659, 660, 665,
 666, 667, 813+, 814, 817+,
 822+, 823+
Richard G. 414, 542
Richard Gardner 823
Robert 294
Robert 2d 294
Ruel 822
Ruth 814, 815, 819, 820, 823

Samuel 328, 560, 579, 819
Samuel G. 348
Sarah ...... 628, 660, 813, 818, 824+
Seth 815, 819, 820
Seth M. 341, 342, 821
Shubael 819, 820
Silas 415
Silvanus .... 241, 818, 821+
Simeon 260, 819
Solomon 408, 414, 418
Stephen 660, 813, 814, 816
Susanna 815, 817, 821, 822
Sylvanus 446, 469, 470

Thaddeus 389, 395, 823
Thomas 821, 823
Timothy 816
Tristram 260, 815, 820, 821
Tristram C. 432
Tristram P. 451

Uriah .... 182, 294, 395, 636+

Valentine 295, 395, 408, 823
Valentine 2d 395

William .. 105, 106+, 393, 404, 405,
 407, 622+, 658, 813, 814+, 815,
 819
William Jr. 182
William B. .... 342, 464, 469+
William C. 329, 347
William F. 347
William H. 347, 348
William K. 347
William T. 480
Wyer 560

Zacchary 393
Zaccheus 816
Zephaniah 824

WORTH

Abigail .... 827+, 828
Adino 830
Andrew 829
Anna .... 826+, 827, 828, 829
Asenath 829

Barzillai 831
Benjamin .. 294, 409, 417, 420, 423,
 431, 447, 581, 647, 831, 832+
Benjamin 2d 443
Bethiah 828

Calvin B. 463
Calvin G. 468
Charles 830, 831
Christian or Christina 830
Christopher 112, 115, 117, 826, 829+
Columbus 502

Damaris 827
Daniel .... 828+, 831
David 272, 294, 414, 831
Deborah .... 828, 831+
Dinah .... 826, 829+
Drusilla 830

Edmund 827
Elihu 831
Elizabeth .... 647, 829+, 830
Eunice .... 828+, 831+, 832
Ezekiel 826

Francis 826, 829, 830, 832
Frederick 574, 576

George 574, 830
George B. 431, 437
George G. 347
George H. 546
Gideon 202, 258, 295, 830
Gorham 348

Hannah 827
Henry Clay 638
Hephzibah 827
Huldah 828

Jedidah 827
Jemima 827, 828
Jethro 831
Job 830, 831
John 182, 193, 197, 260, 395, 574,
 661, 825+, 826, 828+

Jonah 610, 827
Jonathan 395, 825, 826, 828
Joseph ...... 505, 826+, 827, 828, 830
Joseph T. 581
Judith .. 825, 827, 828+, 829+, 830, 831
Lydia .... 543, 570, 826, 827, 828, 830+, 831+
Lyonel 826
Margaret 618
Mary .. 661, 825+, 826+, 827+, 828+, 829, 830+, 831, 832+
Matilda 831
Matthew 610, 827
Miriam 825, 826, 827, 828, 829, 830
Nathaniel .... 825+, 827
Obed 393
Paul .. 257, 389, 400+, 404, 405, 407, 410, 828
Phebe 574, 828, 829, 830
Priscilla 832
Puella 830
Rachel .... 828, 830+

Reuben .... 827, 830+
Richard .. 22, 647, 825, 826+, 829, 831
Ruth 828
Samuel 198
Sarah .... 825+, 826+, 827
Seth 449, 450, 828
Shubael 222, 342, 393, 828
Silvanus 617, 828, 830
Solon 573, 830
Sophia 827
Stephen 828, 831
Sylvia 831
Thomas .. 438, 498+, 504, 828, 831+
Thomas J. 629
Uriah 829
William ...... 27, 33, 43, 50, 52, 54, 61, 64, 70+, 71, 82, 89, 97, 98, 128, 131, 171, 172+, 174, 258, 260, 316, 610, 825+, 826, 827, 828
William 2d 439, 443, 447, 450, 455, 458
Walter 826
Zenas 831

www.ingramcontent.com/pod-product-compliance
Lightning Source LLC
Chambersburg PA
CBHW070300230426
43664CB00014B/2589